SAINTS + SINNERS
2017

NEW FICTION
FROM THE FESTIVAL

Visit us at www.boldstrokesbooks.com

SAINTS + SINNERS
2017

NEW FICTION
FROM THE FESTIVAL

edited by

Amie M. Evans and Paul J. Willis

SAINTS + SINNERS

2017

SAINTS + SINNERS 2017
NEW FICTION FROM THE FESTIVAL
© 2017 BY SAINTS & SINNERS LITERARY FESTIVAL. ALL RIGHTS RESERVED.

ISBN 13: 978-1-63555-004-7

THIS TRADE PAPERBACK ORIGINAL IS PUBLISHED BY
BOLD STROKES BOOKS, INC.
P.O. BOX 249
VALLEY FALLS, NY 12185

FIRST EDITION: APRIL 2017

CREDITS
EDITORS: AMIE M. EVANS AND PAUL J. WILLIS
PRODUCTION DESIGN: STACIA SEAMAN
COVER DESIGN BY SANDY BARTEL

Acknowledgments

We'd like to thank:

The John Burton Harter Foundation for their continued support of the fiction contest and their generous support of the Saints and Sinners Literary Festival program.

Radclyffe & Bold Strokes Books for their talents in the production of our anthology and their sponsorship of the Saints and Sinners event.

Michael Thomas Ford for serving as this year's final judge and for his thoughtful and insightful introduction to this anthology.

Ron Rothbart for his striking photo used in our cover design.

Sandy Bartel for creating the cover with Ron's photo and including the beautiful paintings of John Burton Harter. www.sandybarteldesign.com

The Festival's interns, Drew Jordan and Sean Brennan.

Everyone who has entered the contest and/or attended the Saints and Sinners Literary Festival over the last 14 years for their energy, ideas, and dedication in keeping the written LGBT word alive.

Greg Herren and Wendy Stone for supporting us in countless and humorous ways during our endless projects.

CONTENTS

INTRODUCTION

I once had the pleasure of attending the Westminster Kennel Club Dog Show as the guest of Anne Rogers Clark. Annie, as those in the dog show world knew her, was a formidable presence: a three-time best in show-winning handler, 22-time judge, and the only person to have judged all seven groups and Best in Show. Certified to judge every breed recognized by the AKC, her knowledge of dogs was unmatched. She was also extraordinarily kind and generous and funny. At the time, I was working as an editor of children's books, putting together a series about dog breeds. Annie, whose personal fondness was for poodles, had provided me with photographs of her dogs. When she extended an invitation to accompany her to Westminster, I was of course thrilled, not only to meet her, but to get a behind the scenes look at something I'd watched for years on television.

I'd always found the Westminster proceedings a little baffling, particularly the judging of the seven groups the breeds are sorted into, where a judge is asked to select a winner from among two dozen or more breeds. In the Non-Sporting group, for instance, this might include breeds as disparate as the Shiba Inu, the French Bulldog, and the Xoloitzcuintli. "How can you pick a best dog when the breeds are so different from one another?" I asked Annie.

"You don't judge them against one another," she explained. "You look at them each individually and ask yourself which one is the best example of what its breed is supposed to be. Each dog is first and foremost competing against itself."

I've judged a fair number of writing competitions, and every time I've tried to keep Annie's words in mind, approaching each short story or book as a distinct entity related to the others in the group only by virtue of being something made up of words. Rather than comparing one to another, I try to evaluate each story on its own. Does it accomplish what it sets out to do? Does it do so in a way that's interesting? Is the use of language, structure, and theme particularly effective?

Then, of course, there's the not-inconsiderable matter of the heart.

The judge selected to oversee Westminster's final Best in Show group—which comprises the winners of the seven individual groups—does not know who the contestants are until she walks into the ring to make the final decision on the year's top dog. The idea, of course, being that there should be no preconceived notions, no outside influences. Although each of the final seven has supporters who cheer loudly as their favorite trots around the ring, the judge is supposed to be evaluating them with an unbiased eye, making a selection based solely on breed characteristics, bloodline, conformation.

And yet...

As readers, we have individual tastes, likes and dislikes that are purely personal. The same is true for writers when we peer under the hoods of other writers' stories to get a look at the machinery that makes them run. There are styles and genres I prefer, and story-building devices I find either appealing or distracting. A truly impartial reading is impossible, at least for me. I can appreciate the skill used in crafting a story even if I don't ultimately enjoy it as a reader, but in the end my emotional response to a story usually wins out over my respect for a writer's technical ability. There's a reason I would make a lousy Westminster judge: I'd choose the one who made my heart beat the fastest, even if (actually, especially if) it was flawed in some way.

Finding my top three was surprisingly easy. After reading the 15 finalists, I put them away and moved on to other things, waiting to see which ones would come calling again. Although each story here has something memorable about it (and many thanks to the first-round readers for choosing such a diverse group), ultimately there were three that I found myself thinking about the most over the following days: Alise Wascom's "Bear Food," Michael Chin's "Moonshine," and J. Marshall Freeman's "Curo the Filthmonger."

Apart from solid writing and the requisite "a character discovers something about life/herself/himself and is changed in some way" thing that all great stories mostly have, these three stories have little in common. So how to choose one to take the title? Truthfully, any one of the three would wear the crown well. Wascom's "Bear Food" features an unforgettable main character in Tulip, and when you think the story is going in one direction, it changes course, ultimately taking you someplace you didn't expect yourself (or Tulip) to end up. Chin's "Moonshine" is a shimmering, sweat-soaked look at the beauty and terror of being a teenager filled with longing and overflowing with the need to love and to be loved, only to see the object of your desire drifting farther and farther out of reach. And Freeman's trippy "Curo" is something altogether different, a rollicking sci-fi story that takes all the tropes of the genre and not only pays loving homage to them, but turns them on their head to deliver a clever commentary on the power of art and artists.

Much like a Westminster judge asking the finalists to parade around the ring one last time, I watched these three stories run around the inside of my head, examining them closely to see what it was about each that I loved, what made me return to them again and again, and what each left me with. Truthfully, I also looked for any flaws I could use to take one or another of them out of competition. Also truthfully, I found none. Each story accomplishes what it sets out to do. Each is magical and delightful in its own way. Each deserves to win all the things.

But a winner must be declared, and in the end, my thoughts returned most often to "Curo the Filthmonger," to the language and characters and, ultimately, the way it delighted my heart as both a writer and a reader. And so it takes this year's Best in Show ribbon. Your choice will perhaps be different. That's okay. No story is one size fits all. And as I said, you can't go wrong with any of the contenders. This just happens to be my top dog this year.

Michael Thomas Ford

MOONSHINE

Michael Chin

The night Evie came to live with us, all Zach wanted to do was look at his old *Playboy*, stolen from another boy's father's collection. Before school let out for summer, Zach had bartered baseball cards and half his lunch for it. The sun crept between boards in the treehouse and drew bright parallel lines over his face.

That's when a white SUV pulled up in front. It was Delia—my father's date. She was a big woman—not overweight or obviously muscular, but broad-shouldered, with firmer arms that looked firmer than most women I'd seen her age. She wore a flowing white dress. I had a hard time imagining her driving all the way up from South Carolina in it; had she changed at a rest stop? Her hair reached halfway down her back, the same red-brown color as the checkerboard Zach and I used to spend hours at before Zach got bored with it and called it *kid stuff*.

When Dad had told me six months earlier that he was going to try online dating, I told him it sounded like the stuff of bad comedy. He gave a weak laugh, and I was sure he'd fail—nothing more than a few first dates, then resign himself to bachelorhood. I didn't like the idea of new people in the house, besides which, if he remarried, Mom would never come home. But Dad spent every night on the computer, typing in flurries. Then he started taking his cell phone out on the porch, and I'd hear him laugh. Not the way he laughed at my jokes, but real laughter like when something funny happened on TV or when he had one of his college buddies visit for the weekend.

After three months of that, he told me she was coming. Delia, whom he had never met in person, was going to drive up to New York to spend the summer with us. Then he dropped the bomb: her daughter, Evie, would take my bedroom.

"You can keep your stuff in there, but you're sleeping on the couch, Cal," Dad said. "These are a couple of real southern ladies, and we're going to show them our best hospitality. I expect you to act like a gentleman."

From the moment he heard of the arrangement, Zach started concocting stories of how I would lose my virginity that summer. He'd grown up as a middle child amidst five siblings, and told me how someone was always walking in on someone else in the bathroom, bumping bodies in the narrow hallway that led to their bedrooms. It was a pain in their overcrowded house, but for me—when it was just Evie's body to contend with—proximity and close quarters could work to my advantage. Of course, by the time Delia and Evie arrived, Zach had retreated to more concrete visions of the two of us trying to sneak peeks through the bathroom window when she showered.

I told Zach I wasn't looking forward to having these people moving into our house. I complained about the loss of space and privacy. I didn't care what she looked like.

Zach nodded sagely. "She might be a fattie."

But Evie wasn't a fattie. Zach and I laid eyes on her at the same time, seconds after the SUV settled into park. She had dirty blond hair tied up in a bun, darkly tanned skin, and wore a plaid shirt tied at the midriff. She also had on the shortest jean shorts I'd ever seen, revealing long, skinny thighs. Delia tried to hug her there in the street, before they approached the house. Evie pushed her away and said, "Moooom," in a loud and elongated way that I could hear from the tree house.

The magazine fell to the floor, the pages all curled and bent into each other. Zach elbowed past me to get a closer look.

❖

When Evie made herself at home in the room that had, up until that evening, been mine, she let loose her bun, and her hair fell down to her shoulders. She studied my CD collection, lined up on a makeshift shelf, bracketed to the wall over the bed.

"Your music really blows," she said.

I hated for clothes that had been outdoors to even touch my bed. Mom had always said beds were meant to be sanctuaries. But Evie didn't even bother taking off her sneakers before she stepped up onto the freshly laundered sheets to get closer to the CDs, and pulled out a *Room for Squares*.

I stepped closer to her. "What do you listen to?"

"Anything good." She put the CD back on the shelf but in the wrong spot. In the space for *The Black Parade*, which Zach had borrowed months ago, out of alphabetical order. "The Roots. Radiohead. Nirvana—not that Unplugged shit all the posers wanted to listen to after Kurt killed himself. Real Nirvana."

She turned around and stepped off the bed, pulling the side of the bottom sheet so it was no longer tucked in.

She faced the rest of my belongings and I readied myself for Star Wars and X-Men themed body shots, maybe a knock on the plush elephant that had progressed from a sleep companion to the object I humped three or four times a week, one side now stained with a white cloud shape.

She twisted her hair around her finger. "What do you do for fun around here?"

"Fun?"

"You've heard of it?" She batted her eyes at me in this way that she could have been flirting, but was more likely poking fun at the very idea that someone like her—female, blonde, objectively attractive— would flirt with someone like me—scrawny and unsure of himself. "Back where I'm from, we chip in for a keg, and somebody's older brother buys and hauls it out to the middle of the football field. What do you do?"

"There's Tully's." I set my sleeping clothes down on my desk and didn't know what to do with my hands. I'd never had to think about how to pose in front of someone else in my own room before—no one besides Zach or Dad, or Mom when she was still around. "It was an old drive-in movie theater. They closed it down five years back, but kids still go there to hang out and stuff."

I wanted to tell her about the October night that last fall when Ray Shabots from the AV club smuggled a projector out of the school in his backpack and set it up to show *Ghostbusters* on the big screen. We sat outside there on blankets and beach towels. Somebody brought a grill to make hot dogs and hamburgers. Zach and I ate and ate and laughed and quoted lines from the movie back at the screen. And as the screen turned to black and the credits scrolled, I lay back, hands behind my head, and stared at the almost-full moon. I smelled the dewy grass and the lavender from the detergent Zach's mom used on all of his clothes.

"Stuff," Evie repeated with an elongated *f*. "That's where kids go to hook up?"

It was true that even on that night of *Ghostbusters*, when everyone was invited, a sweetish smoke smell permeated the air, beer bottles clinked and, yes, there were dozens of couples making out. A rumor arose that Johnny Reds had nailed Candice Lawson somewhere in the darkened field, beyond the glow of the screen. It wasn't so shocking that the two would have sex—that much was assumed—but that the sex would happen so close to us boys who had never so much as held hands with a girl.

Apart from that night, I'd only been to Tully's by the light of day. Zach and I used to ride our bikes there every now and then and act out all manner of dragon-fighting, damsel-saving scenarios in the tall grass. Every now and again, enough kids would have the same idea that we could play an impromptu game of football.

Now that I was older than the kids who played there, I still went sometimes to read. Sit down a hundred yards apart from all of the hollering and games and the quiet was remarkable. I could still see the kids but it was like they were on mute.

But after dark, yes. People went to Tully's to kiss. To hump. To hook up.

"It's pretty there," I said. "Peaceful."

She turned around and shimmied off her jean shorts right there in front of me. She wore off-white panties, striped in two shades of pink. The middle of them stuck up her butt just a little. She put on her own pair of gym shorts, then turned looked over her shoulder at me. "Maybe you can show me that place sometime."

Word around town was that a big box store had bought up the lot. That any day there might be bulldozers and a taller fence put in place. I worried about taking her there on the wrong day. But summer had settled in and nothing had happened yet. There were only about six good months without frost to do any sort of demolition or construction in Shermantown, so maybe they'd wait another year. "Sure," I told her. "We'll go there sometime."

"You think your friend Zach will come along?"

The moment would have blown Zach's mind—seeing Evie's underwear and hearing her speak his name within a twenty second span.

"Sure," I said again, and scooped up my clothes again to settle into my exile in the living room. To leave her alone.

The next evening, while Dad grilled, I told Zach that Evie was pretty, but she didn't do anything for me.

He told me, "She's the kind of girl who makes a dude eat her out from behind. You know? So he has to shove his nose right up her crack. Nasty hot."

I didn't know where Zach got this stuff. Maybe his older brother, the degenerate, the only sibling who didn't have to share a room, and who'd graduated high school three years ago but still lived at home. We used to sneak into his room to steal glimpses at his VHS porn collection. The blinds were always drawn and the air always smelled sweet and stale.

Evie leaned in close to the grill maybe to sniff at the charcoal and the ground beef as they cooked. Her mother reached an arm across Evie's chest as if to protect her from the spray of burger grease, or from inhaling too much smoke. Dad didn't seem to notice Evie, just Delia, and he turned his head to give her a peck on her lips, not so different from the way he used to kiss Mom when he was busy doing something else.

"She'll hear you." I tried my best to look like I wasn't listening.

"So what if she does?" he said.

Evie looked over at me. No sign she'd heard anything, but like she was studying me. The same way she looked at me when I forgot I had to bring a change of clothes to the bathroom and left the shower with nothing but a towel around my waist. A quick scan, up and down.

"Nasty, nasty, nasty," Zach chanted.

We headed over to the old red picnic table my father had built around the same time he hammered together the boards of the treehouse. His handyman phase, Mom had called it. Zach had been visiting for dinner a lot. Once a week or so when my mother was around, and more often after. I think he sold his parents on the idea that we needed him around.

By the numbers, it wasn't as though Zach stayed for dinner more often in the two weeks since Evie had moved in. But it sure felt like it.

Dad and Delia sat down on one side of the table, burgers, chicken breasts, and charred ears of corn stacked on platters in front of them. Evie sat down on an end and Zach swooped in to take the middle seat between us. From all of our conversations I had deduced that he saw the two of us in competition for her affections. I wasn't trying, though, and assumed she'd never give either one of us a second look anyway.

Delia blew cigarette smoke out the side of her mouth, away from us. She had been smoking in the house, too, aimed out open windows but inevitably clouding up Dad's bedroom and the kitchen with that stench.

"I thought it would be nice if we said grace." Dad propped his elbows on the table, folded his hands in front of his face, and closed his eyes. Somehow I'd missed that all the little hairs on his forearm had turned as gray as the hair on his head. It was the first time I had ever heard him propose grace. "Cal, why don't you lead us?"

Zach snorted. Delia beamed and pressed her palms and her fingertips together in front of her face.

"I haven't done this much." I put up my fists, knuckle-to-knuckle.

Dad opened one eye and gave me the same look he gave me every time I mouthed off to Mom in front of him, and the same look as when the teacher called home to tell him Zach and I were cheating off each other's math homework.

So I bowed my head. "Thanks for the food, God. We appreciate it. Amen."

Delia repeated the amen. Then my father. Zach and Evie in mumbles.

My father gave me a less pointed version of the same look, as though he weren't sure if I were sassing him or if that were really the best I knew how to say grace. "I think we should also raise a glass to family coming together. You take an assortment of people and they don't always gel. But here we have no fewer than three families represented here."

Zach knocked his knee against mine. Soft enough that no one else noticed. I looked at him but he was looking down at his lap. And there, half-obscured by the red vinyl table cloth, his fingers were interlaced with Evie's. He glanced at me and smirked just enough for me to see it.

"So let's raise our glasses. To the family we choose and to togetherness."

Dad and Delia had wine glasses, cabernet poured from the box on the kitchen counter. The rest of us had blue plastic cups emblazoned with a Coca-Cola logo. We all lifted ours, touching them in zig-zag patterns so everyone made contact with everyone else. Evie hit mine hard enough to splash each of ours, to spill sticky lemonade over our hands, onto the table. Zach and I bumped knuckles, his skin hot and sweaty under the summer sun.

About a week later, Zach suggested we all go to Tully's after dark. He and I hopped the chain-link fence. He had a backpack stocked with a blanket, Granny Smith apples, and a bag of Ruffles sour cream and onion chips, but nonetheless cleared the top of the four-foot enclosure without incident. I was carrying nothing, but managed to bump my knee on the way over. It smarted, but I forced myself not to limp. Evie smirked at me anyway. She handed Zach her tote bag, mysteriously full, then propped herself to sit down on the steel bar at the top of fence, spin on her ass, and take Zach's hand as she dropped gracefully to the ground.

There were fireflies everywhere. Buzzing around, leaving traces of their glow in zig-zag patterns above the high grass. I could hear other voices in the field, but none close enough to make out what they were saying. Silhouettes against the grass, beneath the moon and stars. They could have been anyone.

We walked ten, twenty yards into the dark before Zach stopped. "Here." He unzipped the bag and spread out the red and black checkered blanket over the grass. I remembered a time when we were young enough and bored enough in his living room to take whatever we could find—books, the TV remote, his mother's little ceramic cats—and lay them down on the black squares to play a makeshift game of oversized checkers.

The blanket seemed smaller in Tully's field and it occurred to me that, barring one more growth spurt, the two of us were as big as we would ever be. That the world would soon stop shifting beneath us, and however big things seemed now was how big they would seem for the rest of our lives. The blanket hardly spread far enough for the two of us, much less Evie. I sat down with a whole leg off of it, tickled in the grass and the swarm of mosquitos I smacked at, too late every time.

They sat cross-legged on the blanket, Evie's knee propped on Zach's thigh. There was barely room for me to exist without touching one or the both of them. While Zach unloaded his snacks, Evie opened the tote bag and unveiled a little mason jar full of clear liquid. She held it up to what light there was. "It's moonshine," she said. "There's an old man back home. We all call him Uncle Roger. He makes it in his basement. Once he thinks you're old enough, he'll sell it to you five dollars a jar. No two jars taste the same." Evie tried to loosen the lid but it held fast.

"Give it here." Zach took it from her, tensing his forearms as he tugged and tugged and finally got it to turn. He set aside the lid and lifted the jar to his lips. I recalled dares from years past. I'd dared him to chug pickle juice with a scoop of mayonnaise mixed in. To eat a tooth-paste-frosted slice of American cheese. He'd always do it.

Zach gulped the stuff down as if it were cola. For a second. Then he coughed violently, spitting up half or more of what was in his mouth over the blanket, me, Evie.

Evie rubbed a hand over his back. "You never drank before, huh?"

I rubbed off his spit from my wrist onto a corner of the blanket.

Zach kept coughing and his voice came out raspy. "I've had beer before."

"Uncle Roger says it's 80 proof." Evie took the jar from him. She proceeded to drink from the jar more slowly, evenly, almost as much as

Zach had tried, her neck pulsing as the moonshine poured into her. She offered me the jar.

Zach's eyes were teary from all that coughing. He ran a forearm over them.

Neither one of them said a word, but I could already hear Zach calling me a chicken shit if I didn't at least take a sip, and Evie's laugh.

So, I drank. Just like Evie had, slow and steady. The stuff smelled like my mother's nail polish remover and burned my throat. I had to quit sooner than Evie, but I willed myself not to cough even once, just opened my mouth wide to air out the taste.

"It's good, huh?" Evie took it back and drank some more.

Zach insisted on another swig and took it slower this time. Evie tore open the chips and told us we ought to have something to soak up some of the alcohol or we'd have trouble walking the mile back home.

Evie ended up finishing the jar. Zach lay flat on his back and she propped herself up on him, left elbow on his rib cage, right hand tipping back the jar. I positioned myself half on the blanket, half in the tall grass, swatting at flies, picking off ants as they tickled my skin. Evie lay down again, head on Zach's shoulder, an arm stretched over his chest. I couldn't see what she was doing, but I imagined her massaging his bicep. He'd told me she liked his biceps.

"When my mother first told me we were moving to New York for the summer, I thought she meant the city." Evie moved and pushed out her leg so it touched mine. "I'm glad it's a place like this. Where you can hear the quiet and see the dark."

Evie rubbed her bare calf against mine till she'd pushed up the leg of my jeans, and it rubbed over my shin, soft and slow. I figured she hadn't meant to touch me. That the contact was accidental. Her skin was hot and smooth. My breath caught in my throat.

Zach started pointing out constellations. I could only assume he made up most of them—I'd never known him to have an interest in such things. His voice slurred. His finger traced a pentagon between points of light. He called that one the big house.

"It doesn't look that big," Evie said.

"It's all a matter of perspective. Perspective and distance," Zach said. "If we can see it from a million miles, it's enormous. Big enough for a mom and dad, and as many kids as they want. Guest rooms for aunts and uncles to stay without all being on top of each other. Enough space for everyone to breathe." I'd never heard him this philosophical before. That was new.

My head felt warm and ached. I could feel the weight of it every time I turned it. It occurred to me that the leg over mine could just as easily have been Zach's as it was Evie's, and maybe he was trying to mess with me. We hardly ever touched anymore, but I closed my eyes, and hoped.

I opened my eyes after a minute and looked down. It was Evie. Evie in those cutoff shorts, her legs glistening in the moonlight.

But it wasn't just her leg in motion, out there in the field. In perfect syncopation with that peculiar rhythm, there was a waving motion at Zach's crotch. I propped up my head over my forearm to get a clearer view of Evie's arm disappearing at the wrist, under Zach's belt buckle, pressed against him, stroking and kneading back and forth and back and forth and back and forth.

A minute later Zach shuddered, shaking Evie a millimeter off him, a millimeter into me so she had her butt to my hip. Evie reached a hand over her head and came back to bite into an apple. Too soft to really crunch—the fruit at Zach's house was always just a little past ripe.

Zach reached for the jar of moonshine from his side and picked it up. I thought he'd complain that it was empty—even though he'd already had too much—but instead he just held it up there to the starlight so the glass reflected and refracted all those points of light. He mumbled something about trying to catch fireflies, and then sat up and hurled in the grass.

❖

Moonshine became a fixture between the three of us. Based on how many jars of the stuff Evie produced, I was left to surmise that she was either secretly making it herself in some hideaway she had discovered in our house, or, more likely, that better than half her summer luggage had been those mason jars. She hadn't packed many clothes, for sure, wearing that same pair of shorts every single day, to the point that I could start to smell her from a few feet away—that odor of denim and stale sweat.

Zach told me he loved that smell. He told me I was crazy if I didn't, and I told him that I never said I didn't like it, just that it stood out to me. Of course I like it.

A month passed, full of lazy afternoons of passing jars over games of Monopoly on the kitchen table, or while we watched home design shows on cable. Some days we read. A Bradbury novel for me, while the two of them flipped through magazines—Dad's *Hunting & Fishing* for Evie, an issue of Delia's *Cosmo* for Zach, out of which he spoke in a falsetto, quoting suggestions for how to make sure your colors never clashed again and lines about how to please a man in bed. *Pin him down. Make him tell you he wants you.*

Evie rolled her eyes. "If a woman needs for him to say it, then either he doesn't really want her, or she's doesn't have enough respect for herself." She turned the page, and I caught a glimpse of a man posed with an oversized trout. "She shouldn't need a man to tell her anything."

When Dad got home from work and Delia got back from wherever she whiled away mornings and afternoons, Evie would disappear into the kitchen and return with glasses of her mother's sweet tea for everyone, and pass them out in the glow of the TV screen, somehow keeping straight the glasses that were just tea for the grownups, from the spiked ones for us children. The first time she did it, I purposefully spilled my glass on the floor, sure we'd get caught. But Evie and Zach played it cool, so the next time, two nights later, I did, too, and if Dad or Delia caught on, neither of them ever said anything, either too distracted with cuddling their bodies close together, or with whatever was on TV.

I knew what it meant to be a third wheel, but when neither Zach nor Evie gave me a sign to leave, I'd decided it was all in my head. That we might coexist as a trio. That Evie liked me more than I liked her, and Zach would never turn away his best friend. And no one would ever know why I preferred it to be just me and Zach alone.

The three of us drank together in the treehouse, under daylight, until one day—the end of July, early August—when the wood creaked too badly beneath the weight of our bodies, and I complained it wasn't safe.

Zach took a long swig from the jar. Practiced now. Able to hold his liquor. "If you're so worried about it, you can leave us alone."

Evie reclined, ankles crossed, her neck in the crook of Zach's elbow.

So I climbed down.

A week later, Zach started stocking shelves at Chandler's Grocery. His mom had been bugging him to find a job since school let out, telling him he was sixteen years old and he ought to start earning his keep. Finally, she found the gig for him through a friend. He started disappearing for days at a time to work, with the promise that he'd purpose some of his income for candy bars and potato chips, maybe an outing to the movies for the three of us.

"Not another nudy mag?" I asked him.

He socked me good on the shoulder. Evie laughed.

One afternoon, he was working, my father was at the office, and Delia was window shopping at the mall. I was reading *Brave New World*, when Evie ran up to me where I sat on the couch and punted my book square out of my hands.

"What the hell?" I said.

"I'm bored." She shrugged and folded her hands in front of her and knocked knees. The very image of a pouting school girl.

I recovered the book and smoothed out the yellowed pages. "Why don't you try reading?"

"Boring," she said, dragging out the O-sound. She bundled her hair behind her as if to form a ponytail and then let it drop. "Why don't we go bug Zach at work?"

"How do you think you're going to get there?"

"We could walk."

I scanned the page to figure out where I had left off. I set quotas for my reading. Tried to get through at least fifty pages each summer day. But since Evie arrived, I'd been lucky to get twenty. "It's five miles away."

She tore the book from me. Fast enough that I couldn't even let go of it in time, and the page I'd been open to ripped, the top half dangling at a misfit angle.

I got to my feet and stood close enough to loom. I could smell the moonshine on her breath but wasn't sure if she was drunk. "What's your problem?"

"I told you, I'm bored."

"Give me back my book."

"Make me."

I reached for the book, but she moved it out of the way so I stumbled, and had to put out my hands to the floor to keep myself from falling all the way over. I stood up. Flushed.

And she slapped me. Hard. Across the cheek. Stiffer than play.

And I shoved her.

She fell on her ass.

I was scared I'd hurt her. Ready to apologize. To take my book back and go outside to the treehouse and cede the world indoors.

But she crouched and sprang forward, driving her shoulder into my gut, hooking the backs of my knees with her hands.

My fingers clenched her biceps and I had flashes of the wrestling matches that Zach and I had had in years past. The point when hot skin turned slippery with sweat and we jostled for position in go-behinds and headlocks at an age when I didn't know what a boner meant but instinctively hoped Zach didn't notice mine.

She wrapped her thighs around my ribs and squeezed, got me on my back and scooted up on me until she had her denim-covered crotch poised three or four inches from my chin, where all I could smell was her and I almost retched. "Admit it."

I tried to sit up, but she pressed her full weight on me, had my shoulders pinned to the carpet below. "Admit what?"

"You're jealous of Zach." She scooted off my shoulders, shins still weighing against my upper arms, jean shorts hovering over my mouth and nose. An inch of breathing space. "You want me."

I pressed my feet to the floor and bridged up, arching my back, pelvis in the air. Caught her off balance and rolled. Knelt on top of her left thigh and pinned her wrists over her head. I caught a little of her hair in my fingers in the process and tugged. "I want you out of my house."

She went slack for a second. I let go of one wrist and the tangle of hair from my hand. She moved the hand down and I though she meant to elbow me in the ribs or coil around me and flip me over the way Zach had found ways to do dozens of times in the past. But she moved too slowly for that and touched too softly. Slid her hand under my waist band and felt around. She smiled when she made contact, when she found me hard.

She kicked off her shorts. I was still on top of her, but there was little question that she was in control and that little of what was happening was new for her. She rubbed me the same way she had Zach back at Tully's, until I started to grind against her myself. I heard the pattern of Zach's breathing that night. I tried to match it.

She got my shorts and my boxers off in the same jerking motion. Got on top of me again. Straddling me. Grinding clockwise to my counter. Until everything went hot and wet. Until she hugged me tight and rolled me back on top of her and took my penis in her hand again to guide me inside.

In between sensations, in between blindness and stillness and feeling nothing in the world above my waist, a terror took hold of me— that I might get Evie pregnant. I didn't have any condoms. I didn't even know where to get one. I knew Zach had some. He'd opened a pack of twenty in front of me once, the clear plastic wrapping all connected in a chain that descended from his hand to the floor, unfurling and unfurling. That pang of something like jealousy that I felt in my gut, not because he had condoms and not that he might have sex before me. Jealousy of someone else, someone who didn't yet exist in our world. The way he had smiled, teeth stained with Coca-Cola residue, at the promise of all of that sex that awaited him. A lifetime of orgasms ahead.

Evie recognized what was happening before I did. She took my shoulder in one hand, the base of my penis in the other, and pulled me out. Just as the semen burbled out over the back of her hand and over her pubic hair and on the carpet. Just as I could breathe again.

I expected her to look smug. Superior, that she could make me do this. Vindicated that I had wanted her all along.

But she didn't smile. Her lower lip trembled like she might cry. "Why did you close your eyes?"

My chest heaved. Sweat soaked my T-shirt. I pushed away memories and imaginings. I pushed away Zach and focused my eyes on Evie. "Did I?"

"You didn't look at me." She scooped up her clothes and ran for the bathroom.

❖

One day, Delia and Evie were there. Dad was happy. Zach was my best friend. The next day, the Evie and her mother were packing.

"We talked about it." My father flipped burgers for one last dinner as a family of five.

I stood by him. Inside, Delia fixed a pitcher of lemonade from a pouch and tap water. Zach had his arm over Evie's shoulder, sitting on the ground at the opposite end of the yard.

"It's crazy, I get it," Dad said. "We're grownups. She's got obligations. A summer's fine. A vacation. But she can't just up and move her whole life. And neither can I." He ran a knuckle under his nose and stared into the smoke. I thought he looked disappointed, but also a little relieved—like at least he could go back to wandering the house bare-chested and only have me to worry about if he got a beer with the guys after work. "We had a nice summer, end of story."

Delia had dark rings under her eyes and her hair had grown frizzy in the late summer humidity. She poured the lemonade in careless, sloshing motions, one after the next, each threatening to overflow its glass.

I figured Delia and Evie would stay the night at least, but they had other plans. My father held Delia's elbows, stood chest to chest in the yard after dinner. Said they should wait. Get a good night's sleep.

Delia was crying. But she held firm. Said they could reach Pennsylvania before midnight if they left right then, and her girlfriend would put them up for the night.

Zach and Evie ventured an open-mouthed, sloppy kiss in the driveway. She pulled away from him first. He kept his hand on her hip until he had his arm fully extent, fingers stretched. Until he had no choice but to let her go.

Delia hugged me. Evie didn't say goodbye, or even look my way. And they were gone.

Zach stopped coming over. His excuses varied: he told me he had to work all the time, and then that he had too much homework after school started, and his mom was riding him because he would have to apply to college soon, so he had to get his grades in shape and starting making teachers like him if they were going to write letters of recommendation. Parts of this were true, I was sure.

I pressed him one time, asking him what I had done.

"Dude, she was my girlfriend," he said.

I wanted to tell him Evie hadn't meant anything to me, and I was happy she was gone because he was too good for her anyway. I wanted to tell him I missed him. But it was one of those times when there were too many words running through my head to make space for any of them to come out of my mouth, and he had walked away before I said a thing.

We still had the same circle of friends. We all ate lunch at the same table. But I hardly ever talked to Zach alone anymore, and I never saw him after dark.

My English teacher, Mrs. Chester, said we should start thinking early about college application essays, and offered ten points of extra credit for anyone who turned in a personal reflection about an important place. After a night of chemistry homework, I wasted an hour picking at that paper. I thought of Tully's and remembered a time before I'd met Evie. That night we'd all snuck into the field. The way the moonlight fell over Zach's face and how close we sat—close enough to feel each other's body heat, and for me to imagine that he liked it, too.

But when I finally set pen to paper, I found myself writing about the church I hadn't attended since I was ten. I wrote about the way sunlight got refracted when it shone through stained glass windows. I wrote about kneelers that buckled beneath the weight of growing boys. I wrote about old bibles—those dusty books with the gold edges on every page that I had to assume used to be shiny.

Mrs. Chester read it aloud to the class as an exemplar. I picked my cuticles and only looked at Zach once. He was resting his cheek on his forearms, fast asleep, or at least faking it.

THE GAY RESTAURANTS OF NEW YORK

William Moeck

Café Sphinx
416 Lafayette Street (btwn. Astor & E. 4th)
Dinner, 6:00 p.m. to 3:00 a.m.
Closed Sundays
505-1728
$$

A tow-headed youth solemnly deposits before us an iced cold plate of fish slices floating in a pool of purple liquid. He is dressed head to toe in black, and he disappears into the mist generated by a dry-ice machine near the kitchen door. Banks of fog drift across the dining room where other androgynous servers can be seen moving with hypnotic slowness. The air is filled with voices, their murmur beyond the reach of understanding. For the face of each speaker is obscured by the wing back chair in which it is cradled, and tall tabletop candelabras cast individual features into shadows. In the gloom the chairs, slip-covered to the floor in red muslin, appear as sarcophagi nestling sacrificial victims. Flickering torchères burn strategically on the room's perimeter, and they contribute to the sense of a secret and mysterious rite taking place. For Café Sphinx raises the standards for dining in New York to sublime new heights, I think, and experiences such as these confirm the notion that city's fickle cultural life depends on consuming the past.

"O brave new world," I cried, "with such smoked salmon in it!"

"That looks vile," said Paul Bridgewater, squinting through owlish black eyeglasses at the appetizer. Sampling a slice of fish sitting in a sauce made from *crème de cassis* and raspberries, Paul uttered his verdict with finality: "Not only has the salmon been refrigerated for so long that it has lost all taste, but the currants disguise any flavor it might ever have had. It's a completely disgusting dish, but try it, you must, if only for professional reasons." Paul was wearing a black woolen skirt for men, black turtleneck, and black beret.

I poured Perrier from the bottle on our table into a glass filled with ice and a lime wedge. Paul's position as headwaiter of an upscale American restaurant in midtown entitled him to speak with arrogance about food, wine, and service when the two of us dined out. And since Paul usually paid the bill, I had to take his opinions seriously. But as a budding restaurant critic, I was not afraid to contradict him when I felt he was dismissive about our gustatory experiences, and I frequently disagreed with him in print since Paul seldom read my reviews.

"I should try my liver first," I protested. Re-adjusting the tall candelabra with its five dripping pillars, I took another look at the pistachio- and jalapeño-encrusted *pâté de foie gras* that had been served fifteen minutes earlier. The same sad and solemn waiter, whose tousled blond hair was set off by streaks of blue in the longer strands, had brought me the goose liver in advance of Paul's salmon. But a Beaujolais ordered at the same time was still nowhere in evidence. Paul was meanwhile regaling me with recent exploits in Central Park's Rambles, where his wallet and keys had been stolen.

A stalactite of wax detached itself from the candelabra and fell into the ashtray. With a boredom both exquisite and excessive, Paul lit a cigarette as I held my fork in front of me like a divining rod. First from the top and then from the sides, I gingerly prodded the uneven brown rectangle flecked with red and green, and which was encircled by toast points of a dubious crispness. I silently pondered its medley of flavors before taking a notebook from my breast pocket. Jotting a phrase or two, I gulped down a mouthful of water.

Café Sphinx was the hottest new restaurant below Fourteenth Street. One couldn't expect genteel service or fine cuisine to supplant the thrill of elbowing the style-makers and glitterati vying there for attention. The goal of eating at Sphinx was, after all, not to dine well but to be able to say one had gotten a table at all, and Paul knew the unpublished number needed for procuring reservations. The restaurant was nominally sold out each night except to members of a downtown elect, and while Paul was not any sort of celebrity, his connections in the business lent him authority. Like many employed by the service industry in New York City, Paul envisioned his real center of existence to be elsewhere.

That actors figure prominently among waiters is a myth. Few of Paul's associates sought a career in the limelight, and most were committed to vocations lying outside the traditional boundaries of the arts. True, there was a skilled pianist seeking a livelihood as an accompanist, but there was also a doll collector saving money to open a shop in Paris with her French husband. There was an amphetamine-addicted poker enthusiast, and a railroad buff who applied periodically with the MTA for engineer positions. Most of Paul's colleagues were without professional interest in the food and wine they served, he said, and the only one who planned someday to open his own place was regarded by his peers as a bit of freak. Too zealous a concern with customer service was thought odd even by Paul, who had had unofficial business cards printed identifying his calling to be not that of *Headwaiter*, but *Aesthete*.

Emerging from the billowy mist came the sad-looking waiter, bearing a single wine glass and open bottle of Moulin-à-Vent. Wearing a pout of concentration, he bent low pouring a half glass for Paul to sample. Azure locks of hair separated themselves from the others and dangled down disconsolately before they could be smoothed into place. I lit a Rothman from the open pack on the table and watched, considering how best to forestall Paul's ire. He shooed away an offered nibble of *foie gras* though more than a nibble remained on my plate. Consulting my notes, I praised the dish's original combination of flavors.

"The nut and pepper crust," I said, "creates a piquant foil for the richness of the goose, which is the perfect consistency." The liver unlike Paul's cold salmon had been correctly served at room temperature though I exaggerated the harmony of the flavors.

Paul sniffed from his glass of 1984 Georges Duboeuf Moulin-à-Vent. It was the cheapest bottle on Café Sphinx's list, where it was described as fruity, dry, and light-bodied. Paul thought restaurants had an obligation to educate consumers about wine and that the wine list was the best place to teach novices about the salient characteristics of different varietals. But he also believed that it was important to charge a reasonable price if wine was to become more than a status symbol in the States. The average bottle should cost as much as a typical dinner entrée, Paul opined, a fair mark-up hovering around 100%, or double that of retail. But the $30 Duboeuf at Sphinx would have cost less than $10 at even a high-end merchant like Sherry-Lehman's.

Paul nodded his approval to the waiter, whose eyes failed to register an impression when a giant globule of half-congealed wax dropped onto the uneaten toast points.

"This place is hot in more ways than one," I said, removing my navy blazer to pick at tiny droplets of wax splashed on the sleeve. The waiter unapologetically poured Beaujolais into my water glass, and I said, "I wonder if Sphinx means Odeon's days are numbered." Odeon was another fashionable restaurant.

"Bullshit," Paul snorted. "I'd much rather go to Odeon. That is an abomination," he said, indicating the liver.

Redirecting the conversation, I asked, "What did you tell Stephen about your wallet?" Stephen Western was Paul's older lover, a professor who was more role model than sugar daddy, Paul insisted. Paul moved in with Stephen two years after graduating from the college where Paul and I had met.

"I told the Squire my bag was stolen on the subway," Paul answered, turning the bottle so the label faced him. The Squire was his nickname for Stephen.

"I told him I was going to the Strawberry Fields dedication," he said. The two-acre tract in Central Park commemorated the former Beatles member slain nearby. His widow and Mayor Koch inaugurated the site on what would have been Lennon's fortieth birthday.

"And that I was returning library books on the way," Paul continued. "I put my shoulder bag under the seat, and the six train was so packed at rush hour, I didn't notice it missing until Forty-Second."

Stephen believed all that? I wondered. Like the idea of wearing flip-flops in Times Square, the idea of putting personal possessions on the floor of the subway made me cringe. I shook my head sympathetically.

"The problem wasn't the wallet," Paul continued, fishing two ice cubes with his fork from my glass and transferring them into his own. "It only had ten dollars. The problem was that my keys were in the bag with my wallet and driver's license." He paused. "I had to walk eighty blocks downtown before I could cancel the credit cards and get the locks changed! Forget about Yoko!" With lively brown eyes and long dark hair, Paul had been humiliated by toughs when growing up in Middletown, New York. He wore ugly glasses now as if to make fun of himself.

"Wow!" I wished we had more ice.

"And it's a good thing!" Paul added. "I was already at work when the Squire returned, and he could tell our expensive alarm system had been tampered with. But whoever it was, wasn't able to get in. That's because the super called a locksmith to replace the tumblers when I got home. But the guy—this hunky Cuban number with green eyes—said to reset the keyed alarm would involve a whole new system." Stephen's two-bedroom apartment with roof-deck—but no doorman—was on East Tenth Street off Third Avenue.

"Was it worth it?" I queried, referring to the sex and not the alarm system. Pushing away the salmon, Paul lit another cigarette. Café Sphinx offers a range of main courses from *Magret de Canard* to Monkfish Newburg, but Paul had insisted we commit only to starters and on seeing afterwards how we felt about more food. Our waiter was too dejected to deter us from this strategy, and it seemed unlikely without second courses having been ordered that he was going to clear our appetizer plates strewn with wax. I sensed I was not going to get to try the *Tarte Tatin. Too bad*, I thought, *pastry was my specialty.*

"Best morning fuck in months," said Paul, looking me straight in the eye. "Big Latino postman and with a dick like this," he added, using his thumb and forefinger to indicate a surreal girth. Paul never spared details when it came to describing his anonymous sexual encounters even though he knew how squeamish I was about vulgarity. Yet Paul was strangely reticent when it came to discussing private moments with Stephen, his shyness probably resulting from my familiarity with them as a couple. For Stephen and I shared multiple interests: he was a tenured English professor at New York University, and I was enrolled at the Graduate Center of the City University of New York. Stephen's specialty was in medieval literature, and mine was early twentieth-century poetry.

Stephen's day classes took him out of the apartment early, allowing Paul to fool around before his night shift at the restaurant began. Paul sometimes went to the gym, and he sometimes went to the movies, but on the most recent Wednesday morning in October, Paul said, he slipped on a cock ring after Stephen left. Exchanging his eyeglasses for contact lenses, Paul admired the profile in the mirror of his erect member under a pair of taut jeans. He added a t-shirt, torn denim jacket, and a pair of red sneakers to complete the look. He headed uptown with an orange vinyl shoulder bag containing condoms, postcards, and a paperback copy of *Bleak House*. And at an hour when most New Yorkers have not yet had second cups of coffee, Paul was standing in a wooded grove in Central Park, bent at the waist with his jeans around his knees.

"The Fiorucci bag?" I commiserated, remembering how Paul used to carry books in it at Rutgers. This past Wednesday, however, Paul had unwisely stowed wallet and keys in it, he said, because they interrupted the outline his groin traced on his jeans. And more unwisely yet, he secreted the shoulder bag under low hanging bushes at the entrance to the Rambles, an area in Central Park popular with homosexual prowlers. I marveled at Paul's shamelessness.

"It did enjoy a distinguished history," confirmed Paul, "and I panicked the minute I discovered it missing. I didn't have a dime to call Stephen."

"But why didn't you keep it?"

"For what purpose, Walter?" asked Paul, annoyed at my idiocy when his own vanity was invisible. "So I could whip out my Dickens to show what I was reading?" Paul had hidden the bag because it did not fit the persona he was trying to project. With high cheek bones and delicate features, Paul was too pretty to be a hustler, but that morning he wanted to be seen as rough trade ready for semi-public sex. Paul preferred at other times, paradoxically, to wear Gaultier skirts and read Victorian novels, his fear of being middle-brow resulting in wild oscillations between ultra-fastidiousness and ultra-recklessness.

I held my glass up to the candelabra. "Thibault-Liger it is not," I said, invidiously comparing the Duboeuf to a recherché producer whose Beaujolais we had savored at La Récolte on 110 East 49th Street. But Paul was not paying attention and sat abstracted from his own snobbishness. Looking at his wristwatch, he signaled the waiter unsuccessfully for the bill.

"Look at him. If he went any slower, he'd be moving backwards."

"Don't you want to know the desserts they have?" I asked innocently.

"Like what? Vanilla ice-cream topped with anchovies?" he cracked. "The only thing I want to know is whom you have to fuck around here to get a check," he added sarcastically, emphasizing the m in whom. We had both been English majors at Rutgers.

Mr. Melancholy, who seemed to be ignoring us on purpose, was collecting plates nearby. When Paul finally caught his attention, the waiter brought the bill, and a few minutes later I watched Paul leave him an extravagant tip. As Paul was filling out the voucher, I wondered whether I, too, should be having anonymous sex in the park. There didn't seem to be any other way of meeting eligible bachelors except by having sex, but the very idea made me nervous. The press last week had reported the death from AIDS of Hollywood actor Rock Hudson. Two of Paul's coworkers had been stricken with the gay plague, and when a friend of mine passed away unexpectedly, I could not bury my head in the sand and pretend the disease was not spiraling nearer.

I also had less Paul's personality than that of the Squire, who turned forty before he realized his marriage wasn't working and started sowing his wild oats. I had once toyed with bisexuality under the misapprehension that complexity was sexy in and of itself. And moving to Manhattan emboldened me to think of myself as gay but without accepting all the ramifications. I shied away from going out alone, and when corralled into having drinks at Uncle Charlie's Downtown or The Works, I felt insecure. Guys there seemed they spent their days lifting weights and perfecting their outfits while I had neither money nor inclination to go clothes shopping or join a gym. Most of what I knew about fashion was gleaned from Paul, who edited my wardrobe.

The other problem was that I was average-looking, with only big brown eyes and a disarming smile to my credit. My long smooth neck let me pass for younger than my years, but my ears stuck out and my nose was as beaky as T.S. Eliot's. My hair was thinning, and I lacked the confidence needed for picking up guys. By age thirty my sex life would have made for a poor pornographic novel, and the one person I met recently who interested me I feared to be heterosexual.

"Look, there's Gael Greene," Paul cooed as we made our way haltingly through a dense patch of fog. Presiding over a curtained table near the exit sat a large blousy woman with stringy brown hair and no make-up. Paul was talented at spotting celebrities, and he had once identified to me a hunched-over octogenarian at Rounds, the hustler bar on 303 East 53rd Street, as pianist Vladimir Horowitz.

"Shall I introduce you?" Paul asked.

"Please don't," I pleaded. Ms. Greene was *New York Magazine*'s restaurant critic.

"Why not? She's nothing to be afraid of. She's—oh!—she's with Tom," Paul added with a sharp intake of breath as we drew near. Ms. Greene was surrounded by an entourage of handsome dark men sporting studded leather gear. They must have been making a pit stop on the way to The Saint, said Paul *sotto voce*, who blew air kisses and waved affectedly to one massively muscular man. His ripe lips, opening like a budded flower between unshaven cheeks and chin, called out Paul's name, "Bridgewater!"

The air outside Sphinx's unmarked door was clear and cold. Paul said, "Let's go to Odeon next month. What's the second Friday in November?"

"Wasn't that big guy the underwear model in Times Square?"

"Yes," Paul answered, "and Tom looks best with no underwear."

"How do you know him?"

"From the gym. He used to be an Olympic pole-vaulter. His parents are Polish."

My pulse quickened. "How come you don't want to go out with them?" I asked mournfully. Lurid rumors about the Saint's balcony made me conflate dancing there with sex.

"I'm working lunch. Pete Peterson is coming, and Milton Goldman with Hermione Gingold." He paused. "But you should go. I'll introduce you. Gael's a real pussycat. She writes literary smut."

"I can't. I just collected five sets of student essays. Plus, I need to revise my introduction." Plus, I would have been terrified.

We ambled over to the Astor Place subway stop, and he said

rhetorically, "I trust you're going to give Café Sphinx the shitty rating it deserves?"

"Do you know who designed it?" I asked evasively. Not only could Paul spot every critic, but he could tick off the names of chefs as easily as the persons who designed their restaurants.

"Zachy Sherif."

"He may not be Adam Tihany," I said, "but he has a flair for theatrics. Even if Sphinx's food is lousy, I've never seen any place like it. Remember what Ezra Pound used to say: you have to 'Make it new!' In recreating tradition, every new restaurant destroys the past."

"Sphinx not only destroys the past; it sabotages the future."

"Well, I say it's both good and original."

"Yes, but you know what Samuel Johnson said," Paul retorted. "What's good about Sphinx is not original, and what's original about it is not good."

"Samuel Johnson is dead, Paul, but we're alive, and the energy at Sphinx tonight was palpable! Dining out doesn't get any more exciting! Isn't it the reason you came to New York?"

"Speak for yourself, Walter. I came to New York to be a poet." Paul hesitated as if uncertain whether to head directly north the two blocks to his apartment on Tenth Street. "And, remember, you're an aspiring restaurant critic now," he said, "not a cultural anthropologist. I will never speak to you again if you give Café Sphincter any stars."

It was Paul's idea that I was to be a restaurant critic instead of a college professor, and that the restaurants I reviewed should be gay. While I wasn't about to jettison my unfinished dissertation, I did enjoy dining out if somebody else paid, and I was fairly knowledgeable about desserts, which I had taught myself how to make as an adolescent. But my credentials to be a restaurant critic were scarcely better than those of Seymour Britchky, who famously said his primary qualification for writing reviews was his habit of eating three meals a day.

Paul had moved to New York to be a poet, but something happened once he got here. He spent less time fabricating villanelles than he did going to clubs, where he soon began telling people he was a novelist. After moving in with Stephen, he started identifying himself vaguely as a writer instead of a novelist. And by the time he was promoted to oversee the dining room in midtown where he currently worked, Paul retreated further into obscurity by saying that he was an aesthete. Yet Paul invested less effort in contemplating beauty, it seemed to me, than he did in slinging hash, even if it was hash topped with beluga caviar.

At Astor Place I pecked Paul goodbye on the cheek. He looked lingeringly in the direction of Second Avenue while I consulted the agenda at the back of my notebook to verify the date of the second Friday in November. Standing at the top of the stairs going down to the 6 train, I hollered: "Odeon. Friday. November 8th."

"Nine o'clock," he called back, setting off on the more circuitous route. I meant to ask him about bringing along John but forgot.

❖

Odeon
145 West Broadway (btwn. Thomas & Duane)
Lunch, Monday to Friday, 12:00 p.m. to 2:00 p.m.
Brunch, Sunday 11:00 a.m. to 4:00 p.m.
Dinner, Monday to Saturday, 6:00 p.m. to 1:30 a.m.
233-0507
$$

The blocks below Canal Street are deserted late autumn once the commuters depart for the boroughs and the businesses pull down their gates. Outside, the neighborhood feels chill and desolate, but inside restaurant Odeon, the Bartlett pear poached in red wine and topped with nuts is a dessert guaranteed to warm the heart of every patron. Slightly resistant to the pressure of a knife and fork, the expertly cooked pear is perfectly complemented by the subtle tartness of a red wine reduction, and its crown of toasted walnuts is redolent of autumn.

The limousines double-parked outside the restaurant, which is housed in a former Tribeca cafeteria and named after a London movie-theater franchise, attest to how Odeon is chic as well as authentic. The Depression-era murals are counterfeits, of course, but the menu's bistro food updated with *nouvelle-cuisine* accents is the real McCoy. Delectable country salads of frisée, poached egg, croutons, and lardons, set the stage for two different main courses: five plump sea scallops sautéed in a mustard sauce for me, and a seared tuna steak reposing on a bed of spiced lentils for Paul. What was there not to like?

"Too much cinnamon," said Paul loudly. Poached pear was not a dessert I was qualified to judge, so I did not balk at his scruple.

"I told you to order the *crème brûlée*," Paul said. "I'm going to get one anyway, just in case your pal ever shows up." Flagging down our server, Paul requested the additional dessert and two snifters of chilled Poire Williams *eau de vie*. Paul and I were supposed to have had dinner with a friend of mine who had accepted the invitation but failed to show up.

Excellent food is served at Odeon by solicitous staff members although Paul's late November outfit could not help but command the entire dining room's attention. He wore a red bowtie, white linen suit, and straw boater when the weather called for tweeds. Removing the Corbusier frames to run fingers through his hair, Paul pushed back his chair and crossed one leg over the other. He exuded the air of a contented dandy.

Our server—Paul said *waitress* was frowned upon—was a very short woman whose close-cropped, copper-colored hair warned flattery would be useless. Introduced as an ex-colleague, Jezebel Johnson teetered precariously in platform shoes with the extra dessert, uncertain where to situate it.

"Please, here, darling" said Paul familiarly, pointing to the untouched place-setting. On the seat of the empty rattan chair sat Paul's hat, and over its back was hung the curved end of a mahogany stick. Paul broke the blackened, sugary crust of the *crème brûlée* to scoop out a spoonful, saying, "George won't mind, I'm sure, if I practice some quality control."

"John."

"How long have you known him?"

"Only since last year. I was reading Pound's letters at the library," I said, "and John was helpful at finding his correspondence with Eliot." John Milton was curator of a special collection bequeathed to The New York Public Library by bachelor physicians, Henry W. and Albert A. Berg, who had amassed important holdings in nineteenth- and twentieth-century literature. My dissertation involved researching responses to poetry by Ezra Pound, the expat American who served as midwife to T.S. Eliot's "The Waste Land," less-well known perhaps than *Cats*.

"You should see John's office. He has a desk and chair that once belonged to Dickens!"

"Damn, this is good," Paul said after another spoonful. "You're attracted to him?" Paul knew I had not been with anyone for over a year, and he was always trying to pressure me into having a fling even with people I hardly knew. "What's John Milton like?"

"He's nice. Quiet. Normal," I said, averting my gaze from Paul's woven leather Ferragamo's. "He's from Garden City, but he studied at Cambridge and writes poetry."

"With that name, how could he help it? Of course, you're attracted to him. Why else would you have invited him?"

"Okay."

"Does he work out?"

"How should I know?"

"What does he look like?"

"Your height. Mid- to late-thirties. Long, brown hair. Nice face." John was not as effetely pretty as Paul, but they were not wholly dissimilar. John did something odd when pronouncing his *R*s, though, something in the way of a roll or trill.

"You've been to his apartment?"

"Yes, but I'm not sure he's gay," I said shyly. "He used to be married."

John and I had developed the habit over the summer of walking north on Madison Avenue after the Fifth Avenue library closed. I lived in a walk-up at 1869 Second Avenue, and John had the ground-floor rear in a tenement on First Avenue in the Fifties. One August evening, when John usually turned at Fifty-Third, he asked me to join him for drinks. The hour was still light, but the dry cleaner's and the pet store flanking his building had closed for the day. His apartment had lots of books and a nice stereo, but a bean bag chair and lava lamp in the living room, and popcorn maker and can of Raid in the kitchen, suggested fine dining wasn't a priority.

John showed me his collection of vintage fountain pens and a framed photograph of his favorite daughter, Deborah, and we discussed the effect of the dislocations of the First World War on Modernist writers. The dogs in the kennels at the back of the pet store began barking as the apartment grew dark, and I asked if he was bothered by the sound, audible from both rooms, and which he said lasted all evening. The sound had become a kind of white noise to him, he said, affording an oceanic feeling that connected him to the universe. I gathered John earned a good income, and he was insightful and encouraging about my intellectual work. But he seemed lost and lonely somehow, and it was important to me—I don't know why—that Paul liked him.

"Means nothing," said Paul.

"Jill Krementz used to live in his apartment," I continued. "John gets her junk mail all the time." I don't know why I hoped such trivia would paint him in a more interesting light, yet I didn't want Paul to think I was interested in Milton solely as a sex partner.

"We talked about books," I said. "He knows about music and has *Lohengrin* tickets. Birgit Nilsson is his idol, and I was sure you two would hit it off." I had only started getting to know John, and once the semester began, I saw him less and less. A glance at Paul's shoes made me wonder if he feared not fitting in. He had had a week in which he could have canceled.

"Just remember, plenty of married men like to take it up the old wazoo when the little woman isn't looking," Paul said coarsely, "although I don't know about him." Paul was skeptical since John's sexual orientation was not more visibly imprinted on my description. "How long has he lived in New York? Is it possible he got lost below Canal?"

"I don't know." John was almost three hours late.

"Where does he live?"

"Beekman Place," I said inaccurately.

"Nice," said Paul, taking a cigarette. It was Paul's theory that you could tell as much about someone in New York from his or her address as you could from clothes. "I used to fantasize about living in the Fifties. Bloomingdale's used to be a big pick-up scene."

"John is not as interested in fashion as you are," I said. "But you might get feedback from him if you sent him poems." Paul used to write lyrics on the back of postcards he sent to friends, but the frequency had let up. I had a shoebox full of them, which he referred to as sonnets though they didn't rhyme and the metrical scheme was undecipherable. Their content was also strange: the kind of utterance that might result if the Oracle of Delphi were crossed with *I Love Lucy* dialogue. They made good bookmarks, at any rate.

Sipping his digestif, Paul looked about at, nodding at an Art-Deco sconce. "Flattering lighting. At Café Luxembourg everyone look fabulous, too. They must use pink bulbs," he reasoned. Café Luxembourg at 200 West 70th Street was Odeon's sister restaurant, feeding conductor James Levine and the post-Lincoln Center crowd. Each place was a success, but Odeon's more challenged location below Canal Street gave it a special cachet, and the thick-slatted window blinds created the impression that something risqué was taking place within. Yet diners in New York were notoriously fickle, I argued, predicting Odeon's demise for lack of dependable neighborhood traffic.

"Odeon might have to close if Patrick died," Paul ceded, referring to the chef. "But until that day, it's the center of the known universe." New York City's Commissioner for Cultural Affairs, Henry Geldzahler, was seated at the table opposite with a man in a top hat, who sported an ebony stick too short to be a spear but too long to be a cane. It was even nicer than Paul's.

Glancing at the hat, Paul crowed, "That's Count Smorltork."

"Who?"

"A magician."

"Oh," I said. Eyeing the thin red and blue stripes running through Paul's white suit, I asked, "Did anyone tell you, you look like a circus ringmaster?" I was wearing a blue Brooks Brothers blazer with white button-down shirt.

"It's Kenzo," Paul said. "Don't hate me because I'm beautiful."

"I'll try not to." Paul had dressed ostentatiously at college since New Brunswick was close enough to Manhattan for him to squander his parents' generous allowance on shopping excursions. He was a regular customer at Charivari, a high-end clothing boutique, and he studied *Gentleman's Quarterly* long before menswear news went mainstream. Paul sported black Ray-Ban eyeglasses then, about five years before retro made its comeback, and he would wear unconstructed wool jackets with pleated trousers to the dining hall where he would try to impress upon school chums the revolutionary importance of Armani's first clothing line for Barneys in 1976.

I remembered Paul speaking about up-and-coming designers such as Calvin Klein and Perry Ellis, who used natural fabrics when department store brands were constructed mostly out of synthetics. Older, established manufacturers had been guilty of utilizing inferior-grade materials, Paul said, and Pierre Cardin's line was as phony as Aunt Jemima products. Younger designers, on the other hand, were embracing a whole new aesthetic with all-natural fabrics. The food industry had similarly started demonizing artificial ingredients, and Polysorbate 80 was nothing but polyester writ large, Paul prophesied, at a time when Häagen-Dazs was sold chiefly as health food.

But the use of cashmere and silk in the late 70s represented less the recovery of an artisanal craft to Paul than it did the politicization of the everyday. Newer designers were redirecting the course of fashion with their sexuality as much as with fabric, and quotidian activities such as getting dressed in the morning were opportunities for Paul to proclaim his sexual orientation. His sartorial obsessions were a function of his gay identity, Paul asserted, which informed all his elitist inclinations. His passion for wine, opera, and all things Eurocentric was an extension of what he did in bed, and a corollary of this theory prescribed his flight from the lawn sprinklers and station wagons of suburbia. Paul interpreted the lawlessness of late 70's New York as a blank slate upon which gays were licensed to impose a new world order.

Maybe I had been lucky growing up, or better able to hide behind a shield of invisibility, but I was skeptical about Paul's account of manifest destiny. For the line he drew between cause and effect seemed to me to have been possibly gotten backwards. Perhaps it was a vagary of nurture, rather than nature's iron rule that had inflected Paul's sexuality in one direction rather than the other. Paul's father was aloof, of course, his mother pampered him, and he was bullied by teenagers. But these details may not have signified a homosexual gene at play so much as they were contingent upon Paul's emergent sense of being different, a misfit. An encounter with a Times Square transvestite when Paul was in high school maybe only reinforced more elemental differences—his flair for language and musical gifts—that more truly set Paul apart from peers. When we resumed our friendship in 1980, Paul was shacked up with Stephen and had exchanged Ray-Bans for pink *Colors in Optics* frames.

A frosty bottle of Poire Williams arrived after the first snifters, courtesy of a startlingly tall, Slavic-looking server with luminous blue eyes. "Hi Paul, how are you?" he said coolly.

"Keith is offering you more Poire."

"Thanks, Timmy. I guess this means we're footing the rest of the bill?" Paul asked drily.

Timmy laughed, showing teeth prematurely yellowed with tobacco stains and a front incisor marred by a chip, and refilled our snifters with the icy liquid.

"Let me introduce Walter Grony," Paul said. "He's a restaurant critic."

Timmy looked at me with curiosity, perhaps on account of my Polish name, and I trembled before his beauty. Paul turned to me, saying, "Walter, This is Timmy."

"Hi," I smiled humbly. "Are you from One Fifth, too?" One Fifth Avenue was a restaurant with a nautical theme on the corner of Eighth Street where Paul had worked after Rutgers. Once a hang-out for Andy Warhol and his retinue, as well as a watering hole for the cast and crew members of the television show, *Saturday Night Live*, One Fifth had once been hot. But its popularity was eclipsed by Odeon, which Keith, One Fifth's general manager, had opened with his girlfriend and brother. The three took with them a sizable portion of One Fifth's staff—including Jezebel—while Paul had resisted blandishments to jump ship. When it became clear that One Fifth ceased being a destination restaurant, Paul decamped for midtown.

"No" said Timmy nonchalantly, seemingly indifferent to the chance I was critiquing him.

"Please ask Jezebel for our check," said Paul resignedly, and Timmy retreated.

"Timmy doesn't seem very friendly," I said soothingly. "Does he go to your gym, too?"

"No, friendliness is not part of his persona, at least, not with me. We met a few times at the Mineshaft where I let him piss on me in the tub. We never really outgrew that relationship or its psycho-dynamics."

The Mineshaft was a sex-club located at 835 Washington Street, I knew from Paul's past escapades, and which served no food.

Examining the clear liquid in my snifter with distrust, I asked, "Isn't that a high-risk activity?" Paul's behavior sometimes raised my hackles, for being ahead of the fashion curve exempted him from feeling he had to justify his actions. While I was naïve about places like the Mineshaft, I was aware that *The New York Native* has published a list of practices considered likely to transmit HTLV-3, or LAV, the virus believed to cause AIDS. Unprotected anal and oral sex stood at the top of the list although the hazards of less intimate forms of behavior were disputable. In a recent article warning against the exchange of bodily fluids, *The New York Times* neglected to specify whether urine or saliva was to be included.

"Don't look at me like that. I am always safe," Paul answered defensively. "Piss is not considered high risk according to the GHMC and I never swallow."

Paul was probably telling the truth, I figured, at least about the Gay Men's Health Crisis. But I feared the chances he permitted himself to take, both on his account and on Stephen's. Paul had become a GMHC volunteer when a coworker named Marco had fallen ill. He disseminated pamphlets about safe-sex practices in the Village on days when Stephen wasn't at school. Though Paul frequently reiterated the need for free condoms, I wondered if he used them.

"I don't want anyone else I know getting sick," I said, remembering how the Fiorucci bag with rubbers had been stolen when Paul would have needed one most.

"Don't worry about me," said Paul. "It's your civil rights that you have to worry about. Koch closed down the Mineshaft yesterday, and I am sure St. Mark's will be next to go." St. Mark's was one of the city's largest gay bathhouses, and was located, I subsequently discovered, on St. Mark's between Second and Third.

"My rights? But I never went to either."

"Still, it's an infringement of your freedom, even if it's a choice you don't exercise."

"My freedom to become sick?"

"Your right to have sex with the partner of your choice."

Jezebel brought the bill, and, chewing gum and blowing bubbles, she toyed with Paul's hat while he calculated the service. Squinting at the $196.00 total, Paul peeled bills from a wad of fifties in his wallet and told her to keep the change.

"Thanks," she said, fluttering off. "I'm crazy about your new hat!"

"Do you always tip so much?" I asked afterwards.

"Easy come, easy go," he said, putting away his ostrich-skin wallet. He earned more as a headwaiter than I would ever see as an adjunct instructor, and his income was supplemented by Stephen's, who was promoted to full professor two years ago.

"Take away Odeon's fifth star, will you?" said Paul.

"I don't give out five stars. You're confusing me with the AAA."

"What is your highest rating?"

"Three," I said, "like Michelin."

"That's dull!" complained Paul. "Why can't you do something original? Zagat uses thirty points, and Robert Parker rates wines on a scale from one to a hundred."

"Yes, but what good is it if only the top twenty points count? Any wine ranking in the seventies Parker describes as tasting of wet dog or vegetables," I quipped. "The simplicity of the Michelin's system makes sense, and they don't do New York, so I can tweak it for my own purpose. Three stars are reserved for only the highest level of luxury and comfort," I said as Count Smorltork removed his top hat, out of which leapt a small white rabbit. "Despite your bone for not being comped, Odeon deserves two." The rabbit disappeared under the table.

Paul looked thoughtful. "I have a better idea. Why don't you rank restaurants according to their gayness? You know, one star could mean a place was sisterly in its welcome. Two stars mean it's regal with queenly poise, while three stars denote pure, incandescent flamboyance!"

"I don't know." I usually let Paul pick the restaurants where we ate, but I never really liked the word *gay*, feeling it had been chosen by strangers to describe something intimately mine. And I felt certain Milton would disapprove. "Let me think about it. By the way, the second week in December is no good. It's my mother's birthday, and I have to go to New Jersey. Her photography is being shown at the Friday Afternoon Fine Arts Club." Paul and I routinely dined the second Friday of each month. He and Stephen attended cultural events other Fridays, and Sundays were stay-at-homes evenings the nights when Paul didn't work at The Four Seasons.

Turning my agenda, I asked, "Is Friday, December 20th okay? I want to take you and Stephen to 103 Second." With my salary, Paul hardly expected more than a reciprocal gesture.

"Five-star burgers?"

"With my compliments," I said, rising. "Don't step on the rabbit."

When I got home that night, I felt torn. Whenever I was with John, his company lent a saintly aura to my goals and aspirations, but he had failed me. The siren call of Paul, meanwhile, whose fallen nature could intuit guilty pleasures I secretly dreamed of, drew me ever deeper into a sink. I spent the two hours before going to sleep typing up a review instead of revising my dissertation's introduction.

THE GODS ARE STACKED AGAINST US

Sheila Morris

Baines County Sheriff Tom Owen Reynolds turned to one of two deputies who was on the scene with him and pointed to a shotgun leaning against an antique wooden sideboard in the tiny dining area where the man's body lay face down in a pool of blood that seeped from a gaping wound in his skull. The sideboard was the only piece of furniture in the eating area…there was no dining table. The room appeared crowded as the sheriff and his two deputies surveyed the stage while they tried to avoid touching anything or stepping in the blood. The acrid odor of gun powder lingered in the air.

"Lonnie, take the shotgun and put it in an evidence bag in the truck," the sheriff said to the younger deputy. "And make sure you put your gloves on before you pick it up. I told you boys to wear gloves before we ever walked in and I'm wondering where yours are right about now." The sheriff frowned as Lonnie sheepishly pulled a pair of clear plastic crime scene gloves from his navy Baines County vest.

"Sure thing, Boss. My bad," Lonnie said and retrieved the shotgun with his newly gloved right hand. "Do we have an evidence bag big enough for a double-barreled 16-gauge shotgun?" he asked as he moved toward the door to the kitchen.

"Oh, for God's sake, Lonnie, use the one marked extra-large, will you please?" the sheriff said with more than a trace of annoyance in his voice. "Eugene, go out there and make sure that kid doesn't figure out a way to screw up our evidence chain before we get started, will you?"

"I'm all over it, Tom Owen. Uh, you don't need me to stay here while you talk to that jackleg in there, do you?" Eugene motioned to the bedroom visible through another doorway from the dining room. Russell Cantrell sat in a recliner staring at a small television resting precariously on a short wobbly end table in the opposite corner of the room. The volume was low and the big man changed channels occasionally with a remote he held in his left hand.

The sheriff followed the gaze of his deputy and frowned at the sight. Russell hadn't gotten up or said a word since they'd been in the house except to tell them over his shoulder that he hadn't made the coffee yet.

"Nah, I don't think so," he said with a sigh. "But stay close around in the yard just in case. Now go out there with Lonnie and bring in the coroner when he gets here. We'll need to have statements from the Wasniowski brothers, too. Make sure Lonnie gets details from them before we let them go home."

Eugene left through the same door Lonnie had used and Tom Owen heard the kitchen screen door swing shut. He squatted on his haunches like a baseball catcher and stared at the dead man on the floor.

❖

Sheriff Tom Owen Reynolds was a good-looking man of average height and an acceptable weight for a man in his early fifties—the beginning of a beer belly but not offensive yet. His sheriff's khaki shirt and slacks were neatly ironed. His wife always made sure he looked his best when he left for the office each day. His silver badge shined and he suspected she'd polished it before she'd pinned it to the pocket on his shirt. His black Durango cowboy boots looked brand new. He personally inspected them as soon as he got to work. He kept a shoe shine cloth in his desk drawer to clean them if necessary. The boot color matched his black string bowtie that he'd hastily tied this morning. His beige felt cowboy hat sat at just the right angle on a head of handsome silver hair and his brown holster holding the Colt 45 pistol completed his appearance as a genuine Texas County Sheriff.

He wanted the good people of Baines County to be proud of their sheriff whenever they spotted him at Jim's Hardware or the Wal-Mart or the Mexican restaurant on Main Street or any other place because he needed their votes for re-election every four years. Tom Owen Reynolds was a formidable force in the county, and the good citizens of Baines County respected him—even admired him. He appreciated their support and he loved his job, most of the time.

But, today he didn't like it at all. Deputy Eugene Waller called his house before the sun came up to tell him the 911 operator paged the sheriff's office to report a shooting five minutes ago at the rental house on Janie Grissom's place off Highway 8. A man dialed 911 and said he'd just killed his brother.

Jesus Christ, he'd thought and told Eugene to pick up Lonnie and head to the scene but to wait for him to get there before they went in. He'd gotten dressed quickly but made sure he looked in the mirror for a final inspection before he grabbed his hat, jumped into his official county black Chevy Blazer, and roared out of his driveway with blue lights flashing and siren screaming. *His poor wife*, he'd thought. She'd be worried sick until he called to let her know he was all right.

The ride south of town on Highway 8 took a little over ten minutes and Tom Owen called Eugene to get directions to the rental house once he crossed the cattle guard into Janie Grissom's place. He turned the siren off. No need to draw more attention from the neighboring farms. This was a rural section of the county with houses far and few between and he smiled as he remembered the word mix-up his daughter Cassie made when she was little. He had teased her about it for years and now it was a standing joke in the Reynolds family. *Far and few between is right*, he thought, as he slowed his car on the deeply rutted dirt road winding through the Grissom farm. In the early daylight hour he could see a pasture full of grass almost as tall as his car. He wasn't a farmer, but even he knew it was time to cut and bale it. He wondered who took care of this chore for Janie after her husband Tyler died last year.

He followed the road as it curved sharply to the left and realized he had found his destination when he pulled into a clearing that held the small house he'd seen in the distance when he'd rolled over the Grissom's cattle guard. He saw his deputy Lonnie Moriarty standing in a freshly mowed small yard talking to two men he didn't recognize right away, but then recognized them as the Wasniowski brothers who must live somewhere around the Grissom place.

Lonnie was a young deputy who had recently applied for a part-time position with the sheriff's department after he graduated from Lone Star Community College with a two-year degree in criminal justice. Tom Owen had interviewed him and was impressed with his positive attitude accompanied by a high energy level. The sheriff thought Lonnie had the ability to match his enthusiasm and might make a good lawman one day. Lonnie was a tall thin man in his early twenties with sun tanned skin, a result of spending his off-duty days at his girlfriend's swimming pool. He also worked out at the local gym and was trying to add some bulk to his string bean frame. He told the sheriff he knew he needed to gain weight to be able to scare the bad guys, but it was hard to do.

"Just give it time, son," Tom Owen had advised with a smile, "and you won't need a gym to add weight."

Eugene stood closer to the house but had obeyed his instructions to wait for the sheriff before going in. Eugene Waller was the full-time deputy who had been with the department since before Tom Owen was elected sheriff ten years ago and would be there after Tom Owen was gone. That's what the sheriff liked most about Eugene. The man had no ambition beyond his current position as deputy. He was a loyal, mostly competent deputy who had no desire for the politicking involved in being elected sheriff. Eugene stood six feet tall, had the fair skin of his father, the stocky build of his mother. The meals Eugene's wife prepared for him when he was off-duty had put him well on his way to joining millions of other overweight Baby Boomers. He adored his two teenage girls who were as pretty as any girls in the high school. *He is a good man*, thought the sheriff, *and I'm lucky to have him.*

The house which was hardly more than a shack must have been a sharecropper's home at some point. The paint on the wood had peeled off. The exposed boards revealed cheap lumber and poor construction. Two wooden poles held up a downward sloping piece of corrugated tin from the tin roof to form a makeshift carport offering refuge for an older model white Toyota Camry that had seen better days. A satellite dish was attached to the rear of the tin roof where an old television antenna from the 1950s had miraculously survived for at least six decades, but was hanging on for dear life. Two huge stands of cactus guarded each side of the entrance to the carport. Old tin cans were scattered around the small deck where Eugene stood and Tom Owen imagined they were the Cantrell versions of ashtrays. Shabby chic this was not. Shabby all right, but not two cents worth of chic. He had a bad feeling as soon as he saw the place.

An overly excited Lonnie raced over to meet him when he switched off his engine and opened the door to step out.

"Sheriff, Sheriff, we can't get nobody to come out of there," he exclaimed as he pointed to the house. "Eugene knocked on the door but nobody's come out. Thomas Wasniowski said they'd heard what sounded like gunshots about an hour ago but he and Albert didn't come over until they saw our blue lights. They said Russell Cantrell rents this place from Janie Grissom."

"All right, Lonnie, settle down now. Just settle down," Tom Owen said as he walked toward the house. Eugene shook his head when the sheriff reached him.

"I knocked on the door, looked through the screen door, and saw what must be the kitchen, but there wasn't anybody in there and nobody came out when I knocked again."

"Okay, Eugene," Tom Owen said. "Let's try this door and see if it's unlocked. If it is, you and me will go in first. Lonnie, you back us up." The three men drew their weapons while Eugene reached for the screen door that had several holes in it. The door was open and he held it for the sheriff to go in first. Tom Owen stepped into the kitchen as he took in the scene. He saw that the sink and counters were covered with dirty dishes, empty beer cans, vodka bottles, and a loaf of white sandwich bread. He caught a whiff of cigarette butts from an ashtray sitting on a wobbly kitchen table to his right. Then he looked to his left and saw the body on the floor in the next room. It was a man and he wasn't moving.

"Russell Cantrell? Charlie Cantrell? Either of you boys home?" the sheriff called from the kitchen.

No response. Not a sound.

Tom Owen walked slowly toward the body in the next room and motioned for Eugene to come with him. He signaled Lonnie to stay in the kitchen, but he sensed the younger man was coming with them anyway. *Goddammit*, he thought. *That kid is gonna be the death of me yet.*

The room where the body lay must be a dining area. He could see the old dingy flowery wallpaper that was typical of an ancient dining room. He bent down to the body to check for a pulse but found none. This man was dead, and Tom Owen was shocked as he recognized the corpse was Russell's older brother Charlie. He stood and stepped around the body to peer in the other room through the open door. That's when he saw the large figure of a man sitting in a recliner watching TV.

"Russell, is that you in there?" he called out. "It's Sheriff Reynolds and Eugene Waller. Russell, are you all right?"

"Yes, it's me, Sheriff, and I'm fine," he said. "I haven't had time to make coffee this morning or I'd offer you a cup."

Tom Owen eased quietly to the door of the bedroom and saw Russell sitting calmly in his chair with a TV remote in his left hand, a cell phone in his right. He turned to walk back to the dining room. That's when he noticed the shotgun leaning against a wooden sideboard positioned in the middle of a wall in the room. He ordered the disobedient Lonnie to make himself useful as well as ornamental.

Tom Owen stood up again and surveyed the small room being used for a dining room that would fit into one of the bathrooms in his house. *I am not going to be alright today*, he thought. Charlie, the dead man, was one of his classmates from the local public school kindergarten all the way through high school graduation right here in Fairview which was the county seat of Baines County. Charlie Cantrell, son of Mason and Louise Cantrell who were both deceased. *Thank God they didn't live to see the day that one of their sons killed another one*, he thought. Charlie wasn't a good friend or really any friend at all. Tom Owen remembered him mostly for their brief stint together on the junior high football squad. Charlie played defensive back in the eighth grade for that one year, while Tom Owen stuck with football as a quarterback throughout his high school years on a team that won few games and never made the playoffs. He knew Charlie better on a law enforcement level in their adult years during the past ten years he'd been an officer of the law and Charlie had been a lawbreaker. Their reunion was a strange one for sure.

Tom Owen had been the sheriff for a year when the Texas Rangers contacted him and said they believed they'd tracked a member of a Mexican drug cartel to a place in the deep piney woods at the end of a Baines County dirt road. They wanted the county sheriff's office to be involved as backup with the collar. Tom Owen was flattered to be called in by the Rangers on such an important mission because most of the crimes he worried about to that point in his career had been vandalism at the schools, car break-ins, kids smoking pot, or a cow trespassing on a neighbor's farm. Certainly nothing approaching the magnitude of a possible Mexican drug cartel runner. This was high drama in Baines County.

The plan was for the Rangers to fly over the property in a helicopter at midnight and shine their floodlights from the chopper to illuminate the target which by then had been identified as a single-wide mobile home. Apparently the suspect made regular nocturnal visits to this trailer so unlawful activities were suspected and the Rangers wanted local law enforcement to be available. So the sheriff and Eugene Waller waited with half a dozen Texas Rangers in the pasture past the woods near the mobile home until the helicopter flew over and stopped above them. Bright lights shone through the woods and the whole scene looked like a UFO was about to land in the pasture until a guy in the chopper used a megaphone to shout, "Come on out. We've got you surrounded and we're coming in! Come out with your hands above your head or we'll shoot you dead where you stand."

Just like the movies, Tom Owen had thought and was afraid for his life as he stood next to the other men who had drawn their weapons alongside him. Helicopter blades whirring like tornado winds above their heads. Bright searchlights from the chopper sweeping through the woods like a Fourth of July fireworks display. Eight officers on the ground with weapons ready. The atmosphere was intense and adrenalin pumped at warp speed for Sheriff Reynolds.

And then, with his hands clasped above his head, out came a clearly frightened Charlie Cantrell crying, "Please don't shoot. Please don't shoot me. I give up. Please don't shoot me."

Behind him followed two women who were sobbing uncontrollably and wearing flimsy nightgowns. The obviously younger woman was carrying a baby. It was one of the most pitiful sights Tom Owen had ever seen and he didn't know whether to laugh with relief that it was just Charlie Cantrell or cry at the sight of the baby in the arms of a mother who was probably high as a kite.

He and the other officers on the ground rushed forward to secure the premises. A Texas Ranger asked Charlie if there were others in the trailer and he shook his head. Not taking anything for granted, two Rangers walked cautiously into the trailer with their handguns raised in the fire position.

"All clear," one of the men called as he came back out.

The second Ranger who followed him said, "No Mexicans in here, but we've got ourselves a nice meth lab in the kitchen so the night's not a total waste."

And just like that, Charlie Cantrell became another statistic in the Texas criminal justice system. Both women were also arrested and taken to the county jail in Fairview. The Texas Rangers went home to Houston, and nothing more was ever said about the Mexican drug cartel in Baines County.

Tom Owen knew Charlie served time at the state prison in Huntsville, but he also knew he hadn't gotten the maximum sentence since his sister's brother-in-law was the district attorney. Charlie ended up with a shitload of weekends in community service and had been on parole for several years, but he couldn't stay out of trouble. His driver's license was suspended for a DUI two years ago and from the looks of the empty vodka and beer bottles in the kitchen somebody drank a lot in this little house. The sheriff had heard rumors that Charlie's meth and alcohol addictions had messed up his brain and he had seizures that cost him his last two jobs. His wife ran off with another man before the bad things really started. She left him with three kids who ended up moving in with their mother and her new husband when Charlie began his downward spiral. He'd lost his home and his family, and he was so far behind in his child support payments he'd never have been able to keep any money even if he'd managed to earn some. Good thing the kids were grown, Tom Owen thought, because they'll never be paid now.

With one final gaze at the body on the floor, Tom Owen gave a low whistle and whispered under his breath, "Here lies one fucked-up son-of-a-bitch, but what in the world caused his own brother to shoot him?"

❖

Sheriff Reynolds stepped carefully around Charlie's body and through the door into the bedroom. The big man hadn't moved from his recliner and now was watching an action movie starring Bruce Willis. His features were blond and soft for a man who must weigh close to 300 pounds. His hair was graying and thin, but he wasn't bald. He was dressed in blue jeans and a white T-shirt that was splattered with blood. His shoes were on the floor beside him. The king-sized bed was unmade and messy with pale blue sheets. A bedspread with a floral pattern was bunched up at the bottom near the edge of the mattress.

"Morning, Russell," Tom Owen said. "Looks like we've got ourselves a bad situation at your house this morning. I'm going to have to tell you your rights, and I need you to turn off the TV to make sure you hear me, okay?" Russell Cantrell brought his gaze up to meet the sheriff's eyes and he picked up the remote to click off the movie.

"Yes, okay. Go ahead," Russell responded with a blank stare that looked as dead as his brother's on the dining room floor. When the TV was off, he seemed to lose his composure, and his hands began to shake.

Sheriff Reynolds told him he had the right to remain silent and that anything he said could and would be used against him in a court of law, that he had the right to an attorney and if he couldn't afford one, the Baines County Court would appoint one for him, and asked him if he understood his rights?

"Yes, I do," said Russell. His massive body trembled slightly.

Tom Owen studied Russell, a man he hadn't known when they were children because he was two grades behind him and Charlie. Plus, they hadn't exactly moved in the same circles. Russell was a musical little boy who played the piano at his preacher granddaddy's church in Fairview from the time he was nine or ten years old. When he reached his teenage years, his mother, Louise, made sure he had organ lessons since everybody told her how good he was with the piano. The Sunday School teachers always said what a sweet boy Russell had turned out to be. He was the youngest of her five children—two years younger than Charlie, but seven years separated his older brother Charlie from the middle son whose name was John David. There were two older sisters, too, but the sheriff couldn't remember their names. Charlie and Russell were the second family for the Cantrells. The older siblings left their home before these two boys were in middle school. Russell was the church organist for the First Presbyterian Church in Fairview these days, a fact the sheriff knew because his daughter Cassie and her husband were members there. He'd heard them say at Sunday lunch what a great organist Russell Cantrell was and how they loved to hear him play on Sunday mornings.

"I need to ask you a few questions," the sheriff said to Russell.

At that moment the screen door to the kitchen closed with a whack, and Tom Owen heard the coroner, William Robinson, mutter "shit" when he walked into the dining room. Eugene was with the coroner and Tom Owen left Russell in the bedroom to talk to them.

"Hey, Sheriff," William said. "I would like to say good morning but I see that's not about to happen today. I don't like the looks of this and I'm sure you don't either."

"Morning, William," Tom Owen responded. "No, this isn't any good at all. Sorry to have to call you for a situation like this." The sheriff had confidence in the professionalism of William Robinson who had been a coroner for at least fifteen years. Whenever he was called upon to dissect a crime scene and interpret forensic evidence, he was always thorough; but this one wasn't his typical call. William bent over and took a closer look at the body on the floor.

"I'll do the best I can for you," William said. "Is this Charlie Cantrell? Is that Russell in the other room?"

"Yes and yes," Eugene answered before Tom Owen could say anything. "We think Russell shot Charlie this morning, but we don't know why."

"Ok, Eugene, thank you for helping me," the sheriff said. "We'll leave it to you, William. Eugene, come in the bedroom with me while I talk to Russell. I need you to take notes." The deputy stepped around the coroner who had already opened his bag to begin his forensics work on the body and the crime scene.

"Well, Russell, do you remember what I told you about your right to an attorney?" the sheriff asked. He was standing next to the recliner and Eugene had positioned himself opposite them and close to the now silent TV. "Do you want to have a lawyer present while we ask you a few questions? Or do you waive your right to have an attorney here with you?"

"No, I don't want an attorney," he said flatly. Beads of perspiration formed on his forehead, but the trembling had stopped.

"Okay then. You see Eugene over there? Well, he's going to take some notes for us, aren't you, Eugene?" The deputy nodded and retrieved a small brown notebook from his back pocket. Tom Owen retrieved a pen from his shirt pocket and gave it to Eugene. "The first thing he'll write down is that you declined to have an attorney here while we talk." Eugene scribbled furiously in the little notebook.

"Now Russell, let's start with the phone calls you've made this morning. Did you call the 911 operator this morning?"

"Yes, uh huh, I think I did."

"What did you tell her?" Sheriff Reynolds asked.

Russell looked up at the sheriff as if he thought this was a trick question and didn't answer right away. Then he said, "I told her I killed my brother. Then she asked where I was and I told her I was at the Grissom farm off Highway 8 in their rental house."

The sheriff waited to let the words sink in and for Eugene to write them down.

"Now then, Russell, can you tell us what happened between you and Charlie this morning that made you get your shotgun out and shoot him?"

Again, Russell didn't reply quickly. His face frowned and he shook his head slightly. "The fight started last night really," he began. "When I came home from work about six o'clock, Charlie asked me if I was going to fix the King Ranch chicken casserole for supper and said I'd told him yesterday morning before I'd left for work that I'd fix the King Ranch chicken casserole for supper. That was his favorite meal." He paused and looked at the sheriff.

Tom Owen nodded encouragingly and Russell continued.

"But I said no and that I was tired and that we had leftover pizza from the night before and I just wasn't up to cooking supper. Plus, we had the leftover pepperoni pizza so it wasn't like we didn't have any food. You can see that, can't you, Eugene?"

Eugene almost dropped his pen when Russell spoke to him, but he recovered quickly and said, "Of course I can see how that would be. Who wouldn't want pepperoni pizza?"

"Exactly my point," said Russell and his expression changed to apparent relief at Eugene's agreement. "So we left it at that, and I could see Charlie was mad but I brought out the paper sack with the vodka I'd bought when I left work yesterday and said why didn't we have a drink before we ate anything and just relax for a while outside...you know, smoke some cigarettes, have a drink together which is what we did every night anyway. Charlie didn't talk to me, but we went outside and sat on the porch steps and smoked and passed the vodka bottle back and forth. Charlie rolled his own cigarettes to save money which was nice since he was spending my money every time he bought tobacco." This last comment seemed to generate a flicker of agitation, and the sheriff made a mental note to check out the Cantrell brothers' finances.

"I'd also brought home some Bud Light, and Charlie would go in the kitchen and bring us a beer to drink in between the vodka swigs. I'm not sure how long we sat outside but we finished the fifth of vodka and a bunch of the beers, too, and I told him I was getting drunk and he said he was too, and I said I was going to bed for a little while before I ate supper. At least, I think that's what I said." Russell looked at the sheriff and seemed to hesitate.

"Go on, Russell," Tom Owen said. "Was Charlie still mad at you?"

"I'm not sure," Russell replied. "Yes, I guess he was, but I knew what would make him happy." Eugene dropped his pen and Tom Owen gave him a stern look.

"And what was it that made Charlie happy, Russell?"

All of a sudden tears began to trickle down the big man's pudgy cheeks and his face contorted in obvious pain. He looked again at the sheriff and over at Eugene who had stopped breathing.

Russell Cantrell was a man who carried a heavier burden than his obvious size, the sheriff thought to himself and was afraid of what he was going to hear next. Russell's next words were almost inaudible.

"Me," he whispered. "I could make Charlie happy."

The silence in the bedroom was deafening, and Tom Owen wondered if anyone else could hear his heart pounding in his ears as loudly as he could. He couldn't look at Eugene and then realized the coroner William Robinson wasn't making a sound in the dining room behind them so there wasn't any background noise to fall back on to interrupt the stillness. Somewhere outside he heard a bird sing, but it sounded far away as if it belonged to another world beyond this house where even a bird's song couldn't lessen the Greek tragedy unfolding within these walls.

❖

Russell Cantrell was crying and making a whimpering noise like a puppy on its first night away from its mother and Tom Owen spied a box of tissues on the end table next to the bed. He motioned for Eugene to hand the box to Russell. Eugene picked up the box, promptly dropped it on the floor, and then picked it up again after glancing apologetically at the sheriff who ignored the look. He handed the tissues to the big man who was emotionally disintegrating in front of them.

"Thanks, Eugene," Russell blubbered and took several tissues out of the box and set it on the bed next to his recliner.

"Now Russell," the sheriff said when the man had dried his eyes several times with the tissues, "You take your time and try to remember as much as you can. We're looking for the truth here today, and nobody is judging you or Charlie for anything. We just need to know what happened this morning. Okay? We clear?"

Russell nodded and seemed to relax. His tears stopped and his soft facial features hardened. He looked much older than his fifty years as he slumped back in the recliner which molded perfectly with the contours of his body. The recliner made a slight creaking noise as he settled into it. Russell didn't look directly at the sheriff or Eugene but instead lowered his gaze to the unmade bed which was now the elephant in the room.

"Charlie took a bottle of beer and went to the back room to watch TV and I came in here. I think I had a beer with me, but I'm not sure. Anyway, I took off my jeans and lay down on the bed and must've gone to sleep for a while because I don't know what time it was when I woke up. It was dark in the house and I was hungry and then I remembered the fight I'd had with Charlie about supper. I wondered if he was still mad at me and if he'd fallen asleep, too. I heard the TV in the back room and got up to see if he wanted to eat some pizza with me. When I walked into the den, I saw him sitting there in the dark on the sofa with his tobacco can open on the coffee table. He was rolling a cigarette and drinking a beer. The only light in the room came from the TV. I sat down in the recliner next to the sofa and asked him if he was hungry. He didn't answer and he wouldn't look at me. After a few minutes he said, 'Go put your pants on and cover up that big candy ass of yours... nobody wants to see that whale blubber naked.' Yes, I'd said, I'm sure not just anybody does, but I know one handsome man who likes to look at it. Charlie didn't say anything else to me so I said are you still mad at me and then he said, 'Yes I am, you worthless piece of shit. You're nothing but a lazy lard ass and I wish you'd get out of my face tonight'."

Russell stopped and leaned back in his chair and talked to the ceiling now. He lowered his voice when he started again. "Charlie, let's go lie down on my bed for a few minutes I'd said to him. I want to show you how sorry I am for not making your casserole you wanted for supper tonight. I'll do anything you want if you just won't be mad at me. Please, baby, please. Let's play in the bed for a while like we've always done so I can make you forget about supper." Russell closed his eyes.

The sheriff looked at Eugene to make sure he was still writing. Eugene felt the glance but didn't lift his eyes from his notepad. His hand was shaking, but he was still writing.

"Well, Charlie got up a few minutes later and followed me to the bedroom and after a while, he wasn't mad at me. No, not at me. But he must've been mad at himself because he went into this tirade whenever we had sex lately. He was crying like a baby when he pulled his sweaty body off my back and then he jumped out of bed and started shouting things like 'O God forgive me, you know I'm not like this, you know I'm not a fucking faggot, I don't know why I do this with my own brother, Sweet Jesus, with my own...brother,' and Russell made two words out of the word brother to imitate the way he remembered Charlie's rant. "He said he wasn't like me and that he had three kids and where did I think they'd come from if it wasn't from fucking Sharon and he'd die if his kids ever found out he was their uncle's fuck buddy. Sharon could tell them he was a real man and not some piece of shit faggot and how did I have the balls to touch the organ keys of a church every Sunday when those same fingers touched him the way they did. Then he started zipping his jeans but the zipper was stuck."

At that moment Russell raised himself from the recliner and pressed the remote to his chest. His voice ratcheted up several decibels and he was like a man possessed as he pounded his chest with the remote. "I love you, that's how, I told him. You're not just a random fuck buddy to me, you're my life. You've always been my life. From the time we were little, you've been all I ever wanted. While you were screwing Sharon and making babies, didn't you ever wonder why I didn't have someone in my own life? Didn't you just one time think about how hard it was for me to watch you get married and have children when I couldn't even have sex without thinking about you? And you want to know why I kept playing the organ in different churches for the last forty years? Because I'm usually having sex with the minister of music in the choir room behind a locked door, that's why. So if anybody's going to Hell for anything, it won't be for dirty organ keys." Russell was yelling these last words toward the dining room at the body of his brother who could no longer hear him.

Tom Owen and Eugene reached Russell at the same moment and each one grabbed a thick arm to restrain him. Russell didn't resist. "Ok, Russell, you need to take a deep breath and settle down," the sheriff said and Eugene nodded. "Everything's gonna be okay, but you need to hold on for a little while longer and finish up with us here. Just a little bit more, okay? You still haven't told us about the shotgun." Eugene and the sheriff gently pushed Russell into the recliner again. Tom Owen pried the remote from his hand and laid it on the bed next to the box of tissues.

Russell's eyes filled with tears as he took another tissue from the box and dabbed at his watery red eyes. Then he continued in a more subdued tone. "I kept a shotgun in the corner of my bedroom. Most of the time I didn't have shotgun shells, but Charlie and I did some dove hunting out here around the Grissom place; the season was opening in a week so I'd bought shotgun shells. I don't remember when I loaded it. I really don't," he said apologetically. "All I know is after Charlie's jeans were zipped; he turned to me and said, 'I'm moving into Mama's old house in town with John David tomorrow morning. I can't take sitting out here every day with nothing to do while you're at work and nobody to talk to and no way to drive anywhere and nothing to think about except you and this,' and he pointed to the bed and laughed at me. 'I can't live like this anymore. I'd rather be dead.' Russell hesitated and looked toward the corner where he'd evidently kept the gun.

"So I said well let me put you out of your misery. I rolled off the bed on the side where the gun was and grabbed it and fired both barrels at Charlie. He fell on the floor. The noise and smoke scared me so bad I froze for what seemed like a long time before I walked into the dining room to look at my brother lying on the floor with blood around him. I kneeled down beside him and hugged him and cried and cried and thought about re-loading the gun and shooting myself, but then I thought about Mama and what she would've thought about me and what I'd done and I guess I was a coward. Instead, I stood up, left the shotgun in the dining room, and came back to the bedroom. I put my jeans on and sat down in this chair and called 911."

Tom Owen never forgot the Cantrell brothers and Charlie's murder. Five years passed since that high-profile case put Baines County on a map of notoriety in the state of Texas, and the sheriff still thought about it every once in a while. Russell Cantrell would be in the Huntsville state prison for the rest of his life because his sister didn't try to get her brother-in-law who was the district attorney to ask for leniency for this brother. The two sisters turned their backs on Russell and the sheriff wondered if he would've done that too. Probably. The older brother John David was the only one in the family who tried to help Russell, but there wasn't much he could do.

The scandal of the circumstances surrounding Charlie's death was the talk of the county for a long time, but scandal eventually turns into the mundane and unworthy of further gossip. Time blurs the details anyway. It was a sad story whichever version was told, and Tom Owen tried to control the amount of information from the sheriff's office in the first official statement he'd read on TV. *Good Lord, what a mess that had been*, he reminisced, as he sat in his vehicle across from the

Fairview High School. Better call Eugene, he thought. Looks like vandalism on the football field last night and they'd be needed by the high school's security officers today. Crime and punishment went on as the rest of life did. Good thing for him. He'd be unemployed without them.

JESUS YEAR

Dale Corvino

Marta from housekeeping knocked on the door of room 401 and heard a muffled groan. *"O! Dios,"* she muttered as she opened the door cautiously, remembering all the other inopportune encounters with hotel guests. Her mind indexed every lurid scenario—every drunk wallowing in his own filth, every old man with a lingerie girl half his age. It was a catalog of base horrors she'd assembled in her time working in hotels, and it impacted how she thought about Americans. It was almost enough to make her long for the mushroom farm. They were stern but decent people. *Why were the guests incapable of using the 'do not disturb' placards*, she asked herself as she entered the room.

She found the registered guest, a Mister Chris Tolliver, in one of the hotel's plush bathrobes, slumped against the headboard. His wrists were tied to the wall sconces on either side of the bed with robe sashes. His dark curls were matted to his head with sweat, and his green irises stood out against the pink of his bloodshot sclera, like inverted watermelons. The sconces were illuminated, while the robe was wide open, doing little to conceal his hairy nakedness; and he had what looked like a pair of briefs stuffed into his mouth. Marta rolled her eyes and crossed herself before springing into action.

She held up his arm to put some slack in the sash, and released the slip knot at his wrist. "Sir, are you alright? Were you robbed?" she asked as she removed the briefs with a gloved hand.

"A little," he replied incoherently, stretching his jaw.

On the television, a History Channel program was airing, in which the Norwegian explorer Thor Heyerdahl explained his theory of transatlantic trade between South America and North Africa, via the Canary Current, over a reenactment. The narrator advanced the tale breathlessly, "World sensation, the navigator of the Kon-Tiki, Thor Heyerdahl, built papyrus rafts in the manner seen is Egyptian sepulchral paintings from the fifth century."

Chris Tolliver stretched his freed arm, detecting the aches beneath the numbness.

"He christened the vessel Ra, the ancient Egyptians' name for the sun," the narrator continued. Traders in reed boats had navigated the current, and that's how, Mister Heyerdahl speculated, Egyptian mummies buried inside the pyramids were found to have traces of cocaine.

"See? My shit is pure. I'm like the pharaohs," Chris said to Marta, who turned off the television.

In the last year, Chris had come into a sizable inheritance, though not from a family member. Milo Stewart was a British-born decorator of a certain renown, a style guru for Manhattan's Upper East Side. He'd hired Chris when he was a young design student to draft his interior projects. Over the years of their working closely together for his affluent clientele, Milo had become smitten with his handsome young disciple. Chris had found himself spending more and more of his time at restaurant tables than at the drafting table; Milo was a man of appetites and appearances, so he liked having Chris along as a companion at all the posh eateries frequented by his crowd. He revealed his feelings over dinner at Chanterelle, Chris' favorite.

"I doubt you could love an old wreck like me, but perhaps you can find..." Milo asked, tracing figures with his hand.

"Some affection?" Chris finished his thought. Milo smiled.

❖

Last summer, Milo was on a seaplane to the Hamptons to see the new home of a client, when the craft lost power and crash landed in the Long Island Sound. The pilot and the other passengers were rescued with some injuries, but Milo alone had removed his seatbelt, and had been thrown forward upon impact, sustaining a fatal blow to the head. His funeral was the society neck-craning spectacular of the season. Milo's long-suffering ex-lover was the executor of his will, and surprised Chris with news of his inheritance. "He was really quite fond of you, young man," he said, and Chris was genuinely moved. "Beyond his absurd infatuation," he added caustically.

Chris had checked into the Hotel Bethlehem with a bag full of money. It was one of those ordinary white plastic bags given to shoppers at stores all over the city, printed with the I love NY logo. He'd booked a limo to take him and some friends to the casino, which was built on the grounds of the town's namesake steel mill, now abandoned. The buzz of the gaming floor in that setting brought to his mind maggots swarming an animal carcass.

"You're the lucky one here, Chris, try the blackjack table," the Bulgarian said.

He'd met all of them on a night out some weeks ago and couldn't remember any of their names. He suspected the Bulgarian was some kind of hacker. He knew how to count cards, so all night he sat behind Chris, whispering into his ear what to bet, and whether or not to take a card. Chris won a small fortune and split it with the Bulgarian. They drank martinis until they got thrown out, and on the way out, the crew yelled Chris' praises to anyone they came upon.

After that terrific drinking marathon, he'd sent his friends back to New York in the waiting limo without him. He came to loathe their fawning. The hotel receptionist looked askance at his lack of luggage, so he pulled a twenty out of the bag and managed a smile. In the year since receiving the check from the lawyer, Chris had burned through much of his gay inheritance. What was in the bag was all that was left of it, though Chris was now perplexed to find that bag weighed more than when he'd left New York. He didn't remember winning.

"These sconces are freaking hot. Crucified! Well, it's the end of my Jesus year, so it's the look," he said to Marta, only a bit more coherently.

Marta had suffered drunkenness and she had suffered depravity, but she had never been party to this sort of blasphemy. She summoned her composure and crossed to the other side of the bed, as he seemed incapable of helping himself out of his bondage. "Don't flatter yourself, mister," Marta said as untied his other wrist. "I don't see any nails," she remarked.

"Ugh, they went into my head instead of my hands, dear," replied Chris, rubbing his temples with his free hand. "But that's where I do all my laying and running anyway," he added.

Marta gave Chris a stern look and shook her head, as she worked on his still-bound wrist. Once he was free, he went in for a hug, but Marta backed him off. "Could you…" asked Marta, indicating his nakedness, and to her dismay, he put on the soggy briefs.

She said nails. Chris Tolliver had whispered about nails to himself over and again, whenever pondering Jesus on the back wall. There was this whispered taunt, and it had justified years of bad choices. *Don't worry,* his inner voice would say, *you'll be nailed up like Jesus by the time you're thirty-three.* This intonation had been on infinite repeat since he was an adolescent. Though the Church of his youth had weak currents of Seventies Liberation Theology running through it—he could still remember the words to *Michael, Row the Boat Ashore,* and Sister Regina's awkward guitar lead—the hierarchy was still entrenched in Old-World damnation. This was confusing, so one day when a fuse blew and the lights went out, Chris walked out of catechism. He haughtily announced to his parents he wouldn't be going back. It was then, in a spasm of narcissistic guilt, that the internal whisper campaign started.

"How very Catholic," his therapist had remarked. The prediction had hardened like a stalactite into fatalistic certainty over years of repetition.

In college, Chris adopted the pose of a dissolute. He latched on to Milo Stewart, initially as entrée into the uptown scene, and wound up his companion. Milo was a lover of all things Italian: villas, statues, food, men. Milo nourished his romantic obsession for Chris with elaborate meals and wine. Chris went all over the city with the man— who himself looked like the Pope, with his aristocratic jowls, his large, imposing body, his dainty shoes, his fine blonde hair. He was always enrobed in finery from Roman tailors.

Shortly before his death, Milo took Chris on a tour of Southern Italy—a return to Chris' homeland, and Milo's Romantic idyll. They visited royal palaces, fabulous gardens, and splendid ruins—settings in which he felt Chris belonged. They spent a day at the baroque Reggia di Caserta, constructed in the Eighteenth century for the Bourbon King of Naples. Touring the English Garden, a naturalistic paradise with Vesuvius hovering in the distance, was Milo's main objective. He took a photo of Chris in the garden, with the dormant volcano in the background. Chris felt like an exiled prince, restored to the throne.

Milo expected him to drink wine along with him, in the suits he had made for him. Their nights out were a race to the bottom. Chris wanted him to pass out so he could take a taxi home, and Milo wanted to get him drunk enough to fall into bed with him. He responded to Milo's romantic overtures with increasing cruelty—until one night, when Milo finally wore him down. Milo threw himself on his belly and just sort of held himself there, like a walrus bull warming himself on a rock, and Chris was his sun. *Don't worry,* Chris' inner voice repeated, allaying his shame. *You'll be nailed up soon.*

After Milo's death, Chris embarked on his thirties with an unexpected inheritance. Pope Milo was dead, and he was unleashed. Chris had been regularly getting high, just to be able to put up with the obsessed old man. He found that he had nurtured his own addiction, which was now unleashed, too. Once he came into all that money, he was buying bags of mind-numbing sativa, these excellent strains, from a dealer who lived in his new building. He'd become such a lethargic stoner that he needed some kind of stimulant.

He'd never used cocaine up until then. It was provided by a boyfriend from Venezuela who spoke English with a nearly incomprehensible accent, but had an excellent supplier. His compulsion had escalated to the point where he'd been found by Marta in the hotel room, his pretty mouth stuffed and his thoughts misfiring. His neural network was fried; what crossed his synapses was a spiky tangle. "My very own crown of thorns," Chris said, bringing his hands up to his head.

Marta noticed a cut on his torso, just under his right nipple. The hairy patch below his pectorals was matted with blood. She almost swooned when she realized what it was—she'd always been squeamish in that way, ever since she was made to help her father when he killed the chickens. She steadied herself and made her way over to the house phone.

"Please don't tell anyone—I'm all right," Chris begged. The prospect of medical attention had a sobering effect.

Marta hesitated, and then found some courage.

"Tell me what the hell happened here," she demanded, one hand on the handset.

"Well, uh…what's your name? I can't read your tag," he said, squinting.

"Marta," she replied.

"Thank you for untying me, Marta," he said.

"Of course," she replied.

"I'm Chris. Nice to meet you. You know, the church considers me fallen away. Doesn't that sound pleasant?" he stalled.

Marta picked up the handset again.

"Okay! I picked up some rough trade online. He worked me over," he said.

Marta absorbed this new information, and walked away from the phone. She went over to her cart and retrieved a first aid kit. She was going to just hand him the supplies, but he was so obviously useless that she ended up cleaning and dressing his wound.

"Marta, will you help me get back at him?" asked Chris.

"I don't think that's a good idea. I have to get back to work…" she replied.

"I just want to lure him back to the hotel," said Chris.

"Why would he come back here?" asked Marta.

"Trust me, he'll come back. Could you just let me into a different room?" he asked.

"Oh, no, I couldn't do that. I will lose my job," she said.

"An empty room, one you haven't cleaned yet. Please?" he pleaded. He scrambled to find some twenties, but before he could find any, he saw that he'd already convinced her. Despite his impaired state, Chris was a charmer.

Chris fabricated a new profile on Grindr. He used one of Milo's old photos, and made up a compelling back story for him. His catfish profile was an old-money Philadelphian from Rittenhouse Square who had won big at the casino over the weekend, and had decided to sleep in and spend an extra day at the hotel. He approached Lance, the guy from last night. Lance quickly agreed to meet in a room on the seventh floor.

The room Marta let him use for the confrontation was a suite, sought after for its view of the Bethlehem Star—an illuminated display set on tall scaffolding in the nearby woods. Chris hid in the bedroom closet; he didn't want Lance to catch sight of him. There was a mirror over the desk, and he had worked out the sight lines. Marta stalled Lance, giving him the impression that she'd been called in to freshen up the living room.

Listening through the louvered closet door reminded Chris of his first confession. He'd crossed himself like they taught him in catechism as he entered the confessional and said, "Bless me father, for I have sinned," and waited expectantly.

When the priest whispered, "Well son, tell me your sins," young Chris was appalled. Maybe he hadn't been paying attention, but he expected that the priest would already know his sins. He must be able to divine them through the stamped metal screen, he reasoned. What was the magic in telling? Why did they even bother with this ornate booth? He couldn't even think of any good sins, so if the priest couldn't tell him what was wrong, what good was he?

"I...I don't think that's any of your business," replied Chris.

The priest sighed. "Go back to Sister Regina, ask her to explain Holy Confession, son," he replied. Chris walked out of the booth and straight home in sullen indignation. It was his first confession and his last. His full renunciation of the faith came soon after.

Marta was surprised by Lance's appearance; he was a nice-looking young man, dressed in sweatpants and clean sneakers, and carrying a backpack. He was friendly, and treated her kindly. Unbeknownst to Marta, Lance was one of the Lehigh Valley's most popular escorts. He marketed himself as a college boy, offering the full boyfriend experience, and occasionally took calls in Philadelphia and New York. He really was a college student—though not at Lehigh University, as his sweatpants suggested. He attended a nearby community college and was in his last semester of a degree in Environmental Science. He was finishing up a research project about the impact of hydraulic fracturing of Marcellus Shale on the Valley. He paid his own tuition, and even bought his mom gas cards with the money he made escorting. Chris had been drawn in by Lance's concise profile on Backpage:

Lehigh Valley college stud, 24, 5'11", thick. Athletic lean build. Fetish friendly. Outcalls only. "Sublime natures are seldom clean." Lance.

All Marta knew was that Lance didn't seem like some desperado who would tie a man up and rob him. She wondered why such a composed young man would even want to be around Chris. She had a weakness for blonde men, despite herself. Once Lance was sitting down, and Marta had gotten a good look at him, Chris emerged from the bedroom. He'd cleaned himself up, and dressed in last night's crumpled clothes, though there was still an emptiness in his eyes. Lance caught sight of him and said, "Oh no, not you again," and hustled towards the door, whereupon Marta blocked it with her cart.

"Please, Lance, I just want to say sorry about last night," said Chris.

Marta gave a confused look.

"Let him go, if he wants," Chris said to Marta. "He didn't rob me. It was just a scene gone wrong."

"No, I didn't rob anyone," Lance said to Marta, "I was paid for an hour, and the session went over. Mainly because he wouldn't stop talking." He made the yapping hand gesture, and Marta found herself sympathizing. Then turning to Chris, he said, "Sorry I left you like that—you just annoyed the balls off of me."

"So explain this—how did he get stabbed?" asked Marta.

"He tripped over his pants and landed on a bottle opener," replied Lance.

"Oh, right," Chris said, remembering.

"I tried to help him clean it up, but he wouldn't let me," Lance added.

Marta scowled at Chris. "I should have known better," she said.

"I'm sorry, really. I was strung out. I was tripping on some fractured burial myths. Jesus, the pharaohs, all scramble," said Chris. "There are too many stories in my head," he pleaded. Then he turned to Lance: "I just wanted you to know, I'm sorry. I'll make it up to you, okay? If you'll see me again—a nice, normal date. I mean, I'll give you your full rate, of course. We'll have dinner on the terrace. No bondage, no blow."

Even his kink went back to the man on the cross. He remembered the first time; a session always brought him back to it. It was his older brother and the kid next door, who had a sadistic streak. They didn't like playing with him, but when they deigned to include him, it was only for one game: Batman and Robin. Chris was always Robin, because his brother was always Batman. The next door kid was one of the villains; he was a comic book collector, always pulling out the obscure ones. That day, he announced, "I call Deathstroke," and enlisted a cricket mallet as his weapon.

Playing Robin meant getting ambushed by the villain—being wrestled to the ground while avoiding a fatal blow from the cricket mallet. Deathstroke tied him to the wooden fence between their yards with some bungee cords. Robin watched the battle between his captor and Batman for the cricket mallet, as the fencepost dug into his back. At least he was included. He was even being fought over. He enjoyed being pained and restrained—or at least the way it blanked out all the emotional disorder. After a while, the tedium of the battle set in, his body ached, and he slouched, still bound to the fencepost. His muscles strained against the tightening cords, while an erection pushed against his shorts. The boys' fight spilled into the front yard, and he was left alone for a time, as dusk settled. It should have been frightening, but it registered as serene order. He knew he'd eventually be saved, just like they kept trying to tell him in catechism.

"Okay, sure," said Lance, handing Chris his card. "But keep it cute," he cautioned.

Chris kissed Lance, then crumbled into his embrace. The soapy scent of Lance's skin stirred a reckoning, and he shuddered. The formative myth of the Catholic faith had ensnared him in its thorny, longhaired clutches, though he'd run from it for years, ever since walking out of that confessional. He was mortally embarrassed about enlisting Lance in his jacked-up reenactment. "God, how I've rambled," Chris mumbled into Lance's neck, sobbing. Now the tears flowed, after years of drought. It was the one story he'd sold himself on through years of repetition, and it had run his life.

Lance took his head in his hands and said, "Get it together, man," and walked out the door.

Chris, left hulking towards an absent body in the Star Suite, was engulfed in waves of remorse. He'd bent time, space, geography, history, social order, reason, morality, and judgment to fit a bogus myth. He was thirty-four and wasn't quite dead, just really fucking impaired. Marta looked on with pity.

DALE CORVINO

Chris was seized with panic, suddenly aware that his timeline was not so predetermined. He scrawled a note on the hotel stationery and handed it to Marta. "Safe," he said to her with emphasis. Then he hugged her, and she let him this time, though a little stiffly. He walked out of the suite and down into the lobby, past a tour group which was gathered to peek in on the Presidential Suite, where several American presidents have rested their heads after touring the Lehigh Valley. He walked out of the stately building as the guide started on his spiel about Eisenhower and Kennedy, to make everyone happy. He walked east on Pembroke, and kept walking—through Easton, through Long Valley.

Shortly after crossing into New Jersey, he stopped at a gas station for headache pills and a cola, then continued his hike through Morristown, through South Mountain State Park, where he heard but did not see a waterfall, and through the summer night. He arrived at the bank of the Hudson River in Jersey City in the late morning, and boarded a ferry at Paulus Hook. Thankfully he still had his sunglasses. Upon landing on Manhattan, he walked up Broadway to his apartment. The doorman greeting him with a robust "Good Morning, Mister Tolliver," then as soon as Chris was in the elevator, he called the super to gossip.

The painting over his tufted couch was a depiction of Jesus after the medieval style, coasting out of his crumpled body towards heaven. It was a surprise gift from Milo on their trip to Italy; they'd come across it while hunting for antiques in the Borgo Parioli. After Chris admired the depiction of the heavenly light, Milo circled back and arranged to buy it. Chris shed his filthy clothes, drew the blinds, and lined up some water bottles on the coffee table. Then he sprawled on the couch and slept for three days.

Back at the Hotel Bethlehem, Marta opened the note Chris had written her, which read: 'He is not here. He has risen.' She rolled her cart into the elevator and headed back down to room 401. She opened a window to freshen the air—there was an acrid chemical odor under the muskiness. She resumed her work. When she was finished vacuuming the carpet, she turned on the television for her novella. While she listened to Teresa, the most powerful *narcotraficante* in all of Mexico, confront the handsome police informant, she polished the marble and the nickel fittings in the bathroom. Then she cleaned the mirrors. She changed the sheets, the towels, and the bath robes, lugging all the soiled items to the laundry cart. She restocked the soaps and lotions. The actor who played the informant reminded her of her father, and she winced involuntarily when he spoke his lines.

She stuck Chris Tolliver's note in the clipboard over her work detail, which indicated she was readying the room for the Valastros. She recognized the name; they were regular visitors. They were driving into town for a hospitality industry conference. She recognized the verse too, a regular visitor to her spiritual house, but had to check the bible in the nightstand to find it, in the Gospel of Matthew. Once she had emptied the garbage pails and reset the air controls, she went over to the room safe and tried the combination 2-8-6. It opened for her with a blink of the indicator light, and inside was the bag full of money.

MUST LOVE ANIMALS

Louis Flint Ceci

I knew about the scars before I saw them. When I finally did see them, when I ran my fingers over them, when I embraced them, I thought I knew all I needed to know about Jeremy. I thought I had finally touched something deeper than the surface of things.

The superficial used to be enough. Seeing the taut torso of a young man would keep me dreaming for days. Trouble was, there were too few to be seen. You used to get a good view of the showers from the sauna at the Palo Alto YMCA, but ever since they installed curtains, the view has been disappointing. I swim there regularly, so I saw the decline first hand. The 'New Chastity' struck with a vengeance, and the few young men who still showed up tended to 'deck change,' completely wrapping their lower torsos with a large towel before squirming awkwardly out of their trunks and slipping quickly into underwear. When I was a kid, such behavior would have tagged you as gay. Times change.

Jeremy was different. He was both young and old. The sturdy legs, firm butt, and chest of hard smooth planes spoke of someone in his mid- to late-thirties, but the tight silver-gray curls and deep lines around his mouth suggested a man who had seen quite a bit of life. The timeless blue eyes were tinged with a sharp edge of sadness.

But how did I know about the scars? Because unlike the others, this guy did not hesitate to shuck his shorts. And when he did—well, more on that later. But what he never took off, even on his way to the shower, was his long-sleeved sports shirt. He would bring his towel and button-down Oxford cloth shirt with him to the shower, put both on the hook outside the stall, enter, and close the curtain. A few minutes later, a hand would snake out and grab the towel. Moments later, it would grab the shirt. And then the curtain would part and he would emerge, pantless but shirted, and make his way to his locker.

Clearly, Jeremy had something to hide. A youthful tattoo disaster? A pornographic mole? Or scars? I chose scars.

Okay, so I was making things up. Why not? That's what I do. Not for a living, of course, not here in the heart of Silicon Valley. Here, you need a six-figure income for a one-bedroom apartment with on-street parking, and the biggest grocery chain isn't mockingly called Whole Paycheck for nothing. I managed to hang on by writing Android apps for BigMobileCorp (not their real name). That is, I did until news of a merger with BiggerMobileCorp started circulating and they laid off my entire team.

It takes a lot of discipline to be unemployed. Otherwise every day turns into Saturday, and before you know it you can't tell if it really is Saturday. So I follow a strict schedule. During the week, it's swimming and yoga in the morning; in the afternoon, writing short stories or debugging code for a nifty little 3-D game I've invented that's played on the surface of a tetrahedron. Sundays I review the results of my web bot that goes searching for appropriate job leads.

And when it really is Saturday, I do a three-mile run with the BayLands FrontRunners and join them afterwards for coffee at Peet's on Middlefield. Peet's is also where I hang out during the week after my swim. This is a great location since it's halfway between the Y and home, and has free WiFi with a purchase. I did the math: a cup of chai latte from Peet's four times a week is $32.50 a month; high-speed internet from BigSuckingCableCorp (also not their real name) is $179.00 a month. I got to be a regular at Peet's.

That's where I first saw Jeremy, ordering French roast in his Oxford cloth shirt and khaki pants—typical geek drag, but it looked good on him. I picked up his name when he placed his order. The next day, he showed up in the weight room at the Y. He was intermittent at first, but soon followed a regular routine. I adjusted my swim workouts, hoping I could catch him just as he finished his weights.

After several near-misses when all I caught was the behind-the-curtains wardrobe trick, my timing paid off. I had just finished my 2500 yards and was relaxing in the sauna when he entered the showers. You get a commanding view of the showers from the sauna if you sit across from the door. Like I said earlier, there hasn't been much to look at lately, but one lives in hope.

You could see the spark in Jeremy's eyes even through the tinted glass. Then he dropped his gym shorts and I dropped my jaw. Epic is the word that sprang to mind. My computer geek kicked in a moment later and I started analyzing what I saw. Uncut. No tan line. To get that even a skin tone, he is either Greek or Italian or sunbathes nude. Let's go with Italian *and* nude. He pulled the shower curtain aside and stepped in, still wearing his full-length sports shirt. I'd seen that before. He turned on the water and left the shower curtain open. I hadn't seen that before.

I had to shower too, of course. I was all sweaty from the sauna. And, looky there! The shower right across from his was empty! (Actually, all of them were empty except his, but let's not quibble.) I left the sauna and strolled over to the strategically placed stall, careful not to look in the direction of the spray bouncing off this handsome man's back. Or maybe his chest. As I stepped into my stall, I checked to see which.

He was looking right at me, right in the eyes, blue eyes into brown. I pulled my curtain shut and turned on the cold water. This is the Palo Alto Y after all. I'd paid my annual membership back when I had the six-figure income and I didn't want to be ejected for blatant boners. It would mess up my schedule.

He was gone when I came out. I dressed hurriedly and headed for Peet's, hoping to dissipate my wild fantasies by diving into my latest short story. I got my chai, took my usual place near the outlet, and turned on my Mac. It didn't take long before I was deep into the world I had created, the constant buzz of the cafe a white-noise cocoon around my imagination. I didn't even notice when someone sat down at the table next to me.

"I beg your pardon," said a soft voice with a hard-to-place accent, "but are you on the internet?"

I looked up. There he was, gray curls, blue eyes, tan creases outlining a smile. "Um, yes," I said eloquently.

He held up his phone (an iPhone, I noted). "It says connected to WiFi, but I can't get a peep out of the poor thing."

The accent was resolving itself to somewhere south of Oklahoma, but with oddly-rounded vowels. "You get a password from the cashier," I said. "It's free if you buy something."

"Oh." He nodded at his cup. "I guess I missed my chance, then."

"No, no. Just go up and ask for one. I do it all the time."

"Thanks," he said, rising.

"Tell them Luke sent you," I called out and winced. *Clumsy! Obvious!* I thought, but I wanted to keep it going. I didn't want him to disappear into his cell phone like I had into my laptop. It didn't seem to work, though. He got back to his table and immediately started poking around on his little screen. I stifled a sigh and looked back at the mess of words I had written. My imaginary world didn't seem so lively anymore.

"Ah, there we go," he said quietly. He looked up. "I'm much obliged, Luke." He held out his hand, strong, wide, and big-knuckled with firm tendons that anchored at the wrist and disappeared into his shirt. Where they passed under the cuff was a cross-hatching of raised purple lines. I must have stared for a second because he added, "It is Luke, isn't it?"

I snapped out of it and took his hand. The grip was warm and firm. I felt calluses and wondered if my own hand felt like a skinned fish. "Luke Hammond," I said, omitting the "like the organ" I usually tack on as a pick-up line.

"Jeremy Tollier," he said, grinning. "I hope I didn't interrupt something important."

"This?" I gestured at my laptop. "Naw. Just a story I'm trying to write."

"A story?" He glanced around the cafe at the other regulars busily tapping away at their MacbookPros and ThinkPads. "I thought everyone in Silicon Valley wrote amazingly awesome apps that change the world."

"I used to do that, but it gets old after a while."

"So you quit?"

I shrugged. No need to go into all that just yet. "It was time. I thought I'd try changing myself instead."

"That's quite a move. What are you writing?"

I took a deep breath. "It's a dystopian gay romance about time-traveling monks." There, I'd done it: I'd dropped the G-bomb.

He took a thoughtful sip of French Roast. "You know, there's just not enough of that these days."

"What, time travel?"

That edgy spark twinkled in his eyes. "Gay romance."

Oh, this was going much better than I'd hoped! "Tell me about it. Conversations chopped into tweets, Facebook flooding your inbox, Scruff alerts making your pants dance."

I didn't think Jeremy could get any handsomer, but he did—he blushed. He slid his cell phone over. It was open to Scruff's Nearby page. I couldn't believe it. "What in the name of Steve Kelso are you doing on Scruff?"

He hid his smile with his hand. "I honestly don't know. I just moved here a few weeks ago and I thought it would be a way to find out if anyone was out there."

"And are they?"

He nodded. "I had Hornet and Grindr, too, but it was like having a constant vibrator on my balls."

I nearly squirted chai out my nose. "Oh, man, don't put that image in my head."

"And the worst thing is, I didn't really connect with anyone."

I nodded, closing my laptop before I made a mess on it. "It's like cable TV—400 channels and nothing to watch."

"Do you know what three words I really hate to see in a profile? 'No strings attached.' Everybody has strings attached. That's what makes people interesting."

"I agree. People are messy if you get to know them."

"The mess is where it gets interesting."

Well, I thought, *if we're going there...* "You know what three words I hate? Must love animals. And it's usually in all-caps. I can't love animals. I have a hard enough time with plants. I had an African violet once that committed suicide because it felt neglected."

I was so busy being clever I didn't notice Jeremy's expression change until it was too late. His face was blank and the bright edge was gone from his eyes. "Oh, shit," I said.

He closed his eyes and took a slow breath. When he opened them again he smiled. "Got a moment?"

"I screwed the pooch, didn't I?"

He held up both hands. "Just hold on a minute and come with me. Will your laptop be okay?"

I stashed it behind the counter with the barista and followed him out the door.

Peet's Coffee and Tea is part of a strip mall that is now old enough to be retro. Peet's is at one end and Piazza's Fine Foods (cheaper than Whole Paycheck) is on the other. In between are Mountain Mike's Pizza, a medical supply store, a falafel house, and It Takes All Types, a pet supply store and grooming service. On weekends, It Takes All Types puts up wire cages and fills them with puppies and cats for adoption. The sidewalk overflows with kids and adults oo-ing and aah-ing over the yipping, mewling furballs. We stopped in front of their window.

"This is why I was in Peet's," Jeremy said. "I was on my way to work. I'm a part-time pet groomer here."

Inside, a Labradoodle was getting a shampoo and a rinse. The dog looked as ridiculous as its suds-splashed handler. "Damn," I said. "And we were off to such a good start, too."

"Do you really hate animals?"

I scrunched up my face, trying to squirm my way back into Jeremy's good graces. "I don't hate animals, I just…I wasn't kidding about the African violet. I really don't know how to take care of another living being. I barely know how to take care of myself."

"From what I saw at the Y, you take pretty good care of yourself."

A knife-edge of hope poked me in the chest, but I tried to blunt it. "That's just the outside, the inside is…" I really didn't want to expose myself like this, but that knife hurt. "Look, I didn't quit my job. I got laid off. I'm on a leaky boat that will sink if I don't get another job soon. And I don't mean writing short stories. All my royalties from last year wouldn't buy the two of us pizza."

"That sounds good."

"What?"

"The two of us and a pizza."

I couldn't believe my ears. "So, I didn't screw the pooch?"

"Not unless you keep saying that."

We hugged outside the pet store, the Labradoodle giving us a quizzical yip from inside. Jeremy reported for work and I went back to Peet's. The afternoon flew by (2000 words on the new story) and that evening we had pizza—vegetarian—at Mountain Mike's.

We went on like that for a couple of weeks: knowing looks at the Y, coffee at Peet's, slow walks in Mitchell Park before Jeremy reported to work. I loved watching him at All Types and often trailed in behind him. I'm not a dog person—I'm not really an anything person—but seeing him take skittish, bewildered animals in his strong hands was like watching magic happen. You could see their eyes change as a kind of serenity flowed down his arms, stilling even the yappiest mutts.

"You are amazing," I said one afternoon as I watched him transform a twitchy pug into a little Buddha. "Are you sure you aren't related to St. Francis?"

He stopped—almost froze—his eyes staring at something far from the noisy pet shop. "I'm no saint," he said. Then just as quickly he snapped out of it. "And I'm not a time-traveling monk, either. Shouldn't you be time-warping or changing the world or something?"

I took the hint and went back to Peet's and my laptop.

The truth was, we each were hesitant about bringing the other home. Jeremy said his place was a mess, still unpacked after his move from New Orleans. I didn't want Jeremy to see my place because it would break my heart if he liked it. I'd had no rent payments since my ex moved out, taking his furniture with him, and with no job, and no income stream, the BigBadBank was refusing to refinance. I couldn't let Jeremy see the place until I knew I could keep it.

One day Jeremy postponed our walk until after he got off work. When we got to the far side of Mitchell Park, instead of circling back, he kept going. I kept up my usual chatter, complaining about editors who never answered query letters and boasting about the six—count 'em, six—people who had downloaded my 3-D game. We kept walking until we got to the corner of Curtner and Park and Jeremy took a deep breath. "Well," he said, "here it is. Shoreline Apartments. One and two bedrooms, off-street parking, and a pool."

My heart thumped as I realized we were about to have our first 'hot' date. I covered by quipping, "A pool? Really? Ever use it?"

"No," he said, opening the gate, "I can't swim. Still, it's nice to hear the kids laughing and splashing around."

"Kids, huh? That's too bad."

"Why?"

"If it's got kids, it's probably over-chlorinated. Kids leak."

He nodded and opened the door. "Watch your step," he said.

It was dark inside, darker than you might expect. Only one window faced the covered exterior hallway to let in light. Jeremy flipped a switch and I saw why he cautioned me. There was stuff stacked on every surface and spread across the floor. A narrow path led to a dining table and a single chair. Boxes lined the hallway to the bath and bedroom. I stopped just two steps inside. I couldn't help but think of my empty rooms and how the sunlight gleamed on the kitchen counters in the afternoon.

Jeremy ran his hand through his hair. "I'm sorry for the mess. I really haven't unpacked since I moved." He sighed and spread his arms. "I don't know why I keep this stuff. I don't need it, I just can't seem to—" He broke off and started shifting a stack of file folders from the chair to the floor. "There's a chair under here, somewhere."

I put a hand on his shoulder. "Hey, it's okay. I didn't come for the furniture."

He turned around and looked everywhere but at me. "There's hardly room to..."

"What?" A wicked smile crept up my face. "You weren't about to say, 'to swing a cat,' were you?"

He smiled at the floor and did the blushing thing again. "No, I wasn't. But it's so cramped."

"I know how to make it roomy."

His eyes met mine, the darkness in them shining. "How?"

"Turn out the lights."

He reached over and flicked the switch and I stepped into his arms. "See? Plenty of room."

He hummed and pressed into me. Our lips found each other, and then our tongues. I pulled away and started unbuttoning his shirt. I was determined to see the full length of his torso, unconcealed. Just before I slipped the last button, he pulled my polo shirt over my head and his own shirt slid off his shoulders to the floor. In the dim light from the window I could make out the contours of his skin: the gentle mounds of his shoulders, the smooth plains of his chest, the narrowing valley of his abdomen. Carefully, I ran my hands from his ribcage to his waist; the texture was warm and smooth. "Mmmm," I sighed. "Perfect."

"No, not perfect." He guided my left hand to his shoulder, along the curve of his triceps, then down his forearm to his right wrist. There I felt a knot of twisted ridges and lumps. I had guessed about the scars, even glimpsed them, but here in the dark, my fingertips probing what I had never seen, my urge to know everything felt like a violation.

I gasped and pulled back. "I'm sorry," I whispered.

"It's all right." He led my other hand to his left wrist. There I felt an even larger tangle of scars. His voice was quiet, thin, as though the words could only be said in the dark. "Most people think they're from a suicide attempt. They're not. Just the opposite. But I got tired of explaining."

A writer's imagination can be a curse. Right then, with Jeremy at his most vulnerable, when I should have been in the moment for him, my mind filled with a million stories. I shoved them all aside. "You don't have to explain anything to me," I said. I took his ravaged arms and wrapped them around me and drew him closer.

Would it be too woo-woo to say that because we opened our hearts to each other, the universe opened its heart to us? Yeah, that's a woo too far. But less than a week later, I got a call from a recruiter. Someone had seen my 3-D game and wanted to know if the surface manager was my own design. It was. They thought that was cool, we talked some Android shit, and a week and umpteen interviews later, I got an offer. Finally, I could refinance the house and tell the BigBadBank to kiss my sweet algorithm.

I went around to All Types to tell Jeremy the good news, but the woman behind the counter said he had gone home. "He wasn't feeling well," she said with a look that suggested something more. I dismissed it and drove to his place.

When he answered the door, he did seem a bit off—suspicious almost, frightened—but when I told him I'd signed the offer he broke into a big grin and hugged me. We decided to celebrate at my place. We arrived at 'the smiling hour', when the sunlight hits the tile countertops and makes the kitchen glow.

"Wow," he said, soaking it in. "It's just like grandma's kitchen."

I lit up. I knew he'd love it. And there was something else I knew he'd love. "Come with me," I said, taking his hand and leading him out the kitchen door. We crossed the patio and rounded the corner of the garage and stopped. Jeremy dropped my hand and just stared, open mouthed.

My house is on the corner of a cul-de-sac. It seems like a small lot because the house sits close to the street, but the property fans out behind it. When Jeremy saw it, I'd been working on the back yard for five years. Lupines, borage, ceanothus, and California poppies bloomed in the wildflower garden. Purple Queen bougainvillea climbed the south wall of the house. Two raised beds sprouted tomatoes, peppers, zucchini, and eggplant (my ratatouille garden). A large loquat with small golden fruit shaded the deck at one end of the yard, and a multi-trunked coastal live oak anchored the other.

"It's like a small park!" he exclaimed.

"Nearly a fifth of an acre," I boasted. "Completely enclosed and private, too. I do naked yoga on the deck."

Jeremy swung his arms wide. "A dog would love this."

"Umm, yeah, I suppose."

He turned and smiled at me. "I'm just teasing. You're about as likely to get a dog as I am to swim laps."

"That's different. You can't swim, but I could get a dog." He gave me a skeptical look. "How hard can it be? A bowl of food, a bowl of water, let 'em out when they need to." I shrugged. "They pretty much take care of themselves."

He shook his head, smiling, and hugged my waist. "You're thinking of cats. Dogs need a stable home, a steady presence. It's a relationship. They need to know you'll be there for them."

"Great. Just like people."

"Well, we're animals, too."

"So if I feed and water you on a regular basis, you'll follow me home?"

He leaned in, his words a hot whisper in my ear. "In case you haven't noticed, I already have."

❖

Jeremy never mentioned having a dog again, but because he never mentioned it, it sat there in the back of my mind. I worried over every word he'd said. Oh, I had routines, all right: rigid rules with tight constraints. But that's not what Jeremy meant by 'a stable home.' Maybe that's why he never stayed the night. We'd get entangled in our naked yoga, but I could predict to the second when he would drawl, "Well..." and start reaching for his clothes. His cluttered apartment stayed cluttered and my empty rooms stayed empty.

I wanted Jeremy to be with me in the quiet moments as well as the passionate. I wanted to show him I had room for mess in my life. So I took the next logical step: I adopted a dog.

You're probably saying terrible things about me right now, about being self-centered and manipulative. A pet is a living creature, not a tool for catching a man. And you'd be right. I did it for all the wrong reasons.

But I saw the way Jeremy transformed the dogs in his care, and I saw how they transformed him: the way his solid build would soften without losing any of its strength, the way his focus would shift to something outside himself, and how that saintly aura would surround and suffuse him. I wondered if a dog could work similar magic on me, turn my rigid rituals into something more living and flexible, less superficial than the comfort of repetition.

It was a risk. I'd be putting myself out there emotionally in a way that had failed before. And it was worse for the dog. A rescue dog is at risk to begin with; a returned rescue dog is a dead dog. If I failed again, I could never let Jeremy know.

I decided to do my shopping across the bay to avoid running into any of Jeremy's clients. Surprisingly, I found my match the first place I visited. Her coat was a chaos of bluish-gray, black, white, and tan— colors that don't really go together, but they did on her. "Well, look at you," I said as I squatted down. She came to the front of the cage and looked up at me as if to say, "Well, look at you." Dogs were yapping and scratching at their cages all around us, but she just sat there, looking up at me.

Her name was Roxie but I changed it to Judith. She was a miniature Australian blue heeler. She'd been trained, then abandoned, by a Cal undergrad who skedaddled back to Virginia after getting too much of Berkeley. I took her home that day. Butterflies were flipping in my stomach as I crossed the Dumbarton Bridge. As we waited for the light to change on University Avenue, I seriously thought about turning the car around and going back. Judith was in the passenger seat next to me. I turned to look at her and she looked at me. "Judy, Judy, Judy," I said. She sighed and looked out the window, cool as a cucumber. She was the dog for me.

I worked from home while I set up our routine. Within a month, I was able to bring her to the office. They should have paid her a salary. She seemed to sense when the programming wasn't going right, when my head was jammed with twisted data structures and I was thrashing through one bad design after another. She'd come and lay her head on my thigh and just look up at me. And she was always right: if I took her out for a walk or just played with her in the nearby dog park, the mental fog would lift and I'd be able to attack the problem fresh. Instead of a routine, my life took on a rhythm; instead of a ritual, it was a balanced dance.

Jeremy knew something was up. For one, I wasn't inviting him over to my place anymore. We always ended up at his apartment, shoving boxes aside and causing cascades of manila folders and magazines, more often than not ending up on the musty shag carpet, surrounded by heaps of stuff slouching their way toward entropy.

Then one Saturday after coffee with the Frontrunners, he said, "I think I know why you haven't invited me over in a while."

I gulped. "You do?"

"You've taken a second lover," he said, his eyes twinkling.

I squirmed. "Not exactly."

The edges of the twinkle darkened, but he recovered quickly with a grin. "As if. You and your routines couldn't stand the strain. No, you're waiting to see if I'll ever clean up my act. And I will."

"Your act is fine. I like your act."

"No, I know the mess bothers you. It bothers me, too. So starting next week, I'm cleaning out the junk."

"The only junk I've ever noticed is your junk. I mean, your 'junk', you know? Your—"

"Luke."

"Huh?"

"I'm serious. You won't recognize the place when I'm done. There's even a bed under all that. We won't have to do it on the floor anymore."

I shrugged. "I kinda liked the floor."

"Well, there'll be more of it soon."

I sipped my chai and took a gamble. "I don't know. My new lover might get jealous."

He leaned in and rubbed my cheek with his stubble. "I don't give a rat's ass."

"Would you like to meet her?"

He pulled back, not hiding his shock. "Her? You have a—what? A roommate?"

I giggled all the way back to my place, Jeremy following in his pick-up. We came in through the back gate and entered through the kitchen. Jeremy was standing just inside, a quizzical smile on his face. I leaned over. "Judy!" I called. "Here, girl! I'm home."

There was a clattering of paws on wood floors in the next room and Judy came bounding around the corner and leaped into my arms. I laughed, picking her up and turning around. "This is—"

"No!" Jeremy shouted. He was standing with his arms thrust out, eyes wide, body rigid.

I was dumbfounded. "Jeremy, what—" I took a step forward. Judy wriggled in my arms and whimpered.

"Get away! Get away from me!" he yelled.

I stopped and looked down at Judy. "This is just—"

"I can't!" He backed out the door, tripping over the lintel. "I can't! I can't!" He turned and ran through the gate. A moment later, I heard tires squeal as his truck sped away.

I stood there, holding my dog, facing the open door, not knowing what had happened or why.

❖

Jeremy was not at It Takes All Kinds the next day or the next. I finally asked the woman I had spoken to if he was still working there.

She wobbled her head noncommittally. "I couldn't tell you. You can talk to the manager if you'd like."

And say what? I wondered. "It's just that he was a little upset last time I saw him. I wanted to be sure he's all right."

She raised her eyebrows. "I'm not surprised. He was the moody type."

That didn't sound like the Jeremy I knew. "Moody, how?"

She shrugged. "Sometimes a customer would bring a dog in and he'd just walk out without a word."

I called his apartment but got no answer. Not even voice mail. I threw myself into the new job, dove deep into the code for cover. Judy would come and lay her head on my thigh and we'd go for a walk, but the magic was gone. It was ritual without rhythm.

Then one night a week later there was a knock at my back door. Judy's head jerked up but she didn't bark. When I reached the kitchen, I could see it was Jeremy. He glanced up then away.

I returned to the living room. "Come on, girl," I said and led her to an empty room where her bed was kept. She got in without prompting and looked up at me. "Be good," I said, but it wasn't her I was worried about.

I went back to the kitchen and let Jeremy in.

"I owe you an explanation," he said at once.

"No, you don't. Well, yes you do, but that isn't the most important thing. The important thing is, are you all right?"

He glanced at the kitchen table. I nodded and we both sat down.

"No, I'm not," he said, "But I want you to know I've thrown everything out. Everything I've held onto since Katrina."

I took a deep breath. "You were in New Orleans for Katrina? That's…" But I didn't have the words. I just shook my head.

"I lost things. I lost Joey. And Frankie."

"In the storm? They…died?"

He shook his head, then he nodded. "I kept hoping I'd hear from Joey. But I never did." He wouldn't look at me.

"Look," I said, "you don't…"

He shook his head. "No. I want to." He took a deep breath. "I met Joey at a bar in New Orleans, The Corner Pocket. He was a kind of dancer there."

"Like a disco dancer?"

He smiled ruefully. "Not that elegant. Anyway, I knew the minute

I saw him he didn't belong there. Half the go-go boys there are straight anyway, kids from the country or college dudes looking to pick up some quick cash on the weekend. Joey was different. When he looked at me, I didn't see dollar signs in his eyes. I saw something I wanted to hold, to comfort. When I said I wanted to take him out of that place, he didn't hesitate. He just grabbed this beat-up gym bag and said, 'We gotta take Frankie, too. He's outside.' I wasn't looking to take home two lost boys, but I followed him out back, and there was this Australian blue heeler tied to a post. The dog was really glad to see him, jumping into his arms and licking his face. 'This is Francis,' he said, 'but I call him Frankie. Frankie, this is Jeremy. He's taking us home.'

"My home was on Mandeville in St. Roch, not far. We walked. Joey carried Frankie the whole way. 'Something's wrong with his paws,' he said. That was April, 2005. I can remember the feel of that night, the way New Orleans wrapped around us, the way I wrapped around Joey, the way he wrapped around Frankie.

"Joey was a survivor. His family kicked him out at fifteen when they found him with an older man. He'd been on the street ever since, three years or so. I guess he was a hustler, but he wasn't afterwards. He turned my Creole cottage into a home. He cooked, he cleaned, he fixed up the yard. He made a little doghouse for Frankie under the magnolia tree and fixed the fence so Frankie could have the run of the yard. Once his paws healed up, Joey put him on a chain, but only at night. 'He'd just run off otherwise,' he told me. 'He's a wild one.'

"Late that August, Katrina hit. We heard about it for days. 'Maybe we should evacuate,' I said. 'We'll be fine right here,' he said. 'I'm not going anywhere.'

"And then my momma called. She lives up in Kenner. She's always full of melodrama, but Katrina really put her over the edge. She was hysterical. She wouldn't leave the house. She was going to get washed out to sea, or electrocuted, or a tree was going to fall on her. She wouldn't leave unless I came and physically put her on a bus.

"Joey was furious. He didn't understand my family wasn't like his. We had a helluva fight. How could I leave him? We were supposed to ride out the storm together. 'I'll be right back,' I said. 'No you won't,' he said. Just like that, like it was already a fact. There was no talking to him.

"I went out into the yard and said good-bye to Frankie. He was so glad to see me. I knew Joey was watching from the back porch, so I said, 'I'll be back before you know it, Frankie, I promise,' and he licked my face. I turned to see if Joey was still on the porch, but he'd gone inside. So I left for Kenner. Big ropes of clouds, arms of the storm, were rolling overhead. It began to rain.

"It was much worse when I got there. The wind was worse, the rain was worse, my momma was worse. It took me hours to get her calmed down and into the car and onto the last bus heading out. By the time I got turned around and headed back to New Orleans, it was raining so hard I couldn't see more than a block ahead of me. And then they closed the road and I had to turn back. I went back to momma's to sit out the storm.

"I tried to call Joey but the lines were down. Then the power went. Then Katrina hit.

"It was three days before I got back. I had to walk. There were barricades and guys blocking the roads. I couldn't tell from a distance if they were cops, but I could tell they had guns, so I had to circle around. It took me five hours. It was weirdly quiet. I walked for blocks and didn't see a single person, or a dog, or a cat, or even any birds. Even the trees looked dead.

"There was water in the street, water on the sidewalk. It was up to my ankles when I crossed Claiborne. By the time I got to my block, it was halfway up my legs, and it stank something foul. I grew more and more afraid the closer I got. It was up to my waist by the time I got to the house."

I had been listening in silence, but now I sucked in my breath. "You can't swim!"

"I had to find out! I hadn't heard from Joey since I left. When I got to the house, I was relieved, at first. The water line had gotten as high as the porch, but it didn't look like it had gotten any higher. I climbed the steps, soaking wet, smelling of grease and shit and God knows what. I didn't want to track that inside so I pounded on the door. 'Joey! Joey!' But there was no answer. The storm shutters were closed so I pounded on them. 'Joey!' Nothing.

"I heard barking behind the house.

"I waded back into that filth and made my way around the side.

I couldn't believe the junk that had washed into the yard and was floating around. The fence was gone. The doghouse was gone. But Frankie was there. He was still on his chain. But the doghouse was gone, you see? It was gone and the chain had wrapped itself around the tree. He was in four feet of water. Swimming. Barking. Chained to a tree for three days and no one came for him. He'd been swimming that whole time."

I shook my head, bewildered. "He couldn't have—"

"The whole time! His eyes were huge and he wouldn't stop barking. I had to get him out of there. I waded through the muck and reached for him, but then he—"

He held out his arms as if reaching for the dog and his shirt sleeves pulled up, exposing his scars. "Jesus," I whispered.

"I tried to get at his collar, to unlatch the chain, but he—He clawed, he bit. He tore at my wrists. He wouldn't stop! He'd gone mad from exhaustion."

"Your wrists…!"

"I went crazy. I screamed. I cried. I tried again and again but I couldn't get close enough. Every time I did, he went wild. I tried to get the chain unwrapped from the tree but my hands were numb and slick with blood. Frankie clamped his jaws around my left wrist and wouldn't let go. What could I do? Tell me what to do! I couldn't free him. I couldn't save him. Tell me what to do!"

"Jeremy, listen. There was nothing you could do."

He shook his head violently. "There was. There was something I could do. So I did it."

His hands were shaking, his fingers a tense, tight circle in the air. I covered them with my own and lowered them to his lap. "It wasn't your fault. He would have drowned anyway."

"A saint. You called me a saint. I'm practically a murderer."

I followed a tear as it dropped from his face and landed on our hands. I realized I was crying, too.

I felt something warm bump against my leg, then a weight on my thigh. Judy was there, resting her head on my leg, looking up at me.

Jeremy looked down and I tensed. If he blew up again, would I wrap my arms around him, or try to protect her? I felt torn apart, like he must have.

He took a deep, uneven breath and wiped his eyes with the back of his hand. "That's not Frankie."

"No."

"She's much smaller."

"She's a miniature. She won't get much bigger."

He wiped his face again. "What's her name?" he said in an almost normal voice.

"Judith. But I call her Judy."

"Hello, Judy." He reached out his tear-streaked hand. She leaned forward, sniffed, and licked the salt away.

I stroked her crazy mixed-up fur. "I shouldn't have kept Judy a secret. I just made up all these stupid rules about making everything perfect first."

"And here I thought you stopped asking me over because you thought I'd bring all my mess with me." He took a deep breath and let it out. "I guess I did anyway."

"You don't have to clean up for me."

"And you don't have to make things perfect for me."

I smiled and squeezed his hands. "That sounds…perfect."

People always come with strings attached, a tangle of scars and hopes and broken promises. Jeremy stays overnight sometimes now, and sometime soon I think he'll invite Judy and me to stay the night at his place. There's room now in both our lives, room to enjoy a whole mess of entanglement.

TEMPORARY ADHESIONS

P.D. Walter

After Josh Chang's first experience with speed dating, at the somewhat advanced age of 26, his roommate, Lief Gabrels, asked him if three minutes was really enough time to decide whether you wanted to see someone again.

"Absolutely," Josh assured him. "More than enough. Often thirty seconds is plenty."

Bachelor Number 3, "Hi, I'm Mark and you're…Josh. I like that name."

"Thanks. How are you enjoying this so far?" *This guy is cute. Give him a chance*, Josh thought.

"I'm having a blast. You?"

"Yeah, it's less strange than I expected. A lot of nice people."

"You ticked any 'Yesses' yet?"

"Uh…I think I'll decide at the end. But, yeah, I'll tick a few, I guess. You?"

"Well, there was one. Hu or Who, or something." The fact that he was speaking to another Asian didn't seem to deter him from broadcasting his ineptitude with foreign names. "And he seemed really nice, but then somehow we got onto birthdays and…"

"What? Too old? Too young?" Josh asked.

"No, no, but he's an Aries and I'm a Taurus and I've had very bad luck with Aries. Scorpios too. What's your sign, by the way?"

"Um, I have a mid-December birthday so…" Josh knew nothing about the Zodiac.

"Sagittarius. Yeah, not always the best mix, but then I haven't dated many Sagittariuses, so I'm willing to try. What do you do?"

They were at the one-minute mark, and Josh was done. Indeed, that is how he would remember his interlocutor: One-Minute Mark. He didn't know which was more humiliating, having his romantic options narrowed by an archaic and idiotic superstition on a level with palmistry and tealeaf reading or by the crass measuring stick of worldly success that coloured every other interaction. He tuned out for the rest of the conversation, gave automatic answers, avoided direct eye contact, fondled his pint glass, and awaited the chime that would signal them to move on to the next person.

Bachelor Number 6, "I'm the personal assistant to Mike Newsom," the respected host of a local Sunday afternoon political panel.

"Oh, neat," Josh bleated, sounding a bit glib even to himself. "How'd you get interested in politics?"

"Well, I don't know if you've heard of it, but when I was fifteen I read Ayn Rand's *The Fountainhead*."

The conversation continued from there, but in his head Josh had already checked 'No'. *Disqualified himself in under twenty-five seconds*, Josh thought. That was a new record.

The results arrived in his inbox twenty-four hours later. To his surprise, and trepidation, he had four matches, and spent the next month dating his way through them. But nothing much came of any of these encounters.

There was one delicious slip of a boy, Stefan, who led Josh up the garden path to two or three sessions of easy, playful, guilt-free sissy-sex, which was all Josh was capable of in such basically causal situations. But Toronto held too many other attractions for a boy of such charms to settle on him. Josh, the clumsy butterfly hunter, could only watch him flutter away, and who could complain about being privy, however briefly, to so fine a spectacle?

In retrospect, he appreciated how lucky he'd been to meet his first boyfriend, Roan Gabrels, when he had, in the university darkroom over solutions of developer and fixer. But that was a long time ago, and the two roommates, Josh and Lief, had long since gotten over the awkward fact that Roan was Lief's twin brother.

"If I'd experienced this much difficulty when I was 21," Josh said to Lief, "I'd have gone back into the closet and never come back out."

An aspiring photographer, and retail slave, Josh was not earning enough to launch any of the bigger boats in his fleet of creative ambitions. Sex and companionship, being relatively cheap, were among the few compensations his situation afforded. So every time he felt lonely, horny, or desperate for some male company, he couldn't help thinking another romp with Stefan might be just what the doctor ordered. He wasn't putting his butterfly net away just yet.

Josh had spent much of the previous year insinuating himself into Toronto's thriving alternative queer scene, but not without a push to match the, until then, unanswered pull of his tremulous curiosity. Inept at strategies of homosexual flirtation, it took an older, less inhibited suitor to successfully cruise him outside a gym where Josh was taking maximal advantage of a two-week free trial. That got Josh out into the brash, in your face, DIY queer scene of the early 2000s. It just so happened that the disinhibited 39-year-old with the black leather jacket, shaved head, and half-beard, was Gerold Merretrich, the photo editor of *The Connection*, one of the city's leading news and entertainment weeklies.

For three months, as Gerold's eager protégé, and somewhat more reluctant bedmate, Josh had a backstage pass to any rock concert, art opening, club night, or burlesque show to which he was willing to carry his old Pentax. He met the cream of the local crop of alt-pop indie darlings, avant-garde filmmakers, and pornographers passing themselves off as such. It was through Gerold that he met Daniel Raimer, half-activist, half-urban raconteur, the dandiest of the new flock of queer culture vultures. And, best of all, Joseph Bennett, who, like his forebears Gore Vidal and Elton John, had made a first name out of a last and rechristened himself 'Benny Jo'.

"Benny's the genius behind Jelatine, the best queer party in town," Gerold made the introduction one night at the Tranzac, a run-down Australian-Kiwi social club turned indie music hall off the Bloor Street strip. "You've been, of course?"

"Uh...no, I haven't," Josh admitted to them both. "Where's it held?"

Six shades of horror registered on Benny's face.

"You've never been to Jelatine?" His outfit, Marine Corps chic complete with the gold epaulets, made it feel like a hostile cross-examination in military court.

"No...but I've heard a lot about it," Josh offered in panicked self-defence.

Benny's *Bloody Knuckles* zine and his punk-inspired club nights had more or less single-handedly created the city's enviable homocore scene. An impish little queer, his other favourite look approached total nudity, clad only in juvenile jockey underwear, striped athletic socks, and vintage 1980s Adidas. Retro-fabulous, he was a regular at any event that promised to marry a punk ethos with the possibility of gay sex. He loved the company of well-muscled young guys, regardless of their orientation.

"And I've seen the posters around town. They're beautiful. So authentic and...sort of homespun."

This wasn't the right word, but it *was* the right thing to say. Benny was proud of Jelatine, but much preferred being identified with his art. And the posters *were* works of art, composed of halftone mash-ups of grainy old-school rock'n'roll photos, repurposed Tom of Finland imagery, 19th century illustrations of moustachioed gentlemen, and, of course, 1970s porn. They were hot properties among local collectors of artistic ephemera, but you had to be lucky enough to find them tacked up on café and record shop bulletin boards, or skilled enough to peel them down from lamp standards and construction sidings without destroying them.

"Do you silkscreen them yourself?" Josh asked.

"Yeah, we do them by hand down at Axis PrintWorks."

This place Josh knew. "It's in 401 Richmond," a four-storey brick warehouse converted to house dozens of the city's small galleries, design studios, non-profit arts organizations, graphic design and advertising firms. "It's the same building where I do my printing. At The F-Stop."

"Yeah, that's it. The posters take a lot of time, but the end result is a lot nicer than slick mechanically-printed stuff."

"I totally agree," Josh said, a touch embarrassed by how geeked-out he sounded. But Benny was charmed. "I'd love to see the process some time."

"That could be arranged."

"Sorry, guys," Gerold interrupted, "we should get set up before the show starts." He wanted to give a few pointers to the amateur lensman who'd never shot a live show before.

"Don't be a stranger, now," Benny said. "I'm ready for my close-ups, and I'm single, when Gerold's finished with you."

Josh had no idea how to react, and was sure he just looked inarticulately stunned as Gerold dragged him off. At 25, Josh was still getting his feet wet in the gay world. So he was thrilled to meet someone like Benny, and to have a legitimate purpose for his photographic sorties in and out of this intriguing milieu. He felt like he'd stumbled onto Toronto's version of Studio 54, and all he had to do to secure his entry was to sleep with someone a dozen years older than him. Not a bad compromise. He even convinced himself he might be in love.

Three weeks later, and after a dozen of Josh's candids had appeared in *The Connection*'s weekly 'Out and About' section, he was at the launch party for a queer film festival, relieving himself in a washroom stall, when he overheard two guys talking on the opposite side of the door.

"I see Gerold has a new boy toy," said the one voice.

"Yeah, I wonder how long this one will last," said the other.

"He's cute. And seems to have more than a few brain cells to rub together."

"All the better to get his heart broken."

He waited until they'd left to effect his own exit. There was so much that Josh didn't know about Gerold, and was too afraid to ask. He'd simply taken everything on faith lest the opportunities to publish dry up with the after-hours action.

Lying in bed the next morning, Josh was looking at the large triangular tattoo of barbed wire and a Celtic cross on the small of Gerold's back. It was the sort of thing you might see peeking out from under the upside-down smile of a stripper's thong. He'd been wanting to ask about it since they met, but hadn't had the courage. Until today.

"What, my tramp stamp? You don't like it?" Gerold grumbled, his face still hot, red, and wrinkled from hours of pressing it into a pillow.

"No, it's...it's cool. But...isn't that a bit like..."

"What?"

"Well, like advertising that you're a tramp?"

"But I am a tramp!"

"What are you talking about?" Josh sat up.

"What are *you* talking about?" Gerold clambered up onto his elbows, seeing the hurt look on Josh's face. "What, you mean...you thought...did you imagine this was exclusive?"

"Actually, I did."

"You can't be that naïve. How old are you? Twenty?"

"Don't condescend to me."

"I..." Gerold was speechless, not for shame, but for falling so blindly into the gap between generations. "Oh, god, it would never have occurred to me."

"But I thought you liked me?"

"I do like you. You're beautiful, Josh." He stroked his face. Josh pushed his hand away.

"But so...what is this, then?" Josh asked.

"What is what?"

"This!" Josh gestured helplessly at them both, his voice winding itself around a sterner, less harmonious peg. "What we're doing. What we've *been* doing these past few weeks."

He'd never had the nerve to take Gerold home to meet Lief. Even if he'd lied and said Gerold was just his editor, something about their body language, the way they talked, the postures they adopted with each other would have exposed the rather embarrassing secret. Only the idea that they were exclusive had given the relationship, if that's what it was, any dignity at all.

"This? This is just..." Gerold could see Josh's face dimming.

He didn't need to hear him say it was just sex.

"Josh, these few weeks have been wonderful..."

"But...?"

"But…monogamy is for the big relationship, if at all. I've never made it past two months…with anyone, so it's academic anyway," Gerold said with a mix of self-deprecation and contrarian pride, as if even to dream of it was absurd, pointless.

Josh was drifting further and further away, like a raft swept out to sea, and Gerold was already missing him.

"Well, I'm sorry that I'm not what you're looking for," Josh said, as he got up and started to put on his clothes.

"No, Josh, that's not…Jesus." Gerold was on the edge of the bed now. "Does anybody know what they are looking for? Do you know what you are looking for?"

Pants, shirt, almost himself again.

"Yes, something good. Something serious." Some*one* good, some*one* serious, he wanted to say.

"Serious?" Gerold laughed. "It's only been three weeks."

But Josh *was* serious, and about ready to break.

"I like you, Josh, I really do, but this thing—this relationship—still has its training wheels on, honey."

With that, Josh hopped on his tricycle and sped away as fast as he could. What an idiot he'd been. How humiliating. How fucking foolish. To have trusted, to have expected. It was too stupid to even think about. He felt keenly the lack of anyone to lead the way, the void of elders opened up by AIDS.

Jesus, I don't even know Gerold's HIV status, he thought.

Josh silently vowed to get himself tested as soon as possible, and never to make such an idiotic mistake again.

So, he retreated for a time, stayed out of the 'scene' he'd come to know, and kept working on his own stuff. He focused on more stylized subject matter—the brick walls of back alley garages with rusted eaves and spigots artfully clinging to them like tarnished vine, the odd bit of graffiti framed and decontextualized into pure abstraction, the façades along Queen Street that remained hundred-year-old portraits of the city that was.

One day, he was at 401 Richmond, departing The F-Stop, his backpack heavy with new work, when he ran into Benny Jo en route to his own studio.

"Hey. Josh, right?"

"Yeah. Hi, Benny. What's new?"

"The Hairy Tarantulas are playing Jelatine this week. It's going to be stupidly awesome." Among the few thousand that had ever heard of them, the band was less admired for their musicality than they were for performing naked, save for outsized plush genitalia encircled by equally enormous wigs of pubic hair—handmade by the band, of course.

"Oh…cool," Josh said.

"Don't fall down with excitement." Benny liked Josh too much to lay it on any thicker than that. "Hey, I don't see your pictures in 'Out and About' anymore."

"No, I haven't been very active lately…since, you know…Gerold and I…"

"Don't take it too hard, Josh. Gerold goes through guys like Kleenex." Despite the wild crowd he ran with, Benny was a romantic at heart. He'd had more than his fair share of guys flake out and fuck up on him, and would have dated Josh himself if he could figure out what was going on behind his slightly cool, illegible exterior. "Anyway, keep shooting. You're good."

"Thanks."

"Hey, come and shoot Jelatine this week."

"I'd love to." Those fright-wig crotches with their pantyhose-and-cotton-ball cocks would make hilariously photogenic subject matter. But then who would dare publish the pictures?

"I'll put your name on the list for Friday."

"Th-thanks. That's really…sweet." He winced. So saccharine, so un-hip. But Benny didn't seem to mind.

"You wanna come up and help me print the posters? I could use an extra pair of hands."

"Sure. That'd be fucking awesome," he gushed. His internal censor was on a washroom break.

That's more like it, Benny thought.

And with that to add to his bona fides, Josh made his return to Jelatine, where he met more people like Benny and Daniel, and quickly became a regular face in the crowd. He knew he needed to get himself out there, get his face and his name known, if he was going to keep up the momentum. Soon enough Josh's pictures were appearing in 'Lavender Nights', the local gay paper's social page. The former butterfly hunter was becoming a butterfly in his own right.

He saw Gerold there more often than not. The taste of a little proximity to 'fame' had proved too tempting to Josh, who liked that it probably irritated Gerold to see him getting on by himself. But Josh was always cordial and never consciously tried to rub it in. He was still a decidedly small fish in a pond full of both bigger predators and protectors. He couldn't go too far wrong, he figured, if he swam carefully and always carried a good camera.

And so Josh came to accept, if not entirely to like, that staying on good terms with people who were professionally useful, if personally disappointing, even distasteful, was all part of the big, long game that, more and more transparently, adult life seemed to be.

❖

Counter to type, Josh had few close female friends. But Clarke Anna Coates was different. An activist and recent transplant from Vancouver, as well as being Lief's ex-girlfriend, the fact that Josh had let himself get so close to her was a testament to her many and various charms, not least her impressive knowledge of books and her excellent taste in music, clothing and restaurants. They bonded over the common traumas of losing their mothers to cancer (he at 18, she at 24) and both having dated and been dumped by one of the Gabrels brothers.

On a crisp fall evening, she met him at closing time at his place of employment, Rick Random's, a clothing store-cum-art gallery on Bloor Street, in the heart of the Annex. It was stocked with an ever-changing inventory of discounted and discontinued brand name stuff. Anything good, Josh would grab before the customers had a chance to. It was a fashionable prison for an ambitious creative type, but a prison nonetheless.

"Before we head to the movie," Clarke said, tugging him in the opposite direction, "I want to stop in at Calico's to run off some copies of a poster."

"Sure. What are the posters for?"

"A rally I'm helping to organize."

Josh smiled and turned mechanically on his heel. "When in doubt, always go Left."

Despite its relatively high prices and questionable corporate connections, Calico's Copy Shop was a hub of all manner of dissident activity, like Karl Marx doing the research for Das Kapital at the British Library. No one saw any irony in this. The DIY set appreciated the efficiency and anonymity of their service model. If you could pay and knew how to use the machines, you could do whatever you wanted unmolested by the skeleton staff, who were usually tearing their hair out with architectural drawings or laminated school projects for clients better heeled and more demanding than Clarke and her peers.

No sooner had Josh and Clarke set foot in the door than he ran into someone he knew. A diminutive guy in gas station coveralls, a matching baseball cap, and a silk scarf that Clarke would have thought twice about wearing for being too girly. Josh balked, thought of passing him by, pretending not to see him.

"Josh!"

"Hey, Benny."

He swept Josh up in a one-armed embrace, kissing him on the cheek. A glue stick and a cutout occupied his other hand. He was working at a project table with scissors and a mess of high-contrast photocopies of bands and cultural icons too obscure for Clarke to identify.

She hung back, uncertain of an introduction.

"Where've you been hiding?" Benny asked.

"Nowhere. Just busy."

"Uh-huh," Benny cast a glance at Clarke before returning to his cut-and-paste job, talking over his shoulder. "You coming to Jelatine this month? Psychic Flak Jacket are playing. Not to be missed, Joshie."

She'd never heard him addressed this way and could only guess what sort of relationship permitted this casual intimacy.

"Yeah, sure, if I can."

Clarke was waiting to be included or liberated, she didn't care which.

"I'm just gonna…" She pointed her thumb in the direction of the machines, anxious to get to work.

"Oh, sure," Josh said, then added, "I'll come back and talk to you in a sec, Benny."

"No, it's okay, Josh," she insisted. "You stay and chat." And off she strode.

❖

Five minutes later, they were out the door and on their way to dinner.

"Who was that?" she asked.

"Just a friend."

"Some kind of artist?" She didn't know any gas station attendants who hung out in print shops making poster art.

"Yeah. Artist, deejay, club promoter. Lots of different things."

"How do you know him?"

It would have been simple enough to say he met him through his photographic work, but he chose to tell the whole truth.

"Uh, I go to his club night sometimes."

"Jelatine?" she asked. "What's it like?"

"It's kind of an alternative rock'n'roll party. It's fun."

"I'd like to go. Sounds interesting." She prided herself on being *au courant*, and what was hip in Toronto's underground was unknown on the west coast, a disability she had yet to overcome.

"Yeah...I don't know if it would be your scene."

"What's 'my scene'?"

"It just...it gets a bit wild sometimes."

She understood, and tried to brush off the condescension.

"Well, now I'm really curious. You run in an interesting set."

He didn't recognize himself in this description.

"Benny and his friends like me because I've taken some nice pictures of them, but I am not really of their world."

"No?"

The only way he could participate in something like Jelatine was as an anthropologist. Saying 'yes' to what was on offer there was too scary. His was the power to withhold, to say 'no' (politely), which made him all the more desirable for being unattainable.

Josh led her off of Bloor and onto a quieter side street.

"You don't talk much about your gay life," she ventured to say.

"No, I guess I don't." He wanted to move on.

"So, what's it like?"

"My 'gay' life?" he said, his face cartoonish with incredulity. "It's virtually non-existent."

"Why? You're a good-looking guy. Benny's kind of cute. You never thought of dating him?"

"We were becoming closer for a while there. But I think we both separately came to the conclusion that it wouldn't work."

"Why?"

"I don't know. It's hard to be with someone who *is* someone in the world. There are a lot of agendas and egos and too many opportunities for crossed wires, you know?"

"Yeah, I can imagine." The activist world was not so different.

"People like that are best admired from afar, I think," Josh explained. "Somebody is right for them, someone who can live in the center of the storm with them and not get consumed by it, but it's not me."

❖

Six months later, during a Saturday afternoon shift, Josh came up from the storeroom to find someone whose penchant for black leather made him an unlikely Rick Random's customer. He was intently examining the current photo exhibit, Josh's first, full of abstract graffiti and back alley brick walls. Josh recognized the visitor in an instant, but slipped past him unnoticed.

After the visitor had lingered over one piece for a while, Josh finally lost patience. "You like anything you see?" he called out from the cash register.

Without turning around, "I do. It's good work. I particularly like these two."

A diptych of portraits had been added to the less figurative work that had been up for a couple of months. The first was bleached-out, almost all white. He'd taken it in the aftermath of a bicycle accident that could very easily have cost Clarke her life. She was pictured in her hospital bed with all of its surrounding paraphernalia, an ocean wave of dark hair interrupted by a scar curving around her left ear.

"The textures are so fine," the visitor noted, closely examining the bandage grid of gauze, the paper-like folds of her gown, "and the light values, so diffuse," her face sketched in the subtlest greys, hovering over the white backdrop.

The other was dark and almost geometric. The contrast pushed to blacken the background, only her face and hands caught any of the light. It was Clarke again, her head shaved, lying on her back. She gazed off to the right where an unseen window illuminated her face, her arms raised above her head in a fanciful demi-Arabesque. There was a delicacy and beauty to the portrait that the hardness of the scar and the severity of her haircut might otherwise have denied.

Gerold loved the monochrome pair, the dark and the light. "Who is she?" he asked, coming over to the register. "A friend of yours?"

"Yeah."

"A lot of trust there. They're very vulnerable pictures."

He was right. It hadn't been easy getting Clarke's permission to put them up. But Josh felt it was some of his strongest work, and she didn't want to stand in the way of his career. She was happy to be his muse.

"You're showing your own stuff now," Gerold said.

"Trying to." Also doing his best to look busy, folding t-shirts. "Not getting much uptake, though."

Gerold smiled. "I might be able to use them. Do you have more?"

"Like those two? Maybe." He'd shot a couple of dozen photos of Clarke during her recovery, but these were the only two that had the right mix of formality and ambiguity to give them wider interest. "Use them how?"

"I'm putting together a group show for Plate Glass."

"I don't know it," Josh said.

"It's a new gallery space in an old furniture shop that's just opened on Bloor West. They want up-and-coming shooters. Theme TBD. I can't use the graffiti stuff, but the portraiture…"

"You think it's good enough?"

"It's good, Josh," he said with the confidence age brings.

The photographer eager to graduate from being a store clerk was more than pleased.

"Okay." *Next steps? Next steps?* He had no idea. "You wanna get coffee or something? I'm done at 6:30."

Gerold checked his watch. Twenty-five minutes. "Sure. Let's meet at the Future Bakery," a Ukrainian-owned café just down the street. "I'll wait for you."

❖

What Gerold didn't need to know was that Josh was also sleeping with Clarke. It had started right around the time of her accident. In part out of affection, in part out of curiosity, and in part on the three-strikes theory of entitlement. He figured he deserved some satisfaction after a series of brief same-sex entanglements, what his idol Gore Vidal would have called "temporary adhesions", that had all come to nought. He'd gotten the sense that she was open to it, believed he was capable of pleasing her, learned that he could, and, much as he resisted admitting it to himself, doing so made him feel like a man.

But Clarke was not entirely unselfish in falling into it either. In Josh she had the best of both worlds—a friend and a competent lover—without the strings, without the delusions of 'love' and 'forever'. At least, that was the unspoken spirit in which it began. He let her imagine that she had initiated it, and she let him imagine that he had. It was the only way to conceal from themselves the sheer neediness of this desperate, foolhardy tumble into the unknown that, seen clearly, might have driven either of them away. The idiocy of it. And yet the sweetness too. For Josh was a perfect gentleman. More solicitous of her than he'd been of any previous lover, and more secure in his role. He'd grown up like everyone else with the rightness of a man and woman together reflected everywhere. He knew the script and could play it by heart.

❖

So when he went home that night in June with Gerold, having not seen him in eight months, he was pretty sure he was making a mistake. But it had been so long since he'd been with his own kind, enjoyed the attention of…Well, what could he say? It was fun. Easier to talk now that they both knew where they stood. Coffee led to beer. Beer to dinner. Dinner to dessert. Dessert to…Gerold's place. Josh's dreams opening up. His work in a real show. A door stood ajar. He walked through it. Disorienting, though, when he didn't recognize himself on the other side.

"I'm sorry, Gerold. I just…I can't do this again."

"Then why are we doing it?"

It was Gerold's second failed hook-up of the week. He was about ready to give up on anyone more than five years his junior.

"I felt…grateful. I wanted to thank you for…"

"So thank me." He grabbed the back of Josh's thigh and pulled it into his hip. Josh pushed himself away.

"I'm seeing someone, Gerold."

Charming that this was an obstacle to him. "You've always disappointed me in this department. Nothing's changed."

"I'm sorry."

Gerold waved the apology off as unnecessary, stood up from the sofa, put his jacket on. He wasn't staying home after this. He was gonna go out and get fucked by someone who actually wanted to. That was his right.

"Who is it?" he asked. Never a moral problem for Gerold, but socially awkward if it was someone he too had been to bed with.

"You don't know them."

Gerold caught the odd choice of pronoun, and Josh's stubborn refusal to meet his gaze. A guilty look in the eyes. Something insane occurred to him.

"Not that girl in the photos?"

This was unanswerable, but he answered it.

"No…" Utterly unconvincing, even to Josh's ear.

"My god. What have you gotten yourself into?"

Josh loathed the idea that he had made himself ridiculous in Gerold's eyes. But everything about the defeated posture he'd assumed telegraphed his humiliation as he got ready to leave.

So sensitive these young ones, Gerold thought.

"Well, good luck with that." Gerold jingled his keys. "Time to go."

"So, about the show…?" Josh was afraid to ask.

"Not contingent on your giving me an orgasm, if that's what you're asking. You've earned your place in it."

Thank god. "Thank you, Gerold."

The disemployed Svengali allowed himself to be condescended to with a hug.

"Just get your head straightened out and stop messing with people's emotions, Mr. Chang. It's a good way to make enemies."

Josh's relationship with Clarke finally fell apart in July.

The city fell apart in August.

And in the midst of a protest march turned riot that she'd done everything she could to prevent, she saw a head of black hair she recognized, the face obscured behind a pair of tinted swimming goggles and a bandito mask. She was sure that beneath it was a mouth she'd kissed, and regretted kissing, and thought she loved, and regretted thinking so, someone whose friendship she missed, despite everything, running toward the front, snapping away on a used digital SLR.

❖

In a neighbourhood where every shop front disappeared behind a veil of iron bars at night, where skid row donut shops were fogged with blue cigarette smoke, where neighbourhood pharmacies all declared in bold print 'We <u>Do Not</u> Stock or Dispense Opiates' to any drugstore cowboys who might be thinking of knocking them over, and shabby but respectable ethnic variety stores served only those who could decode their cryptic signage in Ethiopian or Eritrean, infill cafés and humble little galleries with big ambitions were starting to appear.

Plate Glass was one of these. A coat of white paint, a resurfaced wood floor, and some elegantly minimalistic chairs to match the nearly invisible sign were all that distinguished it from the discount furniture store it had been twelve weeks earlier. The pieces of vintage camera equipment in recessed display cases established its credentials as a temple dedicated to the art of picture-making; the magic of lenses, filters, and emulsions; the caprices of the eye, and happy accidents of light.

Two posters in the window, one a blow-up of this week's *Connection* cover, the other an advert for the show itself, announced the arrival of new talent.

It was an iconic image of the chasm the city had plunged into. In the left foreground, a young Muslim mother, a student politician at the University of Toronto, was removing her brightly patterned headscarf to shield her toddler from the drifting tear gas, while behind her on the right a police truncheon was frozen in mid-air about to come down on the helmeted head of a handcuffed cyclist. Dramatic wisps of yellow gas swirled around all four figures, and the sky behind them was an indifferent, pitiless grey.

As the photographer behind that image, Josh had struck gold, and Gerold Merretrich insisted on having it for both the show he was curating and for the cover of *The Connection*. He'd found his theme—the twin spirits of the protester and the photojournalist—and, of necessity, the show became a fundraiser for the Prince Edward Viaduct Legal Defence Fund, supporting those protester and organizers charged in what had come to be known as the 'Riot on the Viaduct'.

So, at 5:30, Josh and the three other featured lensmen and women gathered with Gerold, the gallery owner, and a select handful of the city's top photo editors and collectors for a private viewing. At 6:30 it opened to the public with a short talk and a longer Q&A, and then the whole thing became a lot more relaxed. Josh felt both privileged and out-gunned to be sharing space with these local luminaries. It was a first step, an opening, and he was determined to push himself through it.

He'd just accepted a business card from the publisher of *StreetLevel*, an urban issues quarterly, when in walked his father, Kenneth, clutching a cane, and his brother, Luke.

"You made it," Josh said warmly.

"There was some confusion about which exit to take," Luke said. "Weren't sure where we'd end up, but we figured it out."

Kenneth tugged on Josh's arm.

"What neighbourhood is this?" He'd never been invited to Josh's apartment, and prayed his son didn't live down here.

"This is Bloordale." The name had been newly minted by the real estate industry to sound old and well established, making a desirable area out of a place most middle-class suburbanites drove through with their doors locked.

"It's an interesting space." Luke had an affection for the antique. "The old box cameras are great. Where's your stuff?"

"Some are here," Josh gestured at one large wall dominated by the protest images, to which everyone contributed their best shots. "And the rest are in that corner." Each photographer also had their own chunk of wall space for a broader profile, select images that showed the full range of their work.

There wasn't much chance Kenneth had seen the cover of *The Connection* that week. It was a downtown paper, barely made it as far north as the highway that symbolically divided the city from the sprawl that surrounded it. Josh wondered what his dad would make of it.

Kenneth hobbled over to the group wall as best he could. It wasn't quite what he expected. A lot of police. A lot of smoke. At least one burning squad car. Hippie-looking rioters throwing soft toys and blowing kisses at cops. Others all in black bandanas and masks. A striking image of a woman and a child in a haze of gas. He recognized it from the poster on the window.

"What is all this?" Kenneth asked.

"What do you mean?"

"I left Taiwan to get away from politics. Are you getting mixed up in that stuff?"

"It's art, Dad, maybe journalism, but not politics."

"They're good, Josh. They're really good," Luke said.

"You think so?" Josh wasn't at all confident. He thought the charged subject matter overwhelmed any formal considerations.

"Hey, let me introduce you to the curator." Gerold was wrapping up a bit of business with a collector. Josh waved him over. "Gerold, this is my father, Kenneth, and my brother, Luke."

He shook their hands, said he was charmed, but was already calculating how long he had to invest in these non-relationships.

"Your Josh has quite the eye for small, telling details," Gerold said, "the intimate moments to which black and white lends the necessary weight." The flatness of his tone was the surest sign of its perfect sincerity.

He looked aggressively homosexual to Kenneth, but maybe that's what all photo curators looked like. How was he to know? Kenneth smiled and tried to take his approving comments at face value, not appetized by the idea that there might be something more to this man's relationship with his son.

"Thanks for giving him this break," Luke said. "We've been waiting for the world to discover Josh's talents."

"I'm predicting great things for him," Gerold said in that same confident monotone. And then he hastily excused himself.

Kenneth wandered back over to the framed print of that newspaper cover photo, uncluttered by headlines. Josh followed.

"You took that picture?"

"Yes, Dad. Do you like it?"

Kenneth nodded, said nothing, was inarticulately proud.

LEAVES

James Penha

Halim, who had been lying unconscious in his bed for more than forty-eight hours, opened his eyes and screamed. His wife leaped from the corner chair and tried to hold her husband's hands, but he was flailing them wildly.

"Kill me. Kill me. I cannot stand the pain." He struggled to turn onto his stomach to bury his face in the pillows. "Sit on my head! Smother me!" he screamed, although his wife heard only muffled sounds.

She called for their daughter Yuli to watch over her father while she ran up the street to the local clinic. She was relieved to find Doctor Teguh on duty. He made the rounds among several small clinics and large hospitals in Sibolga, the port city of Northern Sumatra. His presence meant she wouldn't have to recount Halim's medical history to still another practitioner.

"He's awake. Screaming for me to kill him," was all she needed to say.

The doctor swiveled his desk chair to face Ibu Andri. His raised eyes wrinkled his brow. "He awoke. It's hard to believe. When we opened him up last time, the cancer had metastasized so wildly, like a parasite vine in a mango tree. There was little of his own body left. He should be dead. His will to live must…"

"He has no will to live," Andri interrupted the doctor. "He wants to die. He cannot stand the pain. You must do something, Doctor. Please."

The doctor prepared his satchel, told a colleague at the clinic that he needed to attend to a patient, and walked with Andri toward her home. Halfway there, the doctor and Andri and everyone else on the street could hear Halim's agonized, incoherent roars. When they entered the bedroom, Andri told her daughter to leave them alone. The doctor prepared a syringe and injected its contents into Halim. Within a few minutes, Halim's yells modulated into whimpers.

"More," Halim begged the doctor.

"I have given you as large a dose of morphine as I dare without killing you."

"More," the patient repeated, his tears pouring, "More."

"Halim, I am leaving this vial of pills here." The doctor set the plastic container on the bed stand next to a lamp and a bottle of water. "They are pain-killers, opiates. If the injection starts to wear off, you can take one of the pills. I am leaving the vial, Halim. You can medicate yourself. Do you understand?"

Halim grabbed the doctor's hand and brought it to his lips. He nodded his head.

Doctor Teguh patted Halim's cheek and stood away. "I must return to the clinic now, but I will check on you in," the doctor looked at his wrist watch, "in two hours." He turned to Andri. "Leave your husband alone for a while. He needs his rest."

Andri leaned over her husband and kissed his forehead again and again before she accompanied the doctor out of the bedroom and saw him to the front door.

Andri waited nervously with her daughter in the kitchen. She could not stomach the tea Yuli had prepared. Yuli sipped from her cup, but she hadn't been told for what exactly they were waiting. For one hour and fifty minutes Andri stared silently at the wall clock. She blinked with every leap of the minute hand until she jumped from her chair at the sound of the doctor's salaam alaikum in the doorway to which she now ran.

"Alaikum salaam, Doctor. Shall we check on him now?"

"Let me go in first, Ibu," the doctor graciously suggested at the door to the bedroom, but Andri would not wait any longer and snuck in behind the doctor before he had a chance to enter the chamber. The vial was empty, she saw, and Halim looked peaceful. The doctor listened at

Halim's nose and chest. He held Halim's right wrist and turned to face Andri. "He...is sleeping."

"Sleeping? Only sleeping? So painlessly? So peacefully?"

"Ibu, he has taken enough of these pills to kill a water buffalo. They have made him sleep. Deeply. But he will awaken and will again be in agony."

"What is to be done? What is to be done? Shall I smother him after all?" Andri grabbed the pillow from beneath Halim's head and pressed it onto his face with all her weight.

The doctor waited a minute before he took Andri's shoulders and moved her away from the bed. He again listened at Halim's nose and chest. Halim still lived.

"Not long enough!" screamed Andri as she again forced the pillow on her husband's face.

"Stop, Ibu, stop!" Again he removed Andri, screaming hysterically from the bed, and turned her toward him. "Ibu, you cannot kill him. But you can damage him further with even more pain with which he will have to live."

"What are you saying?"

"Halim cannot die. Even if we were to cut his wrists and bleed him dry, I do not think he would die. He would live—suffering not only from the cancer but from the torturous effects of the blood-letting."

Andri collapsed to the floor. "But this makes no sense. This makes no sense!"

"No," said the doctor, sitting next to Halim on the bed. "This makes no sense."

"What can we do?"

"When Halim wakes, feed him more of the morphine. I shall have additional vials sent here. There is no risk that the drugs will kill him, but we can pray they continue to relieve the pain. You will need to explain the situation to him. Tell him what happened here today. Tell him..."

"Yes, Doctor?"

"Tell him he requires medicine of a different kind."

"From God?"

"Perhaps." He paused. "I will send someone who deals in traditional medicines."

"A shaman?"

"She is herself an angel of God, I think, willing to deal with lost causes. I sometimes ask her to ease the transition of a patient from life to death. In this case, we need to hope she knows how to effect the transition."

"Halim does not believe in witchcraft."

"If Halim comes to believe that he cannot die, he may also be willing to try the old ways. You will have to persuade him."

When Halim finally opened his eyes more than a day later and realized that he had failed to kill himself, he did not need much persuasion from his wife to accept a visit from Mbak Tirta who turned out to be, for one in her business, surprisingly young, little older than Halim's own daughter. He had expected a witch out of an old Disney cartoon, but felt, somehow, more comfortable greeting a woman more like Snow White than Queen Grimhilde.

"My knowledge is ancient," she explained, "passed down from mother to daughter, mother to daughter, on this island for 1000 years."

She took a package wrapped in banana leaves from the colorful string bag she had arranged on her lap. She sat next to Andri on Halim's bed. "You want," she said to Halim, "to die."

"Yes."

"Because?"

"Because I am no body but a walking tumor. I should have died weeks ago."

"But you cannot?"

"I cannot. You must kill me."

Tirta laughed uproariously. "No, no, my dear sir. I do not kill."

"Then why are you here?" screamed Halim. Andri moved closer to his face and wiped his brow with the damp cloth she clutched in her hand.

"I am here to let God move you." She opened the banana leaves to reveal a collection of small sprigs of bright-green tear-shaped leaves. "Do you recognize this vegetable, Ibu?" she asked Andri who shook her head. "These are kelor leaves"

"Oh," said Andri. "What is that proverb? My mother repeated it whenever she faced something mysterious."

"The world is not as wide as kelor leaves," Halim intoned.

"Ah, you do remember the old saying," chuckled Tirta. "Aside from the health benefits even modern nutritionists understand, kelor leaves have supernatural qualities. Ibu, please soak these leaves for twenty minutes in boiling water, drain them, and bring them back to me in a pail."

"Must you feed them to me?" Halim objected. "I can barely swallow. It hurts so much even to get the pills down. I do not eat or drink anything else." He moaned, "And still I live."

"No worries," Tirta brightly responded. "I intend to swab you with the leaves. You must remove the bedclothes and your pajamas. I will need to reach every part of your body with the leaves."

"Naked? I must be naked?"

"As the day you were born and as you will be on the day you die and are bathed before being covered in a shroud for burial, Bapak Halim." Tirta laughed. "Don't be shy or embarrassed. Not in front of me who has seen it all already and am unmoved. Anyway, this is how it must be."

When Andri returned with the pail of wilted leaves, she was shocked to see her husband stretched out naked on his bed. She hadn't seen his undressed body for some months. The sallow tint that undulated amidst its protrusions and hollows moved her to tears. She had remembered him as a powerful, ruddy man.

"No time for tears," said Tirta. "Except for these little green tears." She grabbed handfuls of the kelor and, as promised, wiped every aspect of Halim until his body was green as grass, Andri helping to move her husband to make even his most private parts accessible."

"Now," said Tirta. "We wait. If your skin begins to whiten, you will have your wish and can thank me after you kiss your dear wife goodbye. And your daughter of course, but we shall cover you when that time comes."

But after a half-hour, Halim remained green, and his pain worsened enough that he had to submit himself to the agony of swallowing a painkiller.

"Nope," Tirta said. "No beans. Too bad."

"Shall we try again?" Andri asked.

"Oh, no. If it is meant to be, it works like a charm." She giggled. "Well, of course, it is a charm!" She slapped her thighs and stood. "But don't give up hope. It will work once Bapak Halim has atoned for the great sin on his soul."

"What great sin?" Halim asked.

"That's for you to know, not for me to find out. The only reason the kelor leaves won't work is that God needs you to atone. Once you have done so, you'll see, we'll do the leaves thing again, and, bam! you'll be dead! But there is something dire holding things up. So serious, Bapak, I have to think you know what it is. Or can remember it. It's too serious to be nothing. Nothing interferes with death in this way except something really, really serious."

Halim was silent. And thoughtful.

"Hmm," Tirta mused. "I am thinking you have an inkling—Hey, I made a poem there. Anyway, I hope I'm right. Don't want my verse to be worse! Oh, my God, I am so silly today. But this is serious. Bapak Halim, you must seek atonement or at least forgiveness for the sin, and then call me again. You have my cell phone number, right?"

After Tirta departed the house, Andri helped her husband to the stool set up for him in the wet bathroom. She drew water from the barrel sitting there and washed the kelor dye from her husband until he was again a sickly if fresher tawny. She dried him with a clean towel, wrapped him in a sarong, and led him back to his bed.

"No, let me sit in the chair there. I need to strengthen myself for my trip."

"Trip?" The only trip Andri envisioned was the trip to the afterlife, but how was he planning for that now? Andri asked herself.

Ensconced in the well-upholstered corner chair, Halim explained, "I shall be going back home to Batang Toru."

"Batang Toru? You want to be buried in Batang Toru when the time comes?"

"Perhaps, yes. I hadn't been thinking of that. I will return to Batang Toru to find forgiveness."

Andri sat at her husband's feet. "Oh, my dear, do you believe this so-called witch? Her 'inkling'? Ah, she is more like a clown than a shaman!"

"But she is right. I know she is right."

"Who is left to forgive you in Batang Toru? Who there even knows you? You haven't been in Batang Toru for…"

"Twenty-three years."

"Of course. As long as we have known each other."

"We met on the Eid soon after my arrival here in Sibolga."

"I have not forgotten. Anything."

Halim changed the subject. "Andri, leave word at the clinic. I need Doctor Teguh to teach me to inject myself with morphine, and to provide me with enough of the drug to get me through several days in Batang Toru."

"And if you find forgiveness there?"

"I will atone. I will return. I will be bathed in the strange woman's leaves. I will die. And…"

"And?"

"I will be at peace."

Peace was not what the two-hour bus ride from Sibolga to Batang Toru brought Halim. The driver took every turn at top speed and ran over broken, rocky stretches of the road as if he were cruising a newly-paved toll road. Halim touched his arm where, beneath his shirt, he wore a patch of fentanyl.

"One hundred times stronger than morphine," Teguh had explained, "and designed to last twenty-four hours although you may need a fresh patch more often." The three replacements the doctor had somehow managed to obtain were in a pocket in Halim's backpack. Halim smiled to think how, at least, the fentanyl masked the bus-inflicted muscle aches as well as the pain of the cancer devouring those muscles. How was he even able to sit up straight? he wondered. Or walk? A zombie, he replied to himself. He was the walking dead.

When the bus leaped up the awkward incline to the bridge over the river, Halim recognized that he was home for had spent almost every day of his youth swimming or fishing in that river or simply lying on its banks with Tomi. But where was Tomi now? Except for the river and its ancient bridge, the town was so different. Gold had been discovered some years earlier and the mining companies that invaded the town wanted a city.

Using the crutches Doctor Teguh had loaned him, Halim disembarked at the terminal. Tomi had sold cigarettes at this place when it was little more than a bus stop, Halim recalled. They had both lived not far away—close enough for Halim to try to walk to Tomi's old house on a path Halim had trod hundreds of times. How often had he hung over the window ledge of Tomi's room to awaken him for school? How often had he crept over that same ledge surreptitiously to visit his friend at night?

Halim shook his head and all the memories within. But which was the house? The neighborhood was not exactly as he remembered it. But if that mango tree, infested now with its own malignant parasites, was the one he recalled from his youth, then this little house, its facade newly tiled in pink, must be Tomi's.

Halim balanced himself before the front door, knocked, and called, "Salaam Alaikum."

A young boy of about fourteen, Halim guessed, opened the door, "Alaikum Salaam," the boy responded.

"Is your father home?"

The boy closed the door and reopened it moments later in the presence of a woman dressed in the uniform of a civil servant. "Can I help you?" she asked.

"My name is Halim. From Sibolga now, but I used to live in Batang Toru many—more than twenty years ago."

"In this house?" the woman asked.

"No, no. But not far away. This, I think—but it looks so different, I can't even be sure—used to be my friend's house. His name was Tomi. I am looking for him. I came to Batang Toru to find him."

"And his family name?"

"Nasution."

The woman scrunched her nose and mouth. "I don't think I can help. Maybe this was the house. We bought it four years ago from a family named Siregar. I wouldn't know about anyone before that."

Halim sighed.

"Would you like a cup of tea, Bapak Halim?"

"No. No thank you. I need to get along."

"Where will you search now?"

"The place least likely to change, I think. Thank you for your kindness."

The woman wrapped her right arm around her son who hadn't moved from the threshold and closed the door with her left hand.

Halim headed back to the terminal. Pain, like broken shards of glass, cut into his abdomen. Soon, he knew, his whole body would become his greatest enemy. He needed a new patch. When he reached the main road, he hailed a pedicab and, shaking his crutches in explanation as he climbed into the back seat, begged the driver to get him to Masjid Al Ikhlas quickly but with as few bumps as possible. Mosques even more than most buildings in a growing Indonesian city were subject to showy reconstructions, but Masjid Al Ikhlas had been built, more than two centuries earlier, of teak and ironwood without so much as a single nail. It was one of the wonders of the Islamic world. Unless an earthquake had devoured it, Al Ikhlas would await Halim as it had in his youth: cool and beautiful, dark and inviting. And, indeed, in minutes, the mosque's great brown cupola—the magical mound of chocolate, Tomi called it—came into view.

Halim struggled to release himself from the pedicab, paid the driver, and hurried as best he could to one of the toilets at the back of the complex. From his backpack pocket, he extracted a sachet. Fentanyl, the label said. He took off his shirt and replaced the patch he had been wearing on his upper left arm. The traditional toilet had no commode, no place to sit, and so Halim leaned his forehead and hands against the wall until the shards of glass inside him turned into sand.

When he gathered the strength to walk, Halim left the toilet and entered the mosque's office. It served as well as a souvenir shop selling shawls and beads with wooden tags into each of which was burned an etching of the famous mosque. Halim asked the white-robed haji at the counter if he might see the imam.

"Imam Iskandar?" asked the haji. "He is resting in the residence."

"Imam Iskandar? Then he is still imam here?"

"For almost fifty years now. You know him?"

"I grew up in Batang Toru. I spent so much of my childhood in the mosque."

"Praying?"

"Yes. And playing, like all boys."

"They still do." The haji laughed. "I think I recognize you. What is your name?"

"Halim. My father was Asrul Harahap. We moved to Sibolga more than twenty years ago."

"Asrul's son! Halim!" croaked an old man, as ruddy as his robes were white, ambling in to the office.

"Imam!" Halim cried and took the ancient one's wrinkled right hand and kissed it. "Alahu Akbar. Salaam alaikum."

"Alaikum salaam, Halim." The haji got out of his chair to make way for the imam, but Iskandar patted Halim on the shoulder. "You sit, Halim. You look like you need a chair more than I do." Halim demurred, but Iskandar insisted, "You look like death."

"I…I have not been well."

"No, no. I can see that. You are living where?"

"Sibolga. I took the bus."

"To visit the mosque before you die?"

"Well, yes, I suppose…yes." The imam nodded. "And to find my old friend Tomi. Tomi Nasution. You remember him?"

"I remember you both. Typical bad Muslim boys, I think." The imam leaned into a corner of the office. "You used to sneak out of Friday prayers and hide in the rafters beneath the dome."

"We did. Often."

"Not only on Fridays?"

"It was our special place."

"Yes." The imam paused before addressing the haji. "Bapak Haji, can you leave us for a moment to reminisce. I think I can handle any rush of tourists here." The imam smiled and said to Halim, "We are waiting for our first customer in three days."

When they were alone, the imam said, "One of the reasons I remember you is that one evening, I climbed to the dome and found you, you and Tomi."

"You did?"

"I did. There were no lights up there, but the moon was full, and so the two of you were quite visible."

"We were?"

"And quite naked."

"We were, yes, that is possible. Imam, I am here to admit to my sins."

"You were having sex with your friend although I could not discern who was doing what to whom." He paused. "Not that it matters. The following day, I ordered a gate to be built and locked in front of the stairway to the dome." He fiddled in his pocket and removed a key. "It's still there."

"Imam, can you forgive me? Can God forgive me for sinning in his house, for that blasphemy? How can I atone for this abomination?"

"Oh, please! You were young. And you were friends. Do you think you were the first teenagers in this town who ever had sex?"

"But in the mosque!"

"The complex has many private hideaways. You were not the first or the last couple to discover one. And I bet that time I saw you was not the first or last time you had sex with your friend." He waited. "Was it?"

"No. We…we loved each other very much."

"And so what happened that you need to find him now? You must have lost him."

"I came to feel ashamed of what I felt, of loving a boy. Imam, you know, this is not acceptable in our religion, in my family, in our tradition."

"That is so. You felt…"

"Sick. That is what homosexuals are called here. Sick."

"And did Tomi feel the same way?"

"No." No one spoke for some minutes. "He loved me, he said. He wanted us to run away to Padang or Jakarta where there were plenty of people like us." Tears poured from Halim's eyes. He raised his head and shook it back and forth, back and forth. "One night we were lying in his bed in his room where I had so often come to find him. We had had sex before sleeping. No, Imam, let me be honest, more honest than ever. We had made love. But I had already decided—had been trying to decide—to end this immoral behavior. In the middle of the night, I felt his mouth. I told him to stop. I told him he was sick. He was sick, I said, not me. I screamed that I hated people like him. Hated them! And to prove it, I beat him, Imam. Beat him with my fists and dragged him onto the floor to kick him where he fell. He didn't try to defend himself. He just rolled into a ball. I climbed out his window and ran away."

"You never saw him again?"

"I did. I saw what I had done to him. Batang Toru was a small town. But I avoided him."

"Because you told yourself you hated him."

"That is what I told myself."

"But?"

"But I loved him." The imam held Halim's head to his breast. "Can you forgive me, Imam?"

"It is not up to me, Halim, to forgive you. I am not offended."

"Then God? Can God forgive me?"

"I don't think He will…"

"Then I am doomed in ways I cannot even describe, Imam."

"I don't think God will forgive you until you atone."

"How, Imam, how?"

"With Tomi. You must speak to Tomi."

"I came to Batang Toru to do just that. But where is he?"

"He owns the old bread factory. It has a bakery and a café attached now. Tomi is our Starbucks. But he isn't Tomi any more. He calls himself Marissa. Go to Marissa's, Halim. Explain yourself to Marissa."

Halim hailed a pedicab and asked the teenaged driver to take him to the old bread factory. "What old bread factory?" the puzzled driver asked.

"Oh, I mean to say, Marissa's."

The driver smiled. "Marissa's? There's nothing old about Marissa's. It's the trendiest place in Batang Toru."

The parking lot was crammed with motorbikes and cars in front of a colonial-style building looking fresher and friendlier than it did when the Dutch built it in the 1930s.

"Welcome to Marissa's," the driver said as Halim stretched his legs out of the pedicab. The driver looked at his phone. "Hmm. It's already after four—happy hour—half-price drinks with any purchase of a snack. I think I'll have a biscotti and cappuccino myself." The driver grabbed Halim's crutches from the cab of the pedicab. "Let me show you the way."

"It's hard to imagine this is really Batang Toru," Halim said to the driver.

"Friend," said the driver, "it would be hard to imagine Batang Toru without Marissa's."

As they reached the entrance, a young man and woman, clad in fashionable batik sarongs opened wide a pair of double doors. Halim turned to the driver, "Funny these traditional costumes amidst all the neon."

"Maybe, but the coffees and teas are all Indonesian, mostly from Sumatra." A clutch of youngsters at a round table hailed the driver who checked to see that Halim was steady on his feet before telling him that he would be sitting with his friends. "Feel free to join us."

Halim thanked him and asked if he knew where he could find Marissa herself.

"Of course, she is upstairs at the circular coffee bar on the gold stool. She is the queen here, and that is her throne." The driver reminded Halim that if he needed a ride later, he or one of his friends would be happy to provide one.

Halim looked at the circular stairway that led to Marissa's upper floor. He moved his right crutch to join its mate under his left arm so he could grasp the handrail. He had ascended one step when a barista in batik leaped to confront him.

"Please, sir, you can use our service elevator. It's not pretty, but I think it will make your visit to Marissa's more pleasant even so." The young woman led Halim to a door near the kitchen. She opened it and pressed a button. "Have a nice trip!" she said as a mechanical door slid shut, and the elevator moved confidently to the upper level where the door opened onto scenes of conviviality at the center of which was the circular bar and a preposterously ornate gold stool upholstered with purple cushions where, back to Halim, a grand personage draped in a rainbow-colored head scarf and a long black sarong laughed and gesticulated as she conversed with dozens at the bar.

Halim shuffled toward the figure and whispered when he had reached the golden stool, "Tomi?"

Marissa whirled around, her eyes wide and her brow wrinkled. "Tomi? Tomi?" she yelled angrily before her face relaxed in recognition of the man who called her, and she said, slowly and quietly, "Oh. My. God. Halim."

Marissa stared as Halim nodded once. "Tomi," he said, "Yes, Tomi, I am Halim."

Marissa saw that Halim sagged on crutches. "Well, you look like shit. You need a chair. Here, come with me." She spun herself off the stool in a grand gesture, said loudly to her audience, "This fellow is one of my childhood friends, everybody. But he was, as you can see, a much older child than I." She threw her head back as she wrapped her right arm around Halim's shoulders and led him to a banquette in a far corner of the café. A skinny barista carried the creamy concoction Marissa had been drinking at the bar and placed it on the table before her. "Kiki, my friend needs one of the powerhouse juice drinks." She turned to Halim beside her. "You do look like crap, Halim. I'm surprised I even recognized you." Her voice dropped its divaness. "But how could I not? Hmm?"

"You," Halim managed, "look amazing." After noticing Marissa's right eyebrow rise, he added, "Beautiful, actually."

Marissa bowed in gratitude. "You know, Halim, it's because of you that I look," she raised her arms wide, "this wonderful way."

"Me?"

"Remember that time you beat me up?"

"I do. That's why I'm here."

"To beat me up again? This time with crutches?"

"No, of course not, Tomi." He paused to ask, "Is it okay if I call you Tomi?"

Marissa turned away for a moment before answering, "It hurts to hear it from you. To be reminded of how much I loved you. How much you hurt me." She waved her hands, "But enough of that. Enough! The bruises are gone. And that's my point. To cover the bruises you gave my face, I used my mother's make-up. And I liked what that did for me. My family, my friends didn't make fun because they accepted my rationale, the need to look…normal. Ironic, eh? And so, little by little, cosmetic by cosmetic, jewel by jewel, and blouse by gown, Marissa developed and ultimately thrived. And Marissa has you, Halim, to thank for it all—well, not all, the broken ribs were quite nasty bits Marissa could have done without."

"But—but can you can you forgive me for my brutality that day?"

"Halim, I forgave you a long time ago. We were both fucked-up kids trying to understand who we were. Forgiveness came with understanding."

"Then I am damned and damned again."

"Because I forgave you?"

"Because I don't know who else to ask for forgiveness."

"Hello? Can we make a little sense here?"

Halim narrated his story from the onset of the cancer to its ransacking of his body to the helplessness of his doctor to the confidence of a magician in leaves and forgiveness. "The worst sin I ever committed in my life, Tomi, was beating you that day. I was sure that if you granted me forgiveness, I would be able finally to die." He collapsed into his own lap.

Marissa leaned over him and held on to his shoulders, her face against his back. "Do you need the patch again now?"

"I need to die!" Halim moaned.

"Halim, when we were children, did you love Tomi?"

"I did, Tomi. So much. But," Halim sat up again and looked into Marissa's eyes. "I was so afraid of such a love, I wanted to beat it out of myself. And instead I tried to beat it out of you. Can you really forgive me for that? Tomi, have you really forgiven me?"

"Halim, I have, but don't you see; you need to forgive yourself. What is worse than denying love? What sin is worse than that? Can you forgive yourself, Halim?"

"I don't know if I can."

"Halim, let me take you back to Sibolga. It will make me happy to help an old friend, and maybe then you will feel you have atoned for an old, old sin." Halim said nothing. "Come, let me get you to the elevator and downstairs. Wait for me at the entrance to the café. I need to freshen up a bit, and then I'll pick you up in front. Okay?"

Halim allowed himself to be helped to the elevator where Marissa instructed a barista to care for her guest.

In fewer than twenty minutes, a white BMW sedan pulled up to the café, and the barista helped Halim, his backpack, and crutches into the back seat. When the driver moved the car forward, Halim reminded him they had to wait for Marissa. The driver laughed, stopped the car, turned around and said, "Marissa is already here, Halim. I thought it would be too difficult for you to explain her to your wife and daughter. So I dug out my old Guess jeans and shirt. They still fit Tomi!"

Tomi had scrubbed his face free of cosmetics and combed his black bob in a manly fashion. Halim was moved by the lengths to which his friend was willing to go to help him, and he was reminded, despite the years and the scars, of just how beautiful Tomi was in his looks and in his soul. It had not been wrong, Halim thought, to love him.

Halfway to Sibolga, Halim felt the need to replace the fentanyl patch. And he thought to call his wife and Tirta to tell them they should be ready with the kelor again that night.

It was past midnight by the time Halim lay naked on his bed, this time in the presence of his wife and Tomi as well as Tirta who had a pail full of kelor leaves between her and her client. "Okay, then." Tirta looked at Andri sitting with her husband's hand in hers on the other side of the bed, "You have forgiven this man for all his sins?"

"He has done nothing to require my forgiveness," Halim's wife replied.

"Good. Good." She turned to Tomi, sitting next to Halim's wife, his hand gently patting his old friend's knee. "And you?"

"Halim is forgiven," Tomi gripped the knee and looked directly at Halim. "You are forgiven. Isn't that so?"

"It is so," Halim said, slowly blinking his eyes. "It is so. I love you both."

"And me?" joked Tirta. "No love for me? The one who lugged a bucket of wet leaves here?" Her face and voice softened. "The one who will now bring you peace?"

"Inshyallah."

"May God be willing," Tirta said as she bathed Halim everywhere with the kelor leaves. When she was done and Halim lay green and quiet, she listened for his breath. "Call the doctor. He will need to confirm the death." Already, Halim's body was turning pale. "In the meantime, Andri, we can prepare Halim's body for burial with the ritual bath.

Andri said, "Not us. According to Islamic law, a man's body can only be bathed by another man." She turned to Tomi. "Bapak, are you ready and willing to offer this last gift to my husband?"

"Ibu Andri, I came her for this very purpose, for this honor. Indeed, I dressed for the occasion."

CURO THE FILTHMONGER: A TALE OF ART AND SURVIVAL IN THE COLD EMBRACE OF OUTER SPACE

J. Marshall Freeman

I brought the rebellious mining colony to its knees over two excruciatingly quiet weeks of courtly tedium. Orders were penned on actual paper and delivered to my generals on heirloom silver trays; reports on incremental gains were brought to me by only the most well-mannered of couriers, trained to wait patiently for the chamber music to end before delivering their messages. Frankly, I would have preferred two fiery days of bloody carnage—rockets fired in the silence of deep space from my orbiting fleet, raining down cataclysm on the planetoid, and raising screams of agony through its charmless streets and muddy markets. In short, we could have made a spectacle that would have announced to the entire sector that the Waning Lord was not yet ready to bare his neck to the blade of succession.

But those damned, brilliant fortifications.

"Elegant," my Prime Strategist had called them.

"Breathtaking," agreed my Chief Engineer.

Even as I raged and threatened them with public evisceration for making me wait, I secretly shared their admiration. The fortifications were like nothing I had ever encountered. With casual indifference, they repelled direct assaults, forcing us to chip away at them with endless patience (a commodity that has grown scarcer as I've aged). The fortifications were beyond utilitarian, beyond clever. They were—and I never use this word lightly—beautiful.

Truly, none of life's accomplishments is so important as learning to appreciate beauty in all its varied and unlikely manifestations: the dancing filament of cerulean in the cloud expanse of a deep-vid landscape, the final note of garnanberry in a perfect cup of Aurelian liqueur, the magnificent thighs and glutes of a boy who runs marathons, especially when he lifts them high and wide in my bed for the kind of marathon I enjoy. In any case, if some great architect on that sad little mining outpost could build defenses as fine as these, he was to be admired even as he was crushed under my heel.

And so, inevitably, the defenses were penetrated, the bleak industrial towns flooded with my soldiers, the leaders of the insurrection arrested and transported to my command ship. The usual cycle of interrogation, torture and execution followed, my prosecutors collecting intelligence that would lead to further arrests, my historians already penning the legend of my unprecedented victory.

Through these endless days, I sat in my chambers, bored to the molars, emerging only to sign the orders and witness the executions. This was a brief but satisfying thrill; one could find beauty even in the arc of blood splattering across cold concrete. In fact, I was only interested in learning one thing: who had designed those wonderful fortifications? My military and technical experts couldn't stop gushing about the way they distributed force and charge across the length of the structure, etcetera, etcetera. For me, it was all about the moment I first reviewed videos from the reconnaissance fly-over. I had marvelled— actually gasped—at the elegance of the design: two wings, gracefully interlocked, like a fabulous bird of prey displaying both indomitability and serene contemplation. And there was more to it; something which, perhaps, I alone with my practiced eye could see: a wink, a perverse thumbing of a mighty nose. It was the kind of insouciant wit one didn't expect in military infrastructure, much less on a remote colony of uncultured, itinerant miners.

The leaders of the rebellion were all dead now, their broken corpses flashed across every public vid screen on the planetoid. But when I finally asked my Chief Justice who had designed the fortifications, he had the nerve to inform me that the architect had not been the focus of the investigation.

"Just not a key figure in the insurrection," he explained. I had him launched from an airlock, to burn alive in his descent from orbit.

I instructed his replacement that I would begin interrogating colonists in three hours time. In every culture I have encountered, there is some version of the cliché about doing the job yourself if you want it done right.

A new set of witnesses were forthwith brought from the surface. What must they have felt as they viewed my court of a thousand ships growing in the portholes of their transports? The Waning Lord's glittering fleet was a thing of legend throughout the sector. I wanted to ask the fearful men and women as they stumbled before me in terror and awe, "Was the reality more or less than you expected?"

They were universally dirty and pungently unwashed, in the wake of the long embargo and siege. All were wide-eyed at the scale and opulence of the chamber in which they stood. This was the Hall of Justice, by the way, not my throne room. My throne room, though smaller, is one of the great rooms of the settled galaxy—reviewed in countless journals of art and architecture over the decades.

Truly, I had never seen people more ill-at-ease in a royal court. Grandeur and decoration were anathema to these ascetic crows. Worse for them, I think, was the near-nakedness of my courtiers. The season's fashion called for minimal strips of hologram fabric over ruthlessly sculpted bodies, all atop the highest heels seen since the Ion Wars. This blaze of exposed flesh seemed to burn the eyes of the colonists, who blushed and pulled their many layers of coarse, black fabric tighter around themselves.

But their discomfort only made my interrogation easier. "So, you prepared food for the insurgent forces?" I asked one quaking young man who stood before me—comely in his way, but not worth bringing to my bed. My voice, invisibly amplified, seemed to descend from heaven.

"My Lord, I was ordered to bring the rebels..."

The Court Prelate barked at him, "You will address the Waning Lord as 'Unequalled One'!"

"Forgive me, Unequalled One! I was ordered to serve them. I would never have volunteered to..."

"Silence!" I bellowed, discreetly thumbing a control that caused the floor to vibrate with my command. "Who is the designer of the fortifications your rebellious masters raised against me?"

"Sir, please, I was ever true to your heavenly rule. I would never…"

"The architect! His name!"

The pale young man looked up in surprise, like he had only just heard the question. "It-it was the outsider! The newcomer. Curo the Filthmonger."

"Curo," said the next witness.

And the next, "Curo. The Filthmonger."

"That heretic, Curo," said another.

And another, "The Filthmonger. I will not defile my mouth by speaking his name!"

One after the other named this man, painting a picture of an epic degenerate, a man with morals not fit for the rankest pits of the Tharis Slug Market. I was shocked that the very architect who had so brilliantly defended their little world was held in such universal contempt. A pervert! A monster with appetites incompatible with human society! Now, more than ever, I was anxious to meet this Curo.

This was not an easy task. It took my troops two days, searching every abandoned mine shaft on the planet, before they found him. At last, he was dragged before me, more dead than alive—a greasy blob of ordure and grime, scraped from the lowest levels of the colony's dankest sewers. I could barely see a man through those stained robes, under that rat's nest of hair. But in the centre of the shit-smeared face shone eyes that startled: fearful, yes, but ablaze. The eyes of the architect were huge, cunning, seeing everything and everyone around him. Seeing me.

Staring into those eyes, I was silent long enough for the Court Prelate to draw close and say, "Unequalled One, do we torture him and bring you the report?"

I could not reply. Curo the Filthmonger. He had seen something in me and latched on. A weakness? Impossible, I showed none. And yet, what could hide from those wondrous eyes? And a more crucial question: what must it be like to see the world through them?

I waited until I could speak with utter conviction, with self-righteous scorn that I did not feel. "No, he appals me. Clean the prisoner, and dress him appropriately for presentation in my throne room. I will personally interrogate him there, tomorrow after the quarter meal."

I left the hall abruptly, much to the confusion of my retinue, who had to scramble to their feet and rush after me. I had no choice.

Something had fallen; my own battlements were compromised. No one could be allowed to see that.

❖

He was brought before my throne at the ordained hour. I admit to feeling some disappointment, now that he was washed and dressed in fresh garments. True, he was young, and his reddish curls fell appealingly across the pale skin of his brow, but the legs in his tights were too heavy, his stance too stolid, lacking in that lithe, floating vitality that never fails to move me. He was an unprepossessing youth, with neither the charm that came from good breeding, nor a natural, animal appeal. But what was truly fascinating was the way, despite his desperate circumstances, he acted like he belonged in my court, like he had been born to it. If his wrists had not been cuffed, one might have mistaken him for my latest favourite.

Who had dressed him so extravagantly? True, I had asked for him to be presented in my throne room, which request called for a degree of style, but here he was in vermillion and titanium, hologram landscapes scrolling on his cuffs, and a plumed hat of such overblown daring that only career courtier of some standing would dare attempt it.

Myself, I was elaborately armoured—too formally for the interrogation of a provincial criminal. The armour practically doubled my size, making me an almost mythic creature of metal and synthetic muscle. The war helm gave me a frightful countenance—fiery eyes and enormous, curving horns which crackled with arc light. When I had earlier entered the chamber, a surprised silence fell over the courtiers. Why was I dressed as if confronting a surrendering general, or as if I had to meet my son, the Waxing Lord?

Curo could not hide his fear. Who would not be afraid? His crimes against my august rule were no trifling matter. But fear, I could plainly see, had not blinded him. Those remarkable eyes were alive, taking in the details of my throne room in quick, darting glances. And I knew that he saw more than gold leaf and patina—he understood the structures underneath, could likely already sketch the chamber from memory. What did it mean to an architect of his skill and sensitivity to be standing in this storied room?

"You are the one named Curo?" It was barely a question, and the impressive overtones produced by my helmet made me sound all the more intimidating.

His voice quavered but only slightly. "I am Curoditinus Desmeter of Outer Xelphon," he said, adding after a fractional pause, "Unequalled One." I had never heard of this provincial backwater, but in his swamp-tainted accent, he made it sound the most desirable of provenances.

"How did you come to be dressed like a courtier instead of a prisoner on his last day of life?"

I watched the little wave of fear go through him, but admirably, he persevered. "Unequalled One, your servants presumed to dress me in ghastly…" He paused, biting his fat lower lip with uneven teeth. "They meant to dress me in clothes that would have insulted your personage." He looked around at my throne room, more boldly than before. "And the legendary hall in which I am honoured to stand."

Again, I felt those eyes on me, peeling away my defences. I knew he could not see my discomfort through my helmet, but damned if he didn't act like he could. I had to look away. In the far corner of the throne room, the latest in a series of disappointing court artists was starting a new deep vid, stretching rainbow plasma across the work space, every grandiose gesture soaked in pretence. Soon I would need to add another ship to the fleet to house the steady accumulation of mediocre portraits.

I barked at my new Chief Justice, "Well, who is this Curo? He's clearly no miner. What was he doing on this desolate rock in the first place?"

She came forward, moving with the traditional step-bow, step-bow that I increasingly found an irritating waste of time. "Lord, he crashed a Suntide skip-jumper on the planetoid eight months ago. It was unsalvageable. He was trying to raise funds to catch a shuttle to the Central System when you ordered the embargo of the colony."

"A Suntide? Where did such a creature get his hands on that kind of expensive jumper?"

"Registered to Count Bardondry of Avkot, Lord."

My eyes went wide under my helm. Bardondry was an obscenely

wealthy dealer in gravimetric weaponry as well as a shifting fulcrum under the system's political see-saw that sometimes caused events to tilt my way and sometimes into the lap of my son.

"Stolen?" I asked.

"Not clear. We are looking into it, Lord."

I kept my head turned away from the prisoner though I brought up his image in my helmet. I said, "And apparently, while he was raising these funds, he was cutting a swath of perversion across the colony. 'The Filthmonger' they call him. For what actions, exactly?"

"Doodling on walls, Lord," the Chief Justice said, trying to be amusing. She pointed into the air ahead of her, and a dimensional video appeared: alley walls, concrete embankments, bridge overpasses, all decorated with life studies. They were mostly nudes—singles and pairs, drawn delicately or roughly, elaborately shaded or merely hinted at with economical line. The final clip in the montage showed Curo at work, drawing quickly and confidently with a brush, bringing a naked man and woman to life. He never paused in his drawing, or stepped back to contemplate his next stroke. He knew exactly what he wanted. And then the rocks were flying, citizens in the nearby park throwing projectiles and imprecations at the youth, who fled in his grey, threadbare cloak.

"Monster!" They shouted. "Think of the children who will see this filth in the morning!"

But it wasn't filth, and Curo no Filthmonger. It was sublime. Now I wished I had bombed the miners to oblivion. What base idiots, not to recognize the genius among them. The couple he had produced on the wall were clearly lovers in the aftermath of some terrible fight. The slump of the man's shoulders showed his despair, the tenseness of the woman's, her aching resolve. The man reached a hand toward her, but she either didn't see it or didn't want to. All was there in those simple, rough lines: the blood and bone, the disappointment and bitterness, the love that endured despite the pain.

"Villain!" the crowd called after his retreating figure.

I turned to stare at Curo, and he was smiling at this scene from his recent life, a cruel smile, almost a snarl, upper lip curled back. I was taken with an obscene desire to comfort him, tell him that I understood his humiliation. Instead, I startled him out of his reverie with my amplified voice, "On your knees, prisoner!"

He hesitated for only a second, but the guards came forward and pushed him down. He winced as his knees hit the inlaid marble.

I said, "You designed the fortifications that aided the rebellion against my just and fair rule?"

Curo's composure was faltering, but his voice was still strong, "Unequalled One, I deny the accusation. What do I, a mere street-pornographer, know of such lofty architecture?"

But we were more prepared than the boy thought. "Chief Justice?" I called and she produced a small strip of silver.

"Lord, this piece of memory plastic was removed from the prisoner while he was unconscious. It was bonded to the skin between his legs." Curo's bound hands moved downwards, as if to check, but both the restraints and his extravagant codpiece thwarted his efforts.

"Initiate it," I demanded.

A large dimensional display sprang into life above us. The background was a work I knew well, 'The Ascension of Saint Gramla' by T3a'Lita, perhaps the first significant deep-vid of the Second Epoch. The Saint, his breast torn open by his torturers, stands in a circle of fiery stars, looking out serenely at infinity. Scenes of his miracles, depicted in classical dance, flow from the wound like water from a desert spring.

I reached in front of me to manipulate virtual hands in the display space and clicked on an icon near the saint's left eye. The Saint was replaced with a set of nested folders containing plans for the colony's fortifications. I flipped through them, watching Curo's face blanch as I did.

"Treason, Lord," said my Chief Justice.

"Treason," I agreed, even as I paused the display to examine a series of quick sketches: red garnbirds in repose, wings folded, Curo's inspiration for the wings of the fortifications. Thinking of the boy's upcoming torture and execution, I felt something claw at my chest, an uncommon and, therefore, delicious pain. It was regret.

I closed the folder and the Saint reappeared. I was about to shut down the display and render my judgment when I noticed something that made me laugh with delight. Through my war helm, the laugh came out melodramatically sinister, and the entire court turned to stare at me.

"Thirteen stars," I said, and in the whole surprised room, only Curo understood my meaning; his agitation visibly increased.

"My Lord?" queried the Chief Justice.

"Only twelve stars surround Gramla in T3a'Lita's original work," I explained. "But here there are thirteen."

"Don't," said Curo hoarsely, sweat breaking on his brow, as I reached back into the display space and slid the additional sun to the side.

I hesitated a moment before tapping on this icon, hoping against hope for something wondrous to appear, something to pierce the thick skin of tedium that had grown over my life. There had been so much promise before, back when I had been Waxing Lord, and my own father knelt to my blade. An infinity of time and exultation lay before me, and every taste of life was keen with discovery.

I tapped, and I was not disappointed.

A vast portfolio opened, like a hidden treasure room found buried with a long forgotten emperor. I was the exultant archaeologist, or, more aptly, the hungry tomb robber. The works were varied and brilliant, from sketches to fully realized deep-vids. I raced from work to work, overwhelmed and giddy. I was so engrossed, I hardly noticed Curo running at me, screaming curses and incomprehensible threats in the low dialect of his home world. He was tackled by a soldier, who proceeded to attach a tickler to his neck, making the boy scream and writhe in agony.

I let the punishment continue for perhaps ten seconds before I called a halt, and while Curo lay curled and sobbing on the priceless marble floor of my throne room, I continued my tour of discovery through his art. There were portraits, historical renderings, star maps with allegorical scenes in the borders. At first glance, his work seemed traditional, but everywhere there was subtle, brilliant experimentation—twists of time and transition that delighted the eye. And in addition to the fine art, I found more architectural design: churches, estates, and whimsical, twisting structures that might have been dwellings or sculptures.

There was little structure to the archive, but I could already tell what was early work and what recent. The speed with which he had matured—from stiff student exercises to deep-vids of maturity, confidence, and wit—was astonishing. He was now only twenty-four. If I allowed him to live, what treasures might he create? And if he was mine, what unrivalled benefit might I accrue?

My court knew enough not to interrupt me when I was in such a zealous froth, but eventually I grew annoyed with their sideways glances and shut down the display.

"Transfer all the contents to my personal library," I ordered. "All copies are to be kept under level seven lockdown with re-infinitizing code matrices. No one sees these works without my express orders." I paused and deepened the red glow of my eye pieces. "On pain of death," I added, and my inner circle worked to hide their shock.

"I will be in my chambers," I declared, rising from my throne.

The Chief Justice hurried forward. "But the prisoner, Unequalled One! What is your sentence?"

"Have him brought to my chambers in two hours time," I announced and thumped loudly toward the shuttle bay, my armour producing a terrifying soundscape—like the firebombing of a great glass city. "And get rid of that ridiculous hat!"

❖

I was alone in my chambers. "Alone" meant I was accompanied by my valet and his core team of six, by a modest security detail (ten or so soldiers and their officers), and by the eternal, buzzing presence of the cleaning staff. Other than the senior officers, no one spoke unless addressed, and they were all professionally blind. What went on in the Waning Lord's chambers, especially in his bed, was as deeply classified as any military intelligence. I was their Lord, and they were nothing to me. Why, then did their presence today rankle so?

My chambers were arranged in nine concentric circles, separated by shimmering force fields. The fields were of variable permeability, and the higher you were in the chain of privilege, the deeper you could penetrate. Many courtiers spent their whole careers hoping to be allowed a promotion just one level closer to the centre.

I sat in my wide, padded chair in the antepenultimate circle, which I used as my office. I had exchanged my fearsome armour for soft pants and jacket that my Chief Valet subtly suggested was too casual for my upcoming interrogation. I ignored him and continued to pore over Curo's portfolio, now with the luxury of time. And luxuriate I did, immersing myself fully in each work, sometimes literally—expanding the scale until I could promenade through the cascade of colour and movement.

My Chief Curator sat at my side, exultant at the level of access I had allowed him.

"When was the last time you saw such skill?" I asked him, the excitement in my voice all too evident.

"Not in a great while, my Lord. And look how he honours the finest of classical themes!"

"Yes, yes...but no! Don't you see? The true classicist tries to erase himself from the work, but Curo is modern! He is everywhere in the art, commenting, laughing." I myself laughed. "Scandalous. Treasonous!" I exclaimed. I was delighted.

I dismissed the Curator, who slunk out in misery. He knew he had bungled his one chance to cement his reputation with me. But I was not surprised at his myopia. He was a lettered academic, widely respected and celebrated, but his whole life was theory and reference; he probably hadn't fucked in 30 years. And Curo's art was congress and corruption—pissing joyously into the void. No, I alone could see, could feel in my heart and my groin that Curoditinus Desmeter of Outer Xelphon was like me: a helpless acolyte of beauty.

I was reminded just how alone I was. Despite the silent ones around me, despite the entirety of the fleet floating with me year after year through cold space, I had never had an equal. And I knew that Curo, too, was alone, had probably always been alone with his genius. Perhaps in the entire Sector, only Curo could understand my isolation, and I his.

When they brought him to me, I was contemplating his portrait of Count Bardondry of Avkot. I took my time before turning to face him. I saw, with a shiver of disgust, that he had pissed himself in the vermillion tights when the tickler was lighting up his pain centres. A ridiculous flash of anger passed through me that he had been left like that, to marinate in shame. But how should a traitor have been treated? With strewn flowers and accolades?

I turned back to the painting and said, "You exhibit the height of discretion."

"Unequalled One?" Curo inquired, his voice a little shaky.

"Anytime I've met Bardondry, he has never been able to mask the callow connivance in his heart. I imagined it would be impossible to draw him except in caricature—a rat in flashy taffeta."

"My Lord, it is my job to find the nobility in my patrons."

"Your patrons are nobles, after all."

"Or perhaps all people, high and low, are deserving of their dignity?" he suggested daringly. I considered my reaction. There was only so much treason I could allow before I was forced to act. For once, I was aware of all the eyes and ears in the room. Damn them, I thought, I am the Waning Lord.

"Valet!" I snapped. "Clean the prisoner up. Basin, cloth and towel. And bring him a robe to wear!"

The Valet walked Curo through the force fields to an outer circle where the dressers descended on him. I set the opacity on the fields such that I could see out but not be seen, and thus watched the ablutions secretly. Stripped of his courtly finery, Curo was revealed the rough provincial creature he was: no stylish body enhancements, no custom blushes. Working man's muscle, scars—so many scars. There probably wasn't a man in the fleet without some sort of penis augmentation or decoration, but Curo's unadorned sex, nestled in the untamed landscape of coarse, red pubic hair, was obscenely pure. He had hidden this obscenity beneath silk and leather, and this duality, like the duality of image and essence in his art, excited me.

Soon, the guards walked him back through the shimmering walls to stand at my side in a long, loose robe. He was more at ease now, and I considered how I might humiliate him—just as show and reminder. But I was impatient to speak of art to one who understood it. In silence, we looked together at the portrait of Bardondry.

"Why," I asked, "did you place him in the star field?" Curo was close enough to make my Security Chief nervous, close enough that I could smell the fresh soaps on him.

"It is a reference to Third Epoch portraiture of gZarlanter. He was the first to render a noble in his home system."

The Count's face was lit by a stylized sun to his right, a starburst of brilliant red filaments on a circle of dark gold. Above him and to his left, a perfect circle of black cut a hole in the dense star field.

I said, "I suppose that's the red dwarf, Delion 5. But I am aware of no black hole in the cluster. What is its meaning in the composition?"

Curo did not respond, and when I looked over, he was smiling, barely containing his laughter. In one smooth motion, I rose from my chair and pulled a long, jewelled blade from the scabbard hidden in my loose sleeves. I put the point to Curo's throat, and he gasped, tilting his head back in fear.

"You will answer questions when they are put to you, doodler!" I shouted. "Remember, you are mine to use or mine to discard." This studied condescension sounded false to my own ears. Could Curo see through my hollow charade? An urgent voice in my head told me, *Kill him! Kill him before you are undone!* Ridiculous. I was the Waning Lord! What did I have to fear from this swamp-rat? I lowered my knife, and turned from Curo, as if too bored to care.

I called, "Clear this chamber! I wish to be alone with the prisoner!"

My Security Chief came quickly forward. "Unequalled One?"

"You heard me."

My Valet hurried through four force fields to join the conference, "Lord, obviously you have our complete discretion. There is no need to send us out. Anything you...you wish to do with the prisoner is, of course, yours to...yours to..."

The Security Chief jumped in, "Unequalled One, for reasons of your personal safety, I strongly advise..."

"Do you think this boy, this fop, could hope to kill me?" I turned back to Curo, waving the knife lazily under his chin. "Artist, are you planning to kill me?"

Artist. I hadn't intended to say it just yet, but Curo heard it, and he stood taller.

"No, Unequalled One, I am not."

"Leave us!"

When we were alone, I asked, "Bardondry was your patron?"

"Yes, Unequalled One."

"Sit," I told him, waving vaguely. Curo chose a priceless Trielni the Ninth chair to sit in. What else should I have expected?

"Bardondry contracted me as a court artist," he said. "One of fourteen. He had no understanding of the work I was producing for him. I was just another little jewel for his necklace." His tone was insolent. Probably I should not have allowed him to sit on my expensive furnishings; it gave him airs. But I raised my eyebrows, signalling him to continue. "A verbal agreement was all I could get out of him. And when I went to collect even the pittance he had promised, he laughed and told me my services were no longer required."

"So you took his Suntide jumper in payment."

Curo tried unsuccessfully to control his cruel smile. "Yes, that was one way I exacted payment."

"Oh yes? How else?" When he hesitated with his answer, I slowly raised the knife again, belatedly aware of how phallic a gesture it was.

"Unequalled One, I performed some remote programming to the deep vid's AI. Count Bardondry's copy of the portrait has been... degrading since I left." He blushed hotly, a reaction which I found fatally charming. "By now, he looks utterly wasted by Scarfronz Disease, an acute case such as one might find in the dimmest clinics of the Pleasure Markets."

My defenses, such as they had been, crumbled. I laughed until I thought I would fall off my chair, and Curo laughed with me. I turned back to the unsullied portrait and sighed, not hiding my admiration. "That worm doesn't deserve this." I waved my hand at the masterful work.

He was silent a moment, and then said, "gZarlanter perfected this style of portraiture in the court of Klar, the Waning Lord of C-Tharka."

"I know my history, Artist."

"Klar was a great patron of the arts."

I nodded. "He knew talent when he saw it."

"And they say that's why his reign lasted 80 years," Curo continued, so quietly that I had to tilt my head his way. "He wasn't a great general, not even compared to his son, the Waxing Lord, Klar-gir. But the unfolding marvels from his court—the music, the dance, the deep-vid—made him an indomitable figure, decade after decade."

He lapsed into silence, letting his words echo. I could hear the hiss of the cycling air, the low throb of the engines—sounds that were usually drowned out by the droning court. I became uncomfortably aware of endless space hanging beneath us. I was a tightrope walker over a canyon infinitely deep. My life, I knew, depended on never misstepping. My son's blade hung over my neck, gleaming ever brighter.

"80 years, Unequalled One; imagine that," said Curo, his voice a low insinuation, barely rising above the hiss and throb. "How many more years do you think you have?"

"If," my voice was low and rough. I cleared my throat and spoke with more conviction. "If I were to become your patron, what do you imagine creating? A grand portrait? Perhaps a new summer palace!"

"The throne room, Lord..."

I sat up in surprise. "What was that?"

"It must be redesigned," Curo said simply. He was looking not at me, but into infinity, like the martyred Saint Gramla.

"Are you insane? It is one of the great rooms of the quadrant! It is celebrated far and wide. It graces the annals of..."

Curo interrupted me. "It is a relic. And anyone who sits on that throne implies that he too belongs to the glorious past, that he has nothing more to contribute."

I rose to my feet in fury. "You dare!" I sputtered. I slapped Curo backhanded in a desperate attempt to regain some modicum of control. The Trielni the Ninth chair tipped backwards, landing Curo on his backside, one of its priceless legs breaking in half with a gut-churning snap!

Kill him! Kill the traitor now or you will live to regret it!

I was shaking, barely aware of Curo climbing again to his feet, his eyes never leaving me.

"Imagine, Unequalled One, a throne room that at first delights and then disquiets. Every line leads to you, all colour transitions draw the eye to your majesty. You are elevated, but without ostentation. It is your own majesty, it seems, and not the architecture that gives you command of every situation. You are the cause and effect in that room. Everywhere is beauty, but it is just the setting. The Waning Lord, he is the jewel."

He spoke this like an incantation, and I could see it, I could—

though I was barely able to contemplate what wonders might be wrought by the boy.

"Unequalled One," he said in my ear. When had he moved so close? What had I done with my knife? "There is another folder," he whispered as he reached into the display space, tapping a secret icon in Saint Gramla's wound. The swirling human forms filled the space, sweating, mouths straining open in aching ecstasy, copulating with animal fever, stripped not just of clothes, but of shame, of humility. Only hunger remained—gutting, thrusting hunger, and the desire to send one another into the purest oblivion of sensation—to obliterate through liberty.

Astonished and mortal, I watched this shifting orgy, as behind me, Curo the Filthmonger dropped his robe to the floor and walked naked through the last of the shimmering force fields, into the centre-most area of my chambers: my huge, circular bed. I closed the display and followed him, erect to the point of pain, my own clothes falling next to his.

Curo was on the bed, on all fours, his ass open to me. A starburst of brilliant red hairs emanated outwards over the dark gold skin surrounding the hole. Above and to its left, on the ascending crease of the cheek, was the perfect circle of a black mole.

With a vision of my new throne room dancing before my eyes, with the cheers of my court ringing in my ears, I mounted him, making noises of triumph and surrender that I could not contain. He moaned beneath me, letting me know that he was mine, truly and forever.

Bending close to his ear, I hissed, "As I sit in my throne room and watch you work, Artist, I will think of this. I will remember how I conquered you."

"No," he gasped as I thrust deeper, faster, helplessly drawn towards my climax. "I will need the throne room completely vacated for a period of six months."

I was helpless, grasping feverishly for control. "But...I will come and watch you work, Curo. You will work naked for me."

"No, not even you, Unequalled One, must disturb the great work! Tell me you understand, give me your word!"

"Yes!" I screamed, gasping, voice choked, gripping his hips for balance as I toppled over the edge. "Yes! Yes!"

PASSING THROUGH

John Morgan Wilson

I was driving Jesse's '67 Dart GTS that day, on my way to meet the man who killed him. The man's name was Carl Trigg. If things went right, he wouldn't be expecting me.

For all its nice features, the Dart wasn't really my kind of vehicle. I was a hardworking girl, more into pickups than tricked-out muscle cars. But I felt that Jesse's spirit lived on in that car, and I couldn't let it go. Two-door hardtop, four-speed manual trans, four-forty big-block under the hood, five-layer turquoise paint job so glossy you couldn't help but stroke it. A real beauty, but with lots of torque and power. Just like you, Jesse used to tell me, though some would have disagreed about the beauty part, being how unconventional I dressed and carried myself in those days, and still do, for all that.

Jesse had talked about owning a Dart since high school. Had to be a '67, don't ask me why. Finally bought one used in '74 with the pay he'd saved up serving in 'Nam. Customized it down to its flashy rims to celebrate coming back alive. If anybody deserved to be down on life it was my little brother, after what he'd seen over there. But it was always Jesse trying to buoy me up instead of the other way around.

Sometimes on a weekend afternoon we'd pop the lid and tune up the four-barrel V-8 together, while he drew me out of the dark places I drifted into and coaxed me into talking a little. Then he'd take Mom and me for a ride, out past the Dairy Queen where the road opened up and everything was green and peaceful. Me in the back, Mom in the front bucket seat, some righteous rock 'n roll on the FM band and not a worry in the world, at least not right then. Coming back, he'd stop at the DQ to buy us something cold and sweet that we usually denied ourselves. Mom was always on some diet that never helped and I was often cash poor, construction jobs being patchy for females like they were. After the sundaes, he'd switch to an AM oldies station, crank up the volume on his quads, and dance Mom around the parking lot while she protested, loving every minute of it. He'd try the same with me but I wouldn't have it, being tight and guarded like I was. No-nonsense was the word Mom used to describe me if someone commented on my constricted manner, but Jesse knew that was just a cover.

"You only get one life," he told me one time when I was all wrapped up in myself. "And living it halfway is the saddest waste there is."

I guess that was a lesson he brought back with him from the war, the one good thing he got from it, along with that Dodge Dart he treated like a firstborn baby.

Mom passed four days shy of turning fifty, spring of '78. She'd moved to California by then, looking for something she never found. We'd followed her out, Jesse to watch over her, me for a semblance of a home amid my wandering ways. Died in her sleep, bedsheet tucked up neatly under her chin. Massive heart attack is what they said.

At least she didn't suffer like Jesse would when his time came that summer at the hands of Carl Trigg. Those were feverish years when Jesse got lost in a disco dream, determined to squeeze the joy from every moment and chase the ghosts that came back with him from the fighting. Drugs came into it and he fell in with a sketchy crowd, which led him to the trouble with Trigg. I'm not saying Jesse didn't bring some of it on himself. But for all his bad choices he damn well didn't deserve what Trigg inflicted on him when his karmic debts came due.

After it went down, Trigg disappeared and laid low, but his tracks were too deep from the baggage he carried. I bided my time, asked around of the right people, then climbed behind the wheel of the Dart to hunt him down.

It unsettled me some, sitting on the black synthetic leather Jesse had caressed so many times, as if that sleek sedan was another lady who'd tumbled for his smooth looks and charm. I would have happily given it up to have him back, would have given everything I owned, though that wasn't much beyond some power tools and softball gear, and a copy of *Rubyfruit Jungle* he'd gifted me with when he returned from his service. How he knew about that book and what it would mean to me I can't tell you, but he did; he'd always loved and accepted me exactly as I was. But nothing was going to bring my brother back, not the slick ride he'd left me, or my scant possessions, or the fury over his death that coiled inside me like a living, breathing thing.

I could get Jesse some justice, though. That much I could do.

The two-lane highway taking me to Trigg ran long and flat under a high desert sun, hours of heat shimmering off thinning asphalt between any two places you might reasonably call a city.

The glare was fierce, but I didn't mind the miles. I'd logged plenty in recent years, staying put just long enough to bank a few paychecks before moving on. Mom had called me her vagabond child and yearned for me to settle down in a regular manner. She knew about my sexual nature and wished it was otherwise, but she never questioned the fact of what I felt and needed. She just wanted me to find someone who'd help me open up and trust, and get my shot at happiness, same as anybody else. But I favored independence, and never more than that day, traveling to visit Mr. Trigg. It gave me time to think over what I'd learned about him from one of Jesse's ex-girlfriends. I never understood how a woman who'd been with Jesse could end up with an animal like Trigg, but that was how it fell together and how I came by the information I was after. She recounted his drunken boasting of what he'd done to Jesse in his final hours, which I had to steel myself to hear. Then she got weepy telling me how Trigg had smacked her around and sent her packing when he was done with her, as if her sniveling might appeal to some soft part of me.

I grabbed her by the shoulders and shook some sense into her. Don't ever cry over a man that abuses you, I said. Don't give him even that much respect.

Hold back your tears, I told her, and use your anger like a fearsome weapon when the time is right.

❖

The sun was off to the west when I caught sight of a weathered sign she'd told me to watch for. Pete's Chevron; Desert Vista Three Miles Ahead; Next Gas 47 Miles.

Two minutes later I eased up on the pedal, wary of speed traps. A minute after that I pulled in next to a dusty pump and filled the tank with ethyl, waving off the guy who came out to do it for me. Then I scrubbed the bugs off the windshield, paid up, and cruised slowly through town, what there was of it.

Desert Vista seemed a sorry place to make a life but not so bad for hiding out. Years back an interstate had detoured past some thirty miles west, leaving a desolate route for off-grid truckers or the odd traveler in need of petrol or a cup of bad coffee. The main drag was five blocks total, pocked with storefronts boarded up like scabs on parched skin. All the structures were to the east side, facing the highway. Beyond the far shoulder and the billboards was a chain link fence, tumbleweeds clinging to the wire like prisoners dreaming of escape. After that was a set of railway tracks running north and south. Diesel fumes hung in the air when a big rig chugged through. Otherwise, it was nothing but crackling heat and sagebrush all around.

I kept my eyes peeled for a watering hole Jesse's ex had told me about, where Trigg headed each afternoon when he got the shakes. I found it at the end of the last block, next to a narrow side street where the highway left Desert Vista behind like an afterthought. According to the flaking neon above the door it was called the Whistle Stop. The same name was decaled in gold lettering across the window, where a blind was pulled down against the westerly sun.

I drove past and turned right, dodging potholes until I reached an unpaved alley. Another right took me behind the bar and past a dumpster, where I could park less conspicuously and grab some shade. Then I hoofed it back around to the sidewalk, which was nearly deserted of people. Outside the Whistle Stop a dog was chained to a wooden bench, a mix with some shepherd in her and eyes suggesting sadness and submission. Tongue hanging out, no water bowl nearby. I could see the outline of her ribs and scars on her hindquarters. If her name was Lucky, somebody needed to change it.

I pulled open the door and pushed through heavy curtains into dimness and machine-cooled air. Most of the stools along the bar were empty. I took one toward the back to gain a wider view of the place. Somebody had slipped a coin into a Wurlitzer that dropped five platters for a quarter. A tune was playing that was trademark Willie, mellow on the surface but aching underneath, delivered with his laidback Texas twang.

And it's another lonely highway
Through a god-forsaken town
Another long-forgotten byway
And you're nowhere to be found...

A song for solitary drinkers, so I ordered a cold one. The beer went down easy while I eyeballed the other customers. There were three, all male. Sitting midway along the bar were two wrinkled old-timers, pinching unfiltered cigarettes between yellowed fingers while they drained brews from sweaty bottles. Customer number three looked closer to forty, going on sixty. He was wedged into a booth across the sawdust-covered floor, knocking back a double of the hard stuff like a man beset with more troubles than he could comfortably contemplate.

Carl Trigg.

He was right where Jesse's old flame had predicted, getting his fix in the only bar in town, about the time of day he felt the four walls closing in. I wasn't acquainted with the man, except by sight and reputation. Back home, he had a history of hoarding his ill-gotten gains and grievously hurting anyone who tried to trim his action, which had been Jesse's big mistake. From what I could see, time hadn't changed him much, except for a cane across his lap and a handlebar mustache that didn't do much for his pasty face. Otherwise, it was the same stringy hair to his collar, the scuffed Beatles boots, the paisley shirt and flare bottom pants as faded as his rock star fantasies. He was a big man but his bulk looked soft, untested. The kind who likes to throw his weight around until somebody calls him on it.

"How's that beer?"

The bartender propped himself against the inside rail on tattooed arms bunched with cordlike muscle. The tattoos included anchors, so I pegged him for ex-Navy. He was shaved close except for long sideburns, with sparkly eyes in a square-jawed face some women surely would have found attractive.

"Frosty," I said.

He stole a glance at my empty ring finger, then started fussing with napkins and straws that didn't need it. Before long he asked me if I was new in town.

"Passing through," I said.

"That's a shame."

"How's that?"

"We could use a new face around here." He leaned in, lowering his voice. "Especially one as pretty as yours."

"How many times have you used that one?"

He shrugged. "A few."

"Ever work?"

"Once or twice."

"Sorry, but I'm not your type."

"Don't I get to decide that?"

"Not in this case," I said, and gave him a wink I think he understood.

Pretty, not pretty. I tried not to let it burden me, because it was one more way the world had to run you down. What mattered most to me was the dignity I could muster when there was always some small-minded fool around, ready to judge you. Pride was a word you heard a lot just then, and I was working on it. My problem was separating pride from rage, because rage had been wired into my circuitry from the time I realized how many ways people had to revile others for being different. The bartender seemed like a decent guy. He had a nice smile; his taste in the opposite sex apparently drifted wide, given my close-cropped hair and sturdy build. Maybe if I'd been interested in men the way he was interested in me we'd have hit it off and lived happily ever after.

He popped himself a beer and tipped it toward mine until our bottles kissed.

"The way I see it," I said, "we're all just passing through. Trying to stay ahead of whatever's chasing us, until it runs us over."

"You didn't tell me you were a philosopher."

"You didn't ask."

He grinned. "How's it pay?"

"Not as good as construction work, when I can get it."

From his booth, Trigg called for another double. Over the next hour, he downed two more, looking more red-faced and relaxed each time. Then he rose on his cane, tossed some bills on the table, and hobbled out, one hip laboring like an old tire with too many miles on it. I also noticed a bulge beneath his untucked shirt and figured he was packing something besides a swollen liver.

I slid off my stool, sauntered over to the window, and quietly raised the shade. Off in the distance the sky was a blaze of orange. Trigg untethered the dog from the bench and whacked her with his cane when she shrank back, trying to stay behind. I returned to the bar and laid down six bits for the beer and a dollar for the bartender, since he'd been respectful when he could have been a jerk. Then I gave him a small salute and strolled out, hoping Trigg wasn't too far ahead of me.

When I caught sight of him again he was around the corner at the north end, stumbling past the alley where I'd concealed the Dart. I hung back in the shadows and followed. The reluctant dog slowed him down, taking another sting from his walking stick without so much as a whimper.

I'd known a few people like that. Mom was one, too many years of it, until the old man finally left. Not because he wanted to but because he knew if he didn't I'd kill him with my own hands, or at least the business end of my heaviest claw hammer. I would have, too, if Jesse hadn't stepped in and talked to me like he did, about how taking a human life has repercussions way past what the law can lay on a person. Don't get me wrong, Jesse could fight back if the need was pressed on him. But if you take someone's life otherwise, he told me, the best part of you dies with them and you'll never be whole again, with your humanity intact. His lofty words settled me long enough for the old man to pack up and go while he could, and for me to avoid a dead-end stretch in stir. That was Jesse's goodness at work that day, the best part of him. And look where all that goodness got him.

Trigg stopped to pee on an oleander bush, wobbly and wetting himself before he zipped up. The dog squatted beside him and did her duty in the dirt. Then he dragged her eastward again, passing streets to his right where rows of wood-frame stuccos were lined up cookie-cutter style, left over from the boom days that never boomed. Their colors had bled out long ago and their meager yards were choked with weeds and withered shrubbery. No kids out playing, just stillness and silence, except for that hot wind twisting squeaky antennas on sunbaked rooftops.

I figured the heat and distance would do Trigg in but he kept lurching along, leaving the tract behind close to half a mile. All that lay ahead now was a two-story clapboard at the end of the lane, its raw oak siding gone grey from the elements. Outside the old house was a struggling shade tree and low-strung barbwire for a fence, with a rusted gate hanging loose. Toward the back a detached garage stood in the same neglected condition. Beyond that was arid landscape as far as the eye could see. On an average day, Trigg probably ran into more rattlesnakes than people, which I imagine was how he liked it.

I watched him haul the dog up the front steps and into the house. Then I returned to the Dart, where I rummaged in the trunk until I found what I was looking for. It was one of those new aluminum bats that were catching on. Some of the girls I'd played with didn't like the clunky feel of the metal on the ball, but I was okay with it. It could still make serious contact if you had quick wrists and a strong swing, which I did.

❖

Out on the highway, the driver of a northbound rig switched on his lights against the dusk, shifting through the gears as he regained his speed. I stopped to watch his taillights grow smaller in the distance, going over what I intended for Trigg.

I won't pretend that it came easy for me. I'd caused mild harm to men and women who'd crossed me in a way they had no right to, but I'd not yet killed a person. I could have left it to someone else—Trigg had his share of enemies—but nobody I knew of was stepping forward. As for the cops, Jesse's death was just another low-priority 187, barely on their radar. Even if they nicked Trigg for it, I knew how the system worked. Guys with money got the sharp lawyers and the velvet deals, while the rest of us got the shaft. I didn't see how I could live with that.

When I reached the old house a first floor light shown toward the back, behind flimsy window curtains. I slipped through the dangling gate and across the yard as neat as Lou Brock stealing second. The dog was a worry, but she never peeped. I ducked in alongside the house and made my way to the lighted window, which was half open. Stretching up, I was able to peer through the rustling curtains and into a kitchen that looked like a cockroach factory.

Trigg was frying a steak on an iron skillet while he sang "Red Roses for a Blue Lady," keeping time with a crusty fork gripped in his right hand. His cane leaned handily against the stove. The scrawny dog sat up on her haunches, riveted by the sizzling meat, which explained why she'd paid me no mind when I came across the yard.

In between the stove and window was a table. On the table was a gun, a .45 auto by the look of it. Three .45 slugs had been found in Jesse, the ones that had delivered mercy to him from what Trigg had dished out prior.

I hunkered down and collected myself for a confrontation that could go either way. Make no mistake, I'd come to Desert Vista knowing I might not make it out. But Mom and Jesse were gone, and I'd given up on romance a few thousand miles ago, one breakup past my quota. What was left for me now didn't add up to much, not enough to make me cower in the face of an unfavorable ending.

I crept to the rear of the house and up three warped steps to a locked door. The door was mostly splintery plywood on a weak frame and slack hinges. All it took was one good kick to bust it open.

Trigg was caught up drunkenly in his song, turning his dinner with the fork. He seemed more startled at first than fearful, maybe because it was a woman who'd come for him, an unfamiliar one at that. By the time he dropped the fork and went for the gun I was across the kitchen, bringing the bat down on his wrist hard enough to ruin the bones. He let out a wail and swung at me with his other fist, and I crushed that too.

After that I laid into his shins, working my way up from there. The dog crawled quivering under the table. Trigg tried his best to fend me off, but I kept coming at him like a Mexican boxer, one gear, straight ahead. Each time I cut the smoky air with that bat and wrecked another part of him, he cried out in a dreadful way.

He finally crumpled to the floor, begging me to stop, the way I needed to hear it from him before I closed the show.

❖

It was the dog that saved him.

As Trigg curled up moaning at my feet, she ventured out from beneath the table and fixed again on that grease-popping meat. Then she turned her head from the stove to me and back again with starving eyes that jarred me out of the cruel place I was in. I don't know if it was the innocence I saw, or just her raw need. But whatever happened in that moment, it drove me deep through all the tough layers I'd developed since I was old enough to know heartlessness firsthand. I heard Jesse's words again, as clear as if he was standing beside me—what he'd said about taking a life for lowly reasons, even from the vilest creatures. How it turns you into something akin to them, and destroys a vital piece of you that you can never get back. What I was up to was nothing but pure vengeance, and I knew in my heart that Jesse would have wept to see what that ungodly urge had done to me.

I asked Trigg where he kept his keys. He said his front pants pocket. I tapped it with the end of the bat to be sure there was nothing else concealed there. I did the same with the rest of him. He came up clean.

"The keys," I said.

He tried to get at them but cried out, saying it was useless. I raised the bat for another blow. He shrank behind his broken hands.

"Okay, okay." His voice was shaky but also faint with hope. "You want my car, take it. Money, anything I got, it's yours."

"The keys."

He dug gingerly into his pocket again, whimpering worse than the dog. While he worked at that, I turned off the flame under the skillet. There were some small potatoes in with the steak. I put the bleeding meat on a plate, cut it up tiny, mashed in some potatoes, and set the whole thing on the floor. While the dog gobbled it up, I found a bowl and filled it with water, and set that beside the plate.

I had Trigg toss his keys off to the side. Then I made him crawl out of the kitchen and through the house, to put some distance between him and the gun. It went slow and wasn't pleasant for him. By the time he reached the stairs his head hung low; any optimism he might have nurtured seemed left behind with the smear of blood across the floor.

"Who are you?" His eyes were crazy with fear. "What do you want from me?"

I ordered him up the stairs. That went worse for him; every step was more of a struggle than the last. He collapsed at the first landing, weeping quietly like a man facing the last of his illusions.

"Please," he said, "no more."

I came halfway up and threatened him again, but he didn't flinch. He just lay there in a heap, his eyes wet and despairing, pleading with me to shoot him.

I told him the gun would be on the kitchen table, if he wanted to do it himself. Or he could make the long crawl into town for help, if he could take the pain. I'm not sure Jesse would have approved, but I thought it was a passable compromise.

There was one phone in the house, which I ripped from the wall. Then I soaped and rinsed the bat, wiped down anything that might have my fingerprints on it, and cracked his cane in two. Out in the garage, I found his car under a layer of dust. It was a Pontiac GTO, the lame model GM brought out in '74, as if Trigg had arrived late for the party and settled for leftovers. I raised the hood and tore apart the wiring in case he had an extra key he hadn't told me about. After that I threw the set he'd given me out into the desert, where they caught a glint of moonlight before disappearing into a sandy wash.

I'd busted Trigg up bad enough to know he'd never fully heal, not so he could capably handle a gun or threaten anyone with his crippled mitts. Take the power away from a bully and he's got nothing left except the truth of who he is, and there's not enough booze in the world to help a spineless man escape that.

That was good enough for me. I was done with Carl Trigg.

❖

The Dart was waiting for me with a full tank that would take me to wherever I was going, or at least get me on my way.

I pulled out of the alley and back to the main street, where I paused before making my turn. I had the windows down and could hear laughter coming from the Whistle Stop, so I guess there was more companionship in that little town than I'd accounted for. Some danceable music came on the jukebox, the Bee Gees if I remember right. I envisioned woozy couples out on the floor making memories the best they could, hardly the worst you could say of a person.

Across the highway, a freight train rumbled through, heading south. I turned the other direction and hit the pedal, putting the scanty lights of Desert Vista in my rear view mirror. Cooling air flowed comfortingly into the car. When I reached a road sign telling me the speed limit was 55, I pushed the needle to 70 and kept it there.

As I steered the Dart down that highway, I felt more at ease within my skin than I ever had, braced up with a different kind of strength. I couldn't count what I'd done to Trigg as a thing to be proud of, it was too vicious for that, and I was smart enough to know one glimmering moment hadn't magically cured my issues. But in that instant when I'd pulled up short of finishing him off, it seemed like I'd let go of something that had dragged me down for too long. I was on the move again, but it didn't feel like I was running away from myself this time. It occurred to me there might be a good place up ahead after all, a welcoming place where I might begin to know that embrace of life that Jesse had tried to instill in me. Like I said, I could feel his spirit in that car.

Maybe the dog could sense it too.

As we sped north she sat beside me, head out the open window, sniffing wildly, like she knew what freedom smelled like.

Obituaries

Thomas Westerfield

Kurt Woolen has died. And even though I have not seen him, spoken to him, written him, nor made any effort or had any inclination to do so during the nearly five decades since I last sat in front of him in our alphabetically-assigned seats during Coach Wathen's sophomore English class at Owensboro Catholic High School back in Kentucky, I feel...satisfied at this news. There is no second thought or guilty conscience about it either.

A short, squat boy, a second-stringer on the school's football team who rarely played, with a bull-dog build and coal-black hair cut close to the scalp, and almost always wearing a sneering, arrogant little grin when I knew him as a teenager, Kurt Woolen was sixty-two years old at the time of his death. He had lived a hard, mean life of drugs, alcohol, prison, mental illness, and borderline poverty. No cause of death is listed in his online obituary from the old hometown newspaper, *The Messenger-Inquirer,* that I glance at very occasionally, and I don't really need to know how or of what he died. The fact of his death is enough.

There's no doubt in my mind that Kurt Woolen was a psychopath, and always had been. Even as a teenager, I wondered if he had some form of brain damage—dropped on his head by a careless parent, or perhaps severely beaten by one in a rage. But it's hard to have much sympathy for whatever suffering Kurt Woolen endured as a child and a teenager himself given the deep levels of torment, viciousness, and violent assaults he inflicted on me and others he picked as easy prey.

My deep, daily nauseous dread of him in my freshman and sophomore years was not exaggerated and self-dramatizing, as a therapist I saw in my late twenties once tried to convince me. A year or two after I had graduated high school and was attending a college blessedly far away from Owensboro, friends of mine who had remained there told me that Woolen had killed a man with a knife during a mutually drunken brawl. He was quickly found guilty for manslaughter but, for reasons that I have no knowledge of, only served four years in the Kentucky state penitentiary before returning home. I had been intuitive and entirely reasonable in my fear as a high school student that he might murder me.

Besides choking me around the neck and hitting me with hard, striking blows up against my head, slapping me angrily and repeatedly across my face, slamming me up against brick walls, and spitting on me while contemptuously mocking me as "sissy", "faggot", and "queer" (back before the generation after mine had reclaimed the latter word as a vocabulary of defiant pride; something I still bristle against to this day), Kurt Woolen also once punched me in the balls with his full-force fist to where I almost vomited on the spot. The same therapist also tried to convince me this act was Woolen's projected gay-panic over his own same-sex desires, but I've always known that was sheer, unadulterated, grade-A bull-shit. As if I should somehow find comfort or be complimented that Kurt Woolen was probably way, way deep down within a dark, shameful space of himself a cock-loving faggot just like me.

Kurt Woolen's full-force fist punching into my groin was about nothing more than his gleeful expression of how much violence he was allowed to get away with because I was too scared to fight back as a skinny, acne-strewn, withdrawn, and more-than-fey fourteen- and fifteen-year-old. And his status on the football team, even as a lowly freshman and sophomore second-stringer, still raised him up in the school's hierarchy as untouchable by any other student or teacher, save for occasional mild discipline by one of the coaches. The most reprimand he ever got from any teacher who witnessed his torture upon me or any other helpless, friendless boy was a sharp, barked, "Cut that out!" or "Stop it!". Which he would always respond to with an ugly little chuckle and a short break in his happy cruelty until the teacher turned their back on the class again or buried their head in lecture notes or a textbook.

The news of his dying surprises me somewhat in the Pandora's box of old feelings and memories it stirs. Beyond rare mentions of him by the old friends I see whenever I revisit my hometown every six or seven years, I had heard nothing else about him after his prison time except that he was an alcoholic drug addict and obviously mentally ill, still living with his mother in his childhood home. But even that information was a couple of decades old by the time I read his obituary. Kurt Woolen had not been forgotten by me by any means, but there had been no real reason to think of him either.

No wife or children—living or dead—are listed in his obituary, although close to a dozen names of siblings, pre-deceasing or surviving him, take up the bulk of it. I am struck by the fact that, unlike the traditional custom of a small Southern town where family name and history are an all-important and inescapable component of one's life that everyone else is made aware, no identification of any kind, no mention or name, is made of his father.

The other thing that stands out for me in the online write-up is that the upcoming funeral Mass will be said by Father Ray Dunn. Ray Dunn was also our classmate and the first boy I had ever fallen in love, or at least love's closest approximation for a naïve, closeted teenager in late 1960's Kentucky. Ray was tall, gangly, looping—a popular and somewhat skilled basketball player—with thick reddish hair always falling over his puppy-brown eyes, a sweet and shy broad smile, and a painfully awkward disposition outside of the ball court. Almost to the point where I think now he would be considered mildly autistic.

Although Ray no doubt had some sense of my great crush on him, neither of us ever acknowledged it. Except for a brief senior year romance with our high school's resident free-spirit hippie girl Maureen Harris, who wore fringed brown leather vests and purple headbands adorned with peace signs and virgin white peasant blouses, he was never romantically, much less sexually, linked to any girl or boy, known or rumored. Still, one of the strongest erotic memories of my life permanently burned into my psyche is of spending the night at his home our senior year (separate beds, separate rooms) and finding his discarded white jockey briefs bunched in the corner of the family bathroom. I so wanted to pick up that wadded underwear and bring it into my face, breathing in what I imagined Ray's warm crotch musk must smell like. The temptation was a thrilling mix of Catholic sin and shame that I just could not cross the line to know in actuality. But for several years, I would ecstatically jerk off to the heated memory of that resisted fantasy while also visualizing Ray's lanky naked body, with its thin curlicue of just-budding pubic hair and slender, long cock, in the showers after gym class. It was the closest I ever got to having sex with him.

Since Ray had lived in the same neighborhood and gone to the same Catholic grade school on the poorer east side of Owensboro Kurt Woolen attended (whereas I had gone to the Catholic one on the more middle working class south side) and because he was such a good basketball player, but, primarily, because Ray always carried an obvious gentleness that was recognized by both the nuns and his fellow students and their parents as being genuinely religious, he was left untaunted and misused by Kurt Woolen and the other boys of his ilk with whom he shared a classroom for eight years. Though he was not "one of them"—too clumsy and mumbling and prayerful—they left him alone and even cheered and whooped for him as he scored amazing rebounds on the basketball court.

The last interaction I had with Ray Dunn was nearly twenty-five years ago at Owensboro Catholic High School's Class of 1972 Reunion. I was just drunk enough, and just confident enough within myself of both my physical attractiveness and my emotional maturity to handle whatever reaction he might have, to subtly engage Father Ray in intimate conversation. Since I knew I most likely would never see him again for at least another six years or so until I made my next hometown trip—and even that was not a given—I thought, *Why not?* and tried to steer our dialogue into a revelation of secrets and still-held dreams and desires, most pointedly his. I was curious to see if any awareness of sexuality had burgeoned within him since high school and whether he had acted upon any of it. If nothing else, getting my high-school crush, now a priest, into bed during a twentieth-year reunion would make a great story to tell my friends in San Francisco where I now lived.

But somewhere along the lines of a fifth or sixth beer I drank during our talk, which had moved to a walnut-paneled side room of the pretentious small-town country club the reunion was being held, I foolhardily decided to make a heart-felt act of penance, the actual sacrament, in some misguided effort at returning to my spiritual 'roots'. I spoke guiltily of a young man, some ten years younger than me, who I had used and treated shabbily in the first rush of success and big money I had made a few years earlier.

To his credit, Father Ray expressed no shock or judgment, only asking if there was any way I could contact this young man again to tell him directly and decently of my failure to be kind and fair to him, and to see if there was anything I could offer to put him back on track for his education and career, or perhaps any counseling or rehab he may need. I promised I would try to locate this ex-lover and see what I could do, and after a heart-felt stumbling over the old Act of Contrition prayer I surprisingly remembered, Father Ray, as the Catholic Church's ordained representative of Jesus Christ on earth, forgave and blessed me for my great sin of basically having a fucked-up relationship in my early thirties.

The next morning, hungover, I felt far more ashamed at having participated in that self-abasing sacramental act than I did at my cruelty to my former lover. While I still make periodic visits to Owensboro, I've never run into Father Ray again and have done nothing to see or speak with him again. I've never attended another high school reunion either. Nevertheless, once I returned to San Francisco after that drunken, misbegotten confession, I completed my penance and did locate the young man I had treated so badly. I was delighted—and greatly relieved—to discover that he had put things back together his life quite well, having graduated with a Ph.D. in Somatic Psychology from the California College of Integral Studies, and was now with a partner twenty years older than I who was loving and respectful and understanding. He bore no ill will towards me but was very grateful to hear my apology. He even admitted his drinking and drug problems, though exacerbated by our relationship, had, unknown to me at the time, started and been bubbling to the breaking point several months before we had even met.

So, I lost track of Father Ray as I had Kurt Woolen, except once being informed that he had not been able to sustain the pressures of leading a parish community and the myriad and less-than-religious administrative and fund-raising tasks of a day-to-day priest. He had suffered some kind of nervous breakdown and was now assigned to living on the grounds of a small rural contemplative monastery in the diocese to minister to the increasingly aging nuns that survived there. He taught one class each semester at the local Catholic college in Owensboro as well. I also heard from one of my friends who was in Alcoholics Anonymous that Father Ray attended all sorts of twelve-step meetings through-out town in the after-math of losing his parish. The story was that Crohn's Disease had led him to an addiction to pain-killers.

As ridiculous as it sounds, I feel oddly betrayed by Father Ray leading Mass for Kurt Woolen. Who knows if he and Woolen had somehow become life-long friends during his seminary years and Woolen's prison ones, or if they had only re-crossed paths with each other in the recent months or even weeks or days before Woolen's death? But, somehow Father Ray has become involved—perhaps by the Woolen family's request after Kurt's passing—with the final Catholic rites and rituals that signify Kurt Woolen is, in fact, dead in body only; and that his soul, his essence, remains alive and vital and will know God in some form and fashion. There even most likely is a promise of greater forgiveness and compassion in his next life than I would ever allow him—or he ever allowed others—in this one. The more and more I think about it—and as to why I keep turning it over and over in my head I am totally dumb-founded and ignorant—the more I find it all infuriating. Contemplating Father Ray's promiscuous offerings of blessing absolutions to Kurt Woolen's many sins and comforting platitudes to his still-living siblings enrages me.

It is a few weeks later, less entangled and devoured by my rambling, obsessive thoughts and emotions, that I realize what so angers me about Father Ray Dunn's involvement with Kurt Woolen's death. It is because I am not involved. I am not remembered. Of course, why would I be? Until I saw his obituary, Kurt Woolen had not been in my thoughts for many years, decades in fact, and I am absolutely certain that I had never been in his since he disappeared one day from Coach Wathen's English class before the semester ended.

The rumor was he had flunked out, which was highly unlikely given the number of outright idiots who remained as students; most likely, his parents could no longer afford the modest tuition given the multitude of off-spring they were trying to educate in the Catholic school system. Whatever Father Ray's eulogy of Kurt Woolen's life contained, it did not contain any single memory or moment of recognition of me or of his violence against me. As marking as Kurt Woolen was upon my life—at least for a time—I am totally irrelevant to his and always had been.

About seven months after discovering Kurt Woolen's obituary, one night I come across another one listed on the *Messenger-Inquirer* website that is a couple of weeks old. It is a much longer and more detailed one regarding the life of Father Ray Dunn. Although his extensive educational background, his many parish assignments, his expertise in the historical context of the parables of the gospels that he shared as a Professor at the local college, his talent at guitar, his successful sobriety of many years, his great generosity and open-heartedness to all people no matter their social standing, and a long list of surviving siblings and deeply loved nephews and nieces are all detailed in fine form, the obituary omits any facts regarding his death. It is from friends the next day that I learn what pretty much everyone in Owensboro reading Father Ray's obituary already knew: that he died by his own hand, placing a hunting rifle under his chin, firing, and not only blasting out his brains from his skull, but blowing off his handsome, gentle face with its soft, brown eyes.

His body was discovered in his car by early Sunday morning golfers, parked in the course's lot where it was the only car when they arrived. The golf course, which housed the country club my drunken twenty-year high-school reunion had been held, bordered against a beautiful, lush state park and bird preserve with popular, much-walked hiking trails. Father Ray had last been seen at the Saturday evening wedding he had officiated for a couple of former students. He had smiled and mingled and laughed at the reception and there were a number of photos of him posed with the wedding party and with different guests at the reception. He seemed his usual low-key and simple, shy shelf, happy and content—present—and had left around ten o'clock.

For several days after learning all this, and reading and re-reading his online obituary endless times, I am shadowed by an almost breaking sadness. It is the loneliness of Father Ray's act. The self-hate expressed by his blowing off his always gentle face. All that was unsaid within him. It haunts me. The pain he carried is beyond my knowing, beyond my imagining. But, what I can surmise of it, what I can push my heart to emphasize and understand, is crushing.

The memory of his naked, lanky body in the gym shower and the barely sprouted line of hair around his thin, longish cock and images of his now sixty-two-year-old body with his shattered, disappeared face laid out naked on a coroner's table intermingle in my mind. I create elaborate stories in my head where I had somehow reached out to him with a friendly email or out-of-the-blue telephone call which inspires him to share all that he cannot say to any person in his life in Owensboro, Kentucky but that he can say to me now, this time, because I am not trying to manipulate him drunkenly, because this time I care. I am able to see and hear him as him, outside of my teenage desires. I can be there to help him as he struggles in his hell of deep-set loneliness and unspoken self and inwardly turned hate.

And I remember something I had forgotten about the last time we spent time together at that high school reunion. I recall the full, accepting embrace as he said good-bye to me at the end of my drunken confession. He did not linger or move his arms or hands anywhere else around my body during that embrace—there was no subjugated eroticism or unconscious sensuality—just a brief but total holding close; a moment of sincere Christian brotherhood on his part. I feel a great guilt of not recognizing or appreciating it at the time. He was offering true friendship in that moment. But I had not only minimized it, but had forgotten it in my self-contempt at having temporarily fallen back into the trap of Catholicism's self-lacerating mind-set.

For a few days I am even seized with a driving fantasy of making the long multiple-connecting flight to Kentucky. Perhaps I should stand at Father Ray's gravesite at the Catholic cemetery, located right off the interstate highway on the outskirts of leaving Owensboro (or entering it, depending on the direction from which one approaches), the cemetery where my father, mother, brother, grandparents on my mother's side, and many uncles, aunts, cousins, neighbors, teachers, even a couple of good friends I knew when growing up, are all now buried. Perhaps there, in that wide, endless acreage of green and quiet, I might finally know what remains so unknown about the boy I first loved.

As more time passes, the impact of Father Ray's suicide subsides somewhat, though at times it roils and strikes with a shocking immediacy again and I am lost in all the memories and fantasies and sorrows of unanswered mysteries that had consumed me in the first knowledge of it. And, a bizarre and incongruous thing occurs. Another memory comes back to awareness; one I honestly don't think I recalled since the event occurred in the fall of 1970. Except once, about five years later, and the only reason I was reminded of it then was because of some gossip I was being told.

Without the daily torment of Kurt Woolen, and having all summer working outdoors mowing the grass of the golf course and country club grounds Father Ray Dunn would take his life many decades later, I was thriving in ways new and unexpected to me—clear-skinned and tanned, bigger, growing my hair out long, dressing in fashionable bell-bottom jeans and bold-colored paisley shirts bought with my own money. For the most part, I was left alone by most bullies and rarely experienced any physical violence or threats of such from them. A small, tight circle of friends was coming together for me, my first ever in high school.

The only person who picked on me, who tried to show off by making fun of how I sounded and walked and dressed, who would call me names, and who would knock books off my desk and hit me in the back or on my right arm as hard as he could, was another football player, a senior named Bobby Zogg. Like Kurt Woolen, he was rarely brought into the game as he had no speed nor as much strength compared to the other players. Still he had the swaggering-cock attitude of the rest of the team. And he had an imposing, muscular build that might have made him hot and attractive if didn't have such sharp, squinty possum-like face and a real-deal red-neck country boy "hee-haw" laugh.

We were in the same film class taught by the young army wife of a soldier serving in Vietnam. Shiela Buckman was strikingly beautiful with long brown hair and eyes which were an equally lustrous and dreamy brown. She could not have been more than five or six years older than the sixteen and seventeen-year-olds in her class, and, of course, all the straight boys strutted up and smiled eagerly (while often leering behind her back) trying to impress her. But, because I knew so much about both the history and technique of films, and had actually already seen a number of classics mentioned in the textbook, she lavished a lot of attention and praise on me, often deferring to my knowledge in her lessons to the class. She once told me privately that she thought I should be the one teaching it and was extremely impressed that I read Pauline Kael's weekly movie reviews in *The New Yorker*.

As it became more obvious that I was Mrs. Buckman's favored one, Bobby Zogg began to pick up the frequency and intensity of his under-cutting verbal and physical attacks on me. Always out of eyesight of Mrs. Buckman, of course. I have no idea of what had transpired, what action he had taken—it is totally gone with no trace in memory—but one day during class he pulled some stunt or said something meant to threaten and humiliate me. And, out of my mouth, completely unexpected and unplanned—shocking me more than anyone else—I said in a quaking, nervous voice that still remained as matter-of-fact in tone as I could muster, and could be heard by the entire class, including Mrs. Buckman, "What is your problem with me? I haven't done anything to you. What is your problem?"

Mrs. Buckman turned around and smiled amused and quizzical, but saying nothing. A few kids laughed, but most just looked at me looking directly at Bobby Zogg. It probably lasted twenty seconds, if it even lasted that long, but there was nothing but silence from Bobby Zogg before he finally averted his face from mine. And, as terrified as I was for the next few days, tense and alert, steeling myself for some horrifying violent revenge beating, Bobby Zogg did nothing. On occasion he would look at me up-and-down with an emphatic disgust and then turn away. I was fine with that.

I don't know why my moment of…what? Courage? Self-assertion? Just sheer I've-had-enough-ness? Whatever it can be called, it has never been a memory I have returned to for savoring pride or personal inspiration or even as part of the repertoire of favorite stories I like to tell about myself. It has never stood out for me or been recalled by me until now in this aftermath of learning about Kurt Woolen and Ray Dunn's deaths. Somehow, it has sprung a bloom in my consciousness after laying dormant and dark underground all these decades. It is so weird that this significant moment—the moment I took my first faltering steps of "No more" and claim the beginning of the life I was to make for myself as an out gay man as unafraid as possible and make every effort to never allow mistreatment against me ever again—has never been important enough, treasured enough, to become part of those key memories that make up the story of me, my personal legend of self. Remembering Bobby Zogg's flushed face averting my direct gaze in that seemingly long chasm of silence makes me feel happier than I have in many months.

Though I still feel grief and sadness at Ray's self-immolation, life slowly assumes proportion again, which is its wont. I can admit now that Woolen's death upended me with the unpleasant truth that, though I long ago made a hard-won acceptance there is no fairness in this life, I still harbor a deep desire that life did. It shocks me that I have held on to some hope that the old pain from my childhood and teenage years I had wallowed in so destructively during my twenties and thirties remained thirsting for some kind of justice, something to make the physical and emotional traumas all healed or redeemed in the stupid, fatuous Oprah Book Club way. I thought I was at peace in living with the scars, no longer hiding them but no longer scratching at them or high-lighting them either as some kind of of my greater proof of my greater suffering and greater need for love over anyone else's. But I had fooled myself into thinking they no longer *mattered* nor could be felt in any meaningful or necessary way.

What mattered to Ray, the ending of his life, what he held so close and finally could not contain within himself any longer, will remain a grievous and sorrowful mystery to me even though we had not seen or spoken to each other in some twenty-five years. I hate so much that he suffered so viciously alone. But it is my great foolishness and vanity to think that my fantasized return in his life could have in any way "saved" him. The hard, unyielding truth that confronts me is I was as unimportant to Ray Dunn as I was to Kurt Woolen. He will always be the first boy I loved and I will always remember his sweetness, his constant and humble desire to be good, no matter what others demons and confusions, fears and loathings, consumed him. But there can be no escape from the fact: I did not know him at all and was never wanted or invited by him to do so at any point in the time we knew each other or spent together. Somehow I thought I had known this all along and had accepted it, when so obviously and so painfully I had not.

I will never visit Ray's grave. Most likely, I will probably never even visit Owensboro again. It has been six years since my last trip back and in that time the remaining aunts and uncles, at least the favorite ones, have now died. The cousin I am closest to and most enjoy, I meet up with every couple of years on her family's vacations to Las Vegas, New Orleans, or some Florida beach town. My two closest friends from high school that made their lives in Owensboro have children—and most significantly, grandchildren—in other states and are now considering moving closer to them. Also, they are more likely to come visit me in San Francisco now that we will all soon retire.

As for Bobby Zogg, the last thing I heard about him was in the mid-1970s, three or four years after graduation, when Jeannie Scott, a genuinely friendly, popular cheer-leader who always seemed free of the snobbery and status-measuring of most of the other girls of her group—chattering non-stop and good-naturedly to anybody and everybody in her classes and at dances and parties—filed for divorce from him after a short marriage that had given them two children. The gossip was that he, like so many another former Owensboro Catholic High School football player now in young adulthood bereft of his standing among a team, was a raging alcoholic. I don't know anything at all of what happened to him after that. I don't know if he is still living in Owensboro or if he ever re-married or if he ever got sober. I could care less, frankly. But perhaps I will find out some day. Perhaps while reading the online edition of my hometown newspaper I will run across his obituary and think of him again for the first time in many years.

THE FOOL

Ellis Anderson

He still had a few minutes before the couple arrived. Edmund eased into his padded leather chair next to the bookcases. The reach to the bottom shelf was an easy one. He opened a Japanese box with red and white cranes painted on the lid and picked up the deck of cards inside. Unwrapping the amber silk square that protected the cards, he set them on the inlaid table he used for readings. He folded the scarf that had been Harry's favorite, nested it back in the box, and closed the lid, completing that part of the ritual.

Edmund fanned the cards out, face up, across the table in front of him. In the middle, the charger ridden by the Knight of Wands pranced into focus. Extracting that card without moving the others, he held it up and angled it to the milky light flooding in from the French doors.

Most tarot readers believed that the lizards decorating the knight's bright yellow tunic were salamanders that symbolized indestructible courage. Edmund knew them instead as chameleons—masters of deception. They warned of a man who could change his nature to complement any surrounding, to mimic another person in ways so subtle that they'd seem a soul-mate. What could be more alluring than the promise of an emotional twin?

The knight's rearing war-horse carried him toward a barren and mountainous terrain. Edmund's eyes widened and he exhaled a bark of laughter. How had he missed that before? Even a novice reader would have made the connection between the knight's horse and Jake's new white van—the Chevy steed that would shortly be carrying the musician and his girlfriend across the desert toward Los Angeles.

Yet the other parallels between the knight and Jake had been obvious from their first meeting. The cavalier on the card held a staff in front of him, indicating he was a sensual man who led with his passion. The wand also signified a man who rarely looked back—the sort who was quick to discard the past and the people in it. Like the knight on the card, Jake had already forgotten the benefactor who'd made his search for the Grail possible.

Edmund couldn't claim ignorance. If he had been used, it had been with his own full foresight and permission. He'd seen his own role as Fool clearly during Jake's first reading six months ago, perhaps even from the moment the young man stepped into the reading room, having been drawn by the tiny sign hanging on Royal Street.

That particular afternoon, Edmund had been contemplating closing early and going upstairs to his apartment. He'd only had two consultations the entire day. Marking his place in the paperback he was reading, he stood to close up, bringing him face-to-face with Jake when he stepped through the open French doors.

Although the rise from the flagstones of the courtyard was a mere six inches, the step was a commitment. Most first-time clients tapped on the doors and stood on ground level until invited to enter. They would pose the question tentatively: *Are you the fortune teller?* Jake's first parry was a bolder one.

"I want to know my future," the young man said, the question instantly branding him as some sort of Knight.

Edmund recited his standard opening. "No one knows the future. Tarot cards are a tool for the esoteric science of symbolism. If you're looking for someone to tell you you'll be rich, famous, and lucky in love, Jackson Square is just two blocks away."

"So, you're a Jungian, huh?" Jake said. He smiled as if they shared a secret joke. *Maybe the common tourist rube doesn't understand what you're talking about, but I do.* He shucked off his pack and tossed it onto the chair in the corner. Without asking, he slouched into the chair opposite Edmund as if he belonged in the space.

Edmund didn't respond. He sat down in his own chair on the other side of the small inlaid table. He closed his eyes and inhaled through his nostrils.

"I get it," Jake said. "I've read almost everything Jung wrote, so you're preaching to the choir. But I'm short on cash. How much do you charge?"

Edmund couldn't answer immediately. He'd been overpowered by the scent of Harry.

This should have been impossible because Harry's favorite scarf, the one he used to swaddle his deck of cards, had long ago lost the musk of the man. Only one shirt remained, the one Harry had been wearing the last day they'd walked together along the river. Edmund had discovered it behind the washer right after hospice had come in. He'd crushed the stiff fabric around his face like an oxygen mask and inhaled his lover's stale August sweat, sobbing because all the molecules of that scent and all the atoms of Harry himself would soon be dispersed, never to be reassembled. Moved by a prescient impulse, Edmund had stuffed the shirt into a gallon-sized plastic bag and tucked it into the desk drawer that held his journals.

At first, right after Harry's funeral, Edmund indulged daily, opening the bag and drawing the essence of Harry into his body. The smell seemed to assuage the grief that withered him like some kind of soul famine. Then he realized with horror that he needed to ration his indulgences or the scent would be gone before he died. He began strictly limiting the bag openings and inhalations, but he had lived much longer than he'd had imagined. While his lover's olfactory presence had dissipated over the past two decades, the self-imposed miserliness meant there was enough of it still remaining to bring Harry back to life momentarily, twice each year.

And now this lanky, young man across the table from him was manufacturing Harry's scent, fresh, and strong and unsullied by plastic polymers.

The idea of reincarnation flared in Edmund's mind momentarily, but reason smothered it. This man was older than twenty. Not much, but definitely older. The two were nothing alike physically. Harry had been short and on the stout side, a ginger with thin hair and a cherub's face. And he'd possessed a sweet vanilla nature, exuding generosity and compassion. This man was both brash and arrogant; Edmund concluded that pheromones were the only thing the two men shared— and that was only by a whim of fate.

Edmund ended the long pause. "How much can you pay?"

"I can only spare a buck," Jake said.

Edmund frowned, hoping to appear he was debating. Then he looked into Jake's eyes and saw amusement. The handsome scoundrel already knew he'd won a free reading—at the very least.

Edmund unwrapped the deck and handed the cards to Jake to shuffle. He started the recording app on his phone. He normally charged an additional $15 to record readings and email the digital files to his clients. He didn't mention this to Jake.

When Jake looked askance at the device, Edmund said, "You'll want to remember this reading later."

"I'm betting I don't forget," he said, interlacing the cards with thumbs that seemed practiced at stroking fate.

"What do you want to ask?" Edmund said, forcing his eyes away from Jake's hands. "Your question should be one that can't be answered with a simple 'yes' or 'no.' "

Most people took at least a few minutes to work it out. Jake answered immediately.

"How will I achieve my heart's desire?"

They exchanged names and began.

Jake drew the cards, one at a time and handed them to Edmund, who laid them down in the Celtic Cross. The traditional spread always worked best for him. When the third card Jake selected was The Fool, Edmund knew they were going to have some sort of relationship and Edmund would be the agent of the young man's success. He laid the card in the place showing Unknown Influences.

The drawing on the Fool card depicted a little dog barking to warn his young master, who is about to step off a cliff. The Fool must have known he was traveling a treacherous trail, but he's lost in a reverie, gazing up at the sky. Edmund had always imagined the Fool was star-gazing, but realized at that moment that the icon wasn't looking at anything at all. He was smelling—intoxicated by the fragrance of the rose in his hand.

By the time Edmund laid out the fifth card, he knew it'd be a one-sided relationship. Number six showed betrayal. He understood that he would suffer and Jake would prosper by that suffering. The seventh card—representing the one who queries—was the Knight of Wands. The wand itself is a budding stick, and the knight holds it upright, thrusting it forward like a phallic symbol. On the positive side, the wands denote new life, creativity, and energy. They also represent egotism. Narcissism. Self-absorption. Edmund didn't mention the negative aspects. Jake preened.

Card ten, the one carrying the weight of the reading's final outcome, was the Sun. The ultimate card of triumph.

Edmund burned a CD of the digital file that afternoon and gave it to Jake. Six months later, after Jake had moved out, Edmund found it in the bureau he'd allowed the younger man to use. He was certain it'd never been slipped out of the sleeve and it clearly hadn't meant enough to pack. Edmund didn't have to listen to it. By then, he knew the original recording nearly by heart:

You're enormously creative and possess the rare combination of talent and charisma. Few have been gifted with such during the entire history of this earth. Are you a musician? Yes? A songwriter? Ah, that's making sense.

He remembered the layout exactly. It had also contained The Devil card, showing a demon holding a couple in chains, symbolizing erotic bondage of an unhealthy sort. Edmund knew that card spoke to him, rather than Jake.

The cards revealed generalities only, however. Jake supplied more details of his life that night when Edmund treated him to dinner and drinks. After the youth had mentioned he liked Italian, Edmund called Irene's and took advantage of his status to get a table. At the restaurant, the younger man ordered multiple appetizers and top shelf martinis and wine with authority, seemingly born to privilege. But he hadn't been. Jake had grown up in a Florida panhandle tourist town, the son of a plumber. He set his sights for stardom when he started a band in middle school. After high school, his parents convinced him to sign up for an X-ray tech program at the local community college. He lasted through two desultory semesters before dropping out. He played clubs and bars along the Florabama circuit for a year before hitchhiking to New Orleans, in search of influences other than Jimmy Buffet. He told Edmund his original songs needed more grit if he were to ever break through. Earlier in the week, on his second night in the city, Jake had his first true grit experience. He crashed with a girl in the Seventh Ward and while they were at breakfast the next morning, her apartment was robbed. His Martin guitar and bankroll were stolen.

Edmund never did meet the girl and didn't quite believe that she existed, but within a week of Jake's unofficial moving in and infusing the apartment with the scent of Harry, the two went to a music store in the Garden District. After playing nearly every guitar on the wall, Jake settled on a hybrid acoustic and Edmund forked over $3,500 for the instrument.

Jake was not effusive in his gratitude. He accepted the gift as a loan, promising to pay back the investment with interest once he landed some gigs. The two shook hands, manfully. Jake did secure a job in a Bourbon Street joint the next night, and made a show of giving Edmund half of his earnings the next day, $67. After that, he complained bitterly about how the winter crowds were thin and the tips were paltry. Edmund never received another payment and after a few weeks, Jake never mentioned it again.

At first, Edmund showed up at each of the gigs, one of the few grey-haired people at the bar. He would nurse a $5 soda water through each set as his ticket to hear Jake play. During the breaks between sets, Jake would nod at him, but direct his energy to the tourist girls. The women would fawn over him, place their hands on his arms as they talked, or put $20 bills in the tip jar when they requested songs. Edmund eventually stopped going.

❖

As a roommate, Jake exhibited exemplary behavior. He cleaned the shower, washed dishes, and took care of their dirty clothes with weekly trips to the laundromat. He folded Edmund's T-shirts with the fastidiousness of a Brooks Brothers' clerk and hung oxford shirts so skillfully they looked professionally laundered, all the while, chatting amicably. He purchased groceries on occasion and cooked Boy Scout casserole meals over which they'd discuss literature and music. While he did not contribute to the rent or utilities, he displayed his body casually and frequently, and granted Edmund unspoken permission to stare by ignoring the longing looks. He wore no towel after showering and often lay naked on the sofa reading or working on a song. Especially after Edmund had spent a large sum of money.

Edmund's costs mounted; recording sessions, back-up musicians, meals with potential promoters at trendy restaurants, new clothes, and a rack of sound equipment that took up all the space in the living room. Edmund pulled in favors all over town, based on his friendships and the weight of his family name. Doors opened for Jake, depleting decades of inherited and hard-won goodwill. Edmund ignored snide comments from his more sarcastic friends. Bank statements piled up unopened, since he understood there was a fast approaching end date to the situation. He had lived modestly thus far and the trust fund would not be ultimately imperiled.

To justify the expenditures, he thought of all the money he'd saved since sealing his heart in the plastic bag along with Harry's shirt. While he indulged in occasional overnight trysts with an old friend who knew the situation, he would have felt duty-bound to reveal his positive status to any new lover. But that required a degree of trust that never had time to build. Should a vindictive partner delight in linking the name of Edmund's family with HIV, negative reverberations would swell through the upper echelons of the city's social circles. He stood to lose more than the trust fund; most at risk was the relationship with his parents that had been painfully reconstructed over three decades.

For the first few weeks, Jake slept on the sofa. Then, on a particularly Arctic night, Edmund offered to share the queen-sized bed, trying to make it sound like an impulsive thought. Jake accepted, seeming to sleep soundly. Edmund didn't sleep at all. He lay on his side facing Jake, afraid that any movement might drive the man away.

A routine developed. Edmund was only able to actually sleep

while Jake was out playing. The musician never returned before the early morning hours—if at all—and then stumbled into bed. Sometimes Edmund, lying willfully motionless, would close his eyes and imagine that Harry was back and would be smiling, reaching for him in the morning. Other times, Edmund's eyes would rest on the luster of Jake's back or chest, lit by the gas lamps on the balcony and then by the approaching dawn. The man's thick hair would beg for a touch, his skin plead for caresses. Every inhalation sparked a new temptation, yet Edmund understood that to surrender would bring only loss. Often, he'd rise for extended trips to the bathroom, then return to the bed and stay until just before ten, when the reading room opened. Jake seemed unaware of his comings or goings.

The week of Carnival, Jake began exuding a spiky scent that reminded Edmund of rosemary. One woman's name began coming up in conversation, as in *Lilly says this*, or *Lilly believes that*. Jake said she was a chef at a hotel restaurant. After Ash Wednesday, Jake only came back to the apartment to change clothes or take naps in the afternoon. Edmund fretted at first, suffered insomnia, grew testy, and fussed about insignificant things like the folding of bath towels.

Jake didn't notice. He mentioned a van he'd found, one that had enough room for all his sound equipment and still had room for him to sleep. He said it got great gas mileage and was nearly new. It was a great bargain—a friend who was throwing in the towel on the music dream needed the money for college tuition.

Jake's pitch was persuasive. He only needed three grand for a down payment. His parents would co-sign a loan for the balance. If he could buy the van by the following week, he'd be able get some players together and head over to a battle of the bands at a Mississippi casino. The grand prize was $10,000 and a spot in a reality TV show in Los Angeles. If he won—which he was sure to—he'd be able to take care of the band, pay Edmund back, and have seed money to get Lilly and him settled in L.A. Chef jobs were a dime a dozen there; she'd be able to get one in a heartbeat. And they paid a lot better than in New Orleans.

A few days later, Jake invited Edmund for a ride in the new van. The older man accepted, then allowed Jake to treat him to lunch at a Lakeside po-boy café.

"You ought to get out of the Quarter more often," Jake said on the ride back toward the river. "You act like you need a passport to leave." He punched the gas to get through a light as it flashed from yellow to red.

Edmund pushed back the panic rising inside, the sense of impending, unavoidable loss. He forced himself to comment on how smoothly the van rode, even bumping over the wretched streets of the city.

Jake texted Edmund right after the win in Biloxi. The text contained several exclamation points. They'd beat out a dozen other bands, mostly on the strength of his original songs. Edmund sobbed after a solitary glass of wine that night, then finished the entire bottle.

A few days later, another text. They needed to be in California the following week for the reality show orientation. Could he and Lilly stop by tomorrow afternoon on their way out of town? He wanted to pay Edmund back.

They both looked freshly showered, but nonetheless, the girl still stank of rosemary. Shorter than Jake by nearly a foot, her cropped hair and jean jacket added to the waif look. The tats on her neck and hands, the piercings on her eyebrow, were attempts to broadcast moxie. They only added to her aura of vulnerability. It seemed unfair that she had won Jake's affections. She wasn't even very attractive, certainly not a classic beauty like he'd imagined.

An inquisitive creature, she took in every detail of the room: the books on the shelves, the pottery shards, the antique photographs of Egypt on the walls. She shook Edmund's hand, her own cool with an honest grip.

"Great to finally meet you!" Lilly said. "I've heard so much about you."

Edmund had no idea what history Jake had invented for him.

Was he an uncle now? An old family friend? Some sort of personal Kickstarter? He thought it best just to smile in a cordial manner.

Jake shared a few more details about the casino contest, but that was already fading. The future had his full attention now, his shot at being a TV star. When he was in Biloxi, someone had told him about a local kid from Mississippi who won the "America's Got Talent" show back in 2013. He got a recording contract and the works. Edmund had never heard of the show, but nodded. Meanwhile, Jake said, that friend of Edmund's in L.A. had already lined up a job for Lilly at a swank farm-to-table restaurant.

Lilly elbowed Jake. "So ask him already," she said.

"No way. We don't have enough time anyway."

"I'd like a reading before we go," Lilly said to Edmund. "Would you mind? I want to know our future?"

"No one knows the future," Edmund said.

"He always claims that," Jake said to Lilly. "But I'm telling you, the guy's the real deal. He predicted from the get-go that I was going to make it big."

"Please?" said the girl. "I want to know how things are going to go for us out there."

Edmund picked up his deck from the table, shuffled it, fanned them out in front of Lilly. "Since you're short on time, why don't you pick just one? That will give us something to go on."

Lilly settled on one, touched it, and pulled back her hand. She bit her lip and fiddled with one of the rings in her right eyebrow. Then she fluttered her fingers over the fan and chose the one at the very end.

"The best of cards," Edmund said, turning it to face them both. "The Ten of Cups." Lilly's face brightened and she looked up at Jake. He was checking a text on his phone.

"You don't need me to interpret this, Lilly. A happy couple, a rainbow, children dancing, a country scene with a lovely house in the background. What more could anyone hope for?"

He knew then that she was pregnant. She probably didn't even suspect yet. And he saw the next several years of their life roll out before him like a scroll. The rainbow part wouldn't last long. He saw Jake on the road in pursuit of the fame he'd only marginally achieve, he saw Lilly growing lonely and frustrated when Jake didn't stay in touch or send home any of his earnings and finally, angry when she found out about his affairs. He saw her working long hours, sweating in a commercial kitchen, while their daughter was in childcare. He and Lilly were very much alike, stepping stones for Jake. Once he'd climbed over them, they wouldn't exist anymore. Yet, Edmund had known going in. Lilly didn't have a clue.

Edmund tucked the card back into the deck. "You'll have wings on your feet during this trip, my dear," he said to Lilly.

She touched his sleeve. "Thank you," she said, "that means a lot to us both."

Jake was typing into his phone. He glanced up and realized that manners called for some response.

"Yeah, thanks," he said. He fished into his jacket and pulled out a bank envelope, thrusting it toward Edmund. "Hey man, I wish I could be giving you the whole 3,000, but I had to get new tires for the van before we left. But here's 1,500. You know I'm good for the rest. I'll send you a money order as soon as I get my first check from the reality show."

"Not to worry," said Edmund. Jake held his arms out for one of those man embraces, the kind that even homophobic jocks found acceptable. Edmund held him briefly for the first time, and inhaled the heady bouquet from the collar of his jacket, saying goodbye again to Harry, as well as to Jake. Tears pressed on his temples, and he willed a stern withholding. He pulled away and patted Jake on the back.

"My wishes for a fortuitous journey will travel with you," he said, as they stepped out of the room. Lilly smiled at the wording.

Edmund waited until they were nearly at the courtyard passageway before calling out Lilly's name. She turned and he beckoned her. She glanced toward Jake, who flipped his hand out in permission, before turning his attention back to the phone. Lilly came to the step and peered inside. "Yes, Edmund?"

He motioned for her to step into the room, out of Jake's line of sight.

"I have something for you."

He handed her the Japanese box with the two cranes taking flight from the lid.

She stroked the cranes, marveling over their beauty, and looked up at him in askance.

"In Japan, they're symbols of long life and good luck. Cranes mate for life, so they're often used on wedding kimonos."

"I doubt we'll go the kimono route," she joked. He saw in her face that she had already accepted there'd never be a wedding. She wasn't sure why she was being gifted, but she appreciated his goodwill. Before she could thank him, Edmund opened the lid, revealing the bank envelope inside. She looked up at him, eyes wide, the silver row of rings on her brow arching.

"That's for you. No need to mention it to Jake. I daresay it might come in handy someday."

She hugged him then, fiercely, and was out the door before he could react. She called back to him as she skipped across the flagstones to Jake. "You're the best! I'll send a postcard from Hollywood!" She brandished the box toward Jake, who waved an absent acknowledgement for the gift. Then they walked down the dark tunnel of the carriageway.

Just before sunset, Edmund stepped down the splintery dark steps that led into the river. Only ten remained above the waterline. The spring rains had bloated the river, and its surface swirled, stirred by the savage forces below. Thick ropes of chain between pilings served as a railing on the rough staircase. Edmund held on tightly as he stepped down toward the water because he'd lately admitted that his footing had lost the certainty of youth. Standing on the last dry step, he pulled the plastic bag from the tote looped over his arm. When he freed it after two decades of bondage, Harry's shirt billowed. If he had let go, it would have sailed toward the square, over the heads of the trumpet player and the few idling tourists.

He resisted the urge to take a last inhalation. With one hand still gripping the chain, he bent and dipped the shirttail in the water. Once weighted, the river tugged at the prize until he released it. Edmund watched until an eddy swallowed it entirely, then turned to climb.

ONI AND MARIE

Debra Curtis

A new servant walked into the dressing room. Madame Marie Benoist looked up from her book and was struck by the contrast of the servant's dark skin against the white silk stockings draped over her arm.

"Please, step back. No, don't turn, just step back," Marie said, raising her hand and motioning to the other woman. Head down, Oni had turned to walk out of the room.

"Just step back into the light," Marie said.

Oni followed her directions. The morning sun slipped through the window, casting a long line of light on the wooden floor. Marie studied the woman carefully as she stood in the doorway. She fixated on the white stockings and black skin.

"What a challenge it would be to capture the light of blackness," Marie said.

The servant stood, barely moving. She followed her mistress's gaze and scanned the stockings. Marie leaned forward in her chair and studied the woman's arms. Their eyes met and Marie smiled. Oni quickly lowered her gaze.

Oni was a stranger in Paris. She was a slave from French Guadeloupe and now a servant in the Benoist household. Marie was a painter who had occupied a studio in the Louvre until she was forced to move to an apartment after the Director of the French Academy, the comte d'Angivillers, petitioned the King and advised him that he should forbid male and female artists from living in close proximity.

As Marie approached her servant, Oni stepped back. Marie took the stockings from Oni and placed them on a nearby chair. Gesturing to the servant to stay where she was, Marie walked quickly across the room in her bare feet and opened the cherry wood armoire. She pulled out a white muslin morning dress, returned to Oni, and held it up against the servant's chest. Again, she studied the contrast.

"This won't do." Displeased, Marie cast the dress aside and reached for a simple off-white cashmere shawl. When that didn't do, she turned toward the bed sheets. She stripped one from the bed and gathered the whiteness in her arms. Her long brown hair had fallen loose.

Marie untied Oni's light blue neckband and placed the sheet against the servant's collarbone and then slowly slid the sheet down toward her breasts. Oni held her breath and tried not to cringe. She wondered if she had been brought to Paris to be the servant of a mad mistress. In that moment, Marie knew she would paint the woman's portrait. What hadn't occurred to her was how she would explain to her husband that she was starting a new painting, one that no one had commissioned, and of a Negress, no less.

Over the course of the next two days, Oni had a chance to observe her new mistress's routine. Madame Benoist was in the habit of collecting ordinary objects from around the house and bringing them to her studio. She removed candlesticks from the dining room, whole cooked chickens and oranges from the kitchen, and tapestries from the drawing room.

A few weeks later, on a cold morning in January, hearing a sound coming from her studio, Marie stopped at the entrance and peeked through the opening of the pewter-colored drapes, which hung in the entry. She observed Oni across the room, carefully lifting unframed paintings that were leaning against the paneled walls. One by one, she examined the artist's work, holding the smaller ones up in front of her to get a closer look. Sometimes she cocked her head to one side and narrowed her eyes for a keener inspection. As a domestic slave, Oni had seen portraits and other paintings hanging in the grand estates on Guadeloupe, but she had never imagined a painter behind the painting.

❖

Later that day, Marie completed a painting of a child with blond curls holding a bowl of blackberries in his little hands. She put her brush down when Oni entered the studio carrying a tray of coffee and sweets. When Oni set the tray on a table, Marie called her over to her easel.

"What do you think of the berries?" Marie asked, gesturing to the painting.

Oni studied the work before her. "They are the most beautiful, beautiful berries. I can taste them," she said, closing her eyes.

Marie studied her high cheekbones and the lines of her lips. She liked the sound of Oni's foreign French; it reminded her of the color of rusty orange. When Oni opened her eyes, the two women looked at each other and then looked back at the fresh painting. They stood side-by-side in silence until Marie placed her wooden palette on the floor and asked Oni to join her for coffee.

And this is how it began.

❖

Both women's lives had been transformed by the Terror of 1792. Years before they met, spies were ordered to watch the Benoist's apartment. Count Pierre-Vincent, Marie's husband, was a royalist and was later forced into hiding. The police hunted him for months. Some days, she wished he'd been captured. Back in Guadeloupe, Oni's husband, a runaway, was hunted, too.

They had that in common.

Marie had three children. Oni had two, one dead. A month before the French troops landed on the island to enforce the abolition of slavery, her daughter was sold for 200 francs. What Oni remembered of the civil war on Guadeloupe is the blade of the guillotine and the fires in the hills. Early in 1794, Marie's brother-in-law purchased Oni from a man with little mercy and rough hands. There was some dispute about whether the brother-in-law had paid his debts before he sailed to France, taking Oni with him.

Oni had her own truth about the revolution and explained it to Marie, "The Declaration told me I was free but that didn't make it true for five long years. Freedom arrived on a slow boat from France.

There was a planter from Baillif. He bought himself two other slaves, a mother and a child. The next day, he set them free. Two years after that, he married the woman. After that, the woman and her child had the right papers. So I made up my mind to get registered in Basse-Terre. I carried those papers around like a poor man carries gold."

On one of the rare winter days when it snowed in Paris, Marie and Oni passed time in Marie's dressing room in front of a warm fire. Marie read to Oni from Levaillant's latest book, which chronicled his voyage and ornithological discoveries in South Africa. When the naturalist and his companions first went ashore, they were astonished by the array of birds—cormorants, sea swallows, and pelicans. The explorers disturbed hundreds of nests; flocks of birds darkened the sky. Marie read aloud Levaillant's description of how he could not walk on land without crushing fragile eggs and baby birds with his heavy boots. Oni wept. Marie read on. The naturalist returned to France with caged birds, and Oni was reminded of the caged children she had seen at the auctions at Point-a-Pitre on the main platform, and her own lost child.

"She was seven, when they sold her. I didn't even know it was coming. She sucked on another woman while I was working in the house. But I got to her every few days. She was a light-hearted girl with big round eyes that saw everything. I was hoping she could learn the laundry and work in the house with me. She was gone one day before I even knew it."

"Wasn't there any way you could have asked the mistress of the house to help you find her?" Marie asked.

"Don't you see? I'm like the mama birdies that couldn't defend their nests."

Marie reached over and covered Oni's hand with hers as tears filled Oni's eyes.

Staring at the fire Oni said, "If I had known better, I wouldn't have made more slaves." Her voice was soft as the flakes falling outside.

❖

It was one of the coldest nights of the year. A little before midnight, Marie checked on her children and then went to the kitchen where her small staff, with the exception of Oni, sat gathered around the stove playing cards. Standing at the threshold of the kitchen, she pulled her shawl tightly over her shoulders as a draft moved through the house. Concerned for Oni, Marie went to her own bedroom and removed the heavy silk covered quilt from her bed. She didn't anticipate running into anyone as she made her way to Oni's room on the third floor because she assumed the staff was still socializing. She would have collided with a young servant had the girl not been carrying a small candle.

"May I help you Madame?" The servant glanced down at the expensive quilt in Marie's arms.

"No, thank you," Marie said, passing the girl on the stairs. When she reached the top step, she turned around and the girl was gone. She waited a few seconds only to see the servant girl peering around the corner at the bottom of the stairs.

"That will be enough," Marie said sharply.

The narrow hall was dark except for a candle lit on a table outside of Oni's room. She and the cook had their own bedrooms and the others shared one of the larger rooms above the kitchen, which benefited from the rising heat of the stove. The door to Oni's room was cracked open just a bit. Marie pushed it open. The entire room wasn't much larger than the size of Marie's own bed. She couldn't see Oni through the darkness, but she could hear her breathing. Marie stepped into the small room and immediately felt a rush of icy air coming through the cracks in walls. As she covered her servant with the quilt, Oni stirred and opened her eyes.

"Madame, what is it? Is there something wrong?"

"No, it's just cold out." Marie said, tucking the blanket under Oni's shoulders.

❖

Around the time the gardens bloom, Marie took Oni to a salon hosted by her former teacher, Mme. Vigee-Lebrun, who had just been allowed to return to Paris after living in St. Petersburg for some time. The gallery in her house on the rue du Gros-Chenet was filled with émigrés, surviving royalists, republicans, and the Russian Princess Dolgorouky—all of whom were engaged in polite and not-so-polite conversations. In the corner of the room, a young novelist with an impressive cleavage was stretched out on a chaise-longue reading aloud from her book, surrounded by beautiful men in silk stockings and buckled boots.

Oni copied mannerisms, gesture by gesture, like a public scribe copied a document, word by word. After the guests dined on beef and oysters and plenty of Burgundy, a blind man recited poems about love and loss. Over dessert, the widow of a great mathematician announced a new essay contest sponsored by the Society of Sciences and Arts. The guests debated the essay topic: whether the education of women would lead to an increase in men's happiness or be a deterrent to it.

When the conversation turned to the antislavery movement, Oni heard the widow say, "Women and slaves are just the same. I'm no different from Mme. Benoit's new servant from the West Indies."

Oni's eyes narrowed. Marie studied her carefully. While returning home in the carriage, Marie asked, "Well, what do you think? Should women be educated?"

"To what end?" Oni replied.

Marie was taken aback by Oni's reply and waited for her to say something else.

"Education brings freedom, right?" Oni asked. Without waiting for a response, she added, "Then education and freedom go together like hummingbirds and banana blossoms."

Marie smiled but turned to gaze out the window. Oni's response stunned her. As a child, her father had taught her the latest scientific facts: that Africans were the missing link between Europeans and primates. *If this is so,* Marie thought, *then why does Oni seem so utterly human?* She was genuinely curious to hear Oni's opinions on the other topics of salon conversation as well.

"What did you think of Mme. Condorcet's insight that women and slaves are the same?"

Oni looked down at her lap and ran her hands over her full skirt, smoothing out the wrinkles. She was wearing a new pink and yellow-stripped linen skirt that Marie had made for her. Marie couldn't figure out why Oni wouldn't answer her. They had become close over the last several months and Marie had grown fond of Oni's honesty.

"Well?" she prodded.

Oni pressed the back of her hand to her nose and said, "The stench of the streets is unbearable today." Marie laughed.

"Why won't you answer my question?"

Oni looked at Marie for what seemed like a long time.

"I'm sorry," she began. "I'm sorry that her husband died in prison, but when her children are shackled and collared and sold, then we might be the same."

❖

"Mother, look! Mother, look!" It was Marie's only daughter Genevieve. When Marie looked up from her sketchpad, her five-year-old was teetering on top of a stack of books that the little girl had placed on the seat of an old wooden chair. Marie rushed to her daughter.

"This isn't safe, my love." She wrapped her arms around the child and lifted her to the ground. Immediately, she thought of Oni and all of the unimaginable horrors from which her new friend couldn't protect her own daughter.

She left her sketchpad on the ground and played dress-up with Genevieve for the rest of the afternoon. More and more, thoughts of Oni infiltrated the time she spent with her children. It was that afternoon, in the midst of her daughter's costumes and toys, that Marie decided that for Oni's portrait she would fashion a sheet around her, tied with a red ribbon at the waist, so that it would appear as though Oni was wearing a tunic; a neoclassical effect, inspired by her teacher, master painter Jacques-Louis David, and reminiscent of the Sabine women in one of David's most popular paintings.

She laid out some red chalk, a pen, and brown ink. She had one of the dining room chairs moved into the studio. A midnight-blue satin evening gown was draped over the back of the chair. It was Oni's idea to use a piece of white linen as a head wrap. Standing in front of the canvas, Marie studied her model. *Something's not right*, she thought. The white sheet overwhelmed the composition. Marie's first solution was to expose more of Oni's black skin. *How do I convince her to let the sheet fall around her waist?* Marie wondered.

"What is it? What's upset you?" Oni asked as she sat up straight in the chair.

"There's too much white," Marie said.

Without hesitating, Oni reached behind her neck to untie the sheet and pull it down to her waist, revealing her shoulders and full breasts. Oni gathered the sheet with her left hand, which she then rested on her lap. Without thinking, Marie moved toward Oni, cupped her hand under the other woman's breast, lifted it and exposed Oni's nipple. Neither spoke. But Marie was taken off guard by a new form of desire that had invaded her like a foreign army. It moved deep within her—somewhere between her heart and just below her belly. She went back to her stool and tried to focus on sketching.

This long period of sitting was tiresome for Oni, but she soon recognized this kind of fatigue as a luxury. Her mind wandered. One hot afternoon, when she was a child, she stood in the yard, waiting for her mother to return from work. It was dark by the time another woman, one with short incisions on her face that reminded Oni of tears, came to her and told her that her mother had lain down in the cane fields and gone to sleep. Oni remembered how the woman stood in the yard with a cutlass still in her hand. Her other hand had only three fingers. The rollers had taken the other two while she was feeding sugarcane into the mill. For weeks, Oni stood at the door of their hut, looked out into the darkness, waited for her mother to wake up and walk out of the fields.

About three hours into the session, a young servant girl carried in a tray of coffee and pastries, which she set down on a table in the corner of the room before leaving. Thinking they were alone, Marie took one of the macaroons from the tray and brought it to Oni. When Oni reached out to take the little sweet, Marie pulled her hand back, teasing her. They both laughed.

"Open your mouth," Marie said.

Oni tilted her head back and parted her lips. Tenderly, Marie brought the pastry to Oni's lips and fed it to her. A drop of buttercream appeared in the corner of Oni's mouth. Marie wiped it away with her fingertip and as she did, she couldn't help but glance down at Oni's breasts. They both heard the little gasp of the servant girl who was peeping through the drapes. Marie shooed the girl away with a wave of her hand, but knew instantly that if others learned of this small incident, there would be no stopping the vicious gossip.

❖

"Tell me something, are you appealing to men's desires or your own with your latest portrait?" asked Marie's husband.

Marie was taken aback, relieved that the canopy hid the expression on her face. Count Benoist had visited his wife in her bedroom that night. Holding a candle over the day's sketches, which were lying on a desk across from Marie's bed, he traced the model's breast with the tip of his finger, smudging the nipple just a bit. Then he picked up one of her charcoal pencils and used it to scratch his back. This irritated Marie. She was tired of him—tired of his hacking and spitting, but grateful for his string of mistresses, especially the most recent one who was rich and demanded a lot of his time. But still she felt obligated to please him. So moments later, she tried her best to allay her husband's suspicions.

A woman's body can hide the truth in all sorts of ways, Marie thought.

Marie knew of this kind of attraction between two grown women. When she was 15 years old, her mentor painted the Duchess of Polignac. Everyone knew of the rumors that this woman, with eyes the color of violets, was the Queen's lover. That night, while lying next to her husband, rousing and uncontrollable images filled Marie's mind—the gold hoop earrings that Oni wore, the elegant line of her neck. In the middle of the night, she had erotic dreams of Oni's breasts. Closer to dawn, however, she dreamt of Marie Antoinette's severed head. Oni dreamt of orange skies and pale green waters.

For the weeks that followed, Marie neglected her children, ignored invitations from friends to attend salons, and postponed her husband's evening requests. Her only companion during this time was Oni. The artist worked feverishly. Stretching the canvas, grinding and mixing the paints. She was careful, as usual, to purchase and prepare her own pigments. She wouldn't risk using inferior, adulterated products, which might fade or crack.

Marie took Oni to a small shop off of the rue du Faubourg Saint-Honore' on the edge of the city. While she was looking at a new Prussian blue, she observed the shopkeeper's eyes wandering on Oni. He slid the tip of his tongue over his top lip. The only thing that Oni seemed to notice that day was the man's polished silver shoe buckle. The vulgar man's display of desire conjured up an image in Marie's mind that incited her own desires—an image that she desperately fought to erase and one that didn't include the shopkeeper, but most certainly involved Oni.

There was to be trouble in the Benoist home. The special attention Oni received from Marie incited jealousy. The overly curious young servant girl, who had spied on Maria and Oni in the studio, reported what she saw to the cook, who was known for loving gossip as much as she loved wine. Soon the scullery maid was making ape noises whenever Oni appeared in the yard. Someone placed a page from an obscene pamphlet on Oni's bed. It depicted a plump naked woman sitting on a plush stool. Kneeling between her legs was a second woman. Shocked by the image, Oni's first impulse was to destroy it. Yet, she couldn't take her eyes off of the lewd drawing. So instead of tearing it up, she hid it between the cracks of the floorboard in her third-floor bedroom.

❖

"You'll be sitting for a while; you should use the toilet before we start."

Oni headed toward the entrance of the studio.

"Where are you going?" Marie asked.

"Just as you said, up to my room, to use the chamber pot."

"Use the one over there," Marie said, pointing to the corner of the room.

"But that's yours."

"Now it's yours, too."

The artist lined up her brushes, palette knives, and charcoal while Oni stepped behind a decorative dressing screen and removed her clothing. When she took her seat, she lowered the sheet, exposing her breasts. Marie moved back and forth, needing to see both model and painting in the same light. She painted bold strokes.

Hours passed. Oni grew tired and her shoulders ached. Marie shook her head, put down her brush, and walked to her. She gently rubbed Oni's shoulders and the top of her arms. Gradually, she allowed her fingers to rub the spot just below Oni's clavicle bones. All at once she wanted desperately to reach around and grab the fullness of Oni's breasts. As the palms of her hands grazed Oni's nipples, Marie felt the other woman grow tense and leaned forward to cross her arms in front. Just then a loud cry came from the hall, startling them both. Marie pulled her hands back.

"Mamma, Mamma!" Genevieve ran into the studio carrying a broken doll. Marie closed her eyes and sighed. It was Oni who knelt before the child and held the girl's small wet face in her hands as the white sheet cascaded down around her waist spilling onto the floor.

❖

That night Marie was disturbed by her dreams. She lay awake thinking that she'd be locked away in the Salpêtrière for what she was dreaming of doing. In her own bed, Oni recalled how, as a child, she had played mommy and baby with another girl in a nearby hut, each sucking the other's breast. But those were games children played. Somehow Marie's caresses felt different. Unsettled but aroused, Oni rose from her bed, lit a candle, and retrieved the pornographic image from the floorboards.

The next day, while Oni was dressing Marie, something she had done many, many times before, her hands trembled as she rolled one of the silk stockings up Marie's calf. Marie spread her legs and Oni searched for the top of her thigh. The dressing process ceased, the stocking was forgotten. Oni buried her face between Marie's legs. Moments later, Marie moaned, low and round, and made a sound like a child's whimper.

They ended up in Marie's bed that morning and the morning after, behind locked doors. Over the course of the next year, Marie looked forward to the days and nights when her husband traveled. On these occasions, she shared her evening meals with Oni in the dressing room. Oni called her "Petal" because her skin was whiter than the flower of the frangipani tree.

One night, with the candlelight flickering, Oni studied count Benoist's collection of maps. She drew a line with her fingertip across the Atlantic, from the west coast of Africa to the islands of sugar. Naked, Marie watched her from the bed.

"What foods do you miss the most?" Marie asked.

"Mangos," Oni told her.

"What do they taste like?"

"You."

"Then how could you miss them?" Marie said smiling as she flung back the sheets and beckoned to Oni. As she did, she bent her knee and let her leg fall off to the side.

The finished painting of Oni was exhibited at the Louvre. Upon seeing the painting, an art critic named Boutard was taken aback by his own response—a quick stiffness in his trousers, which he concealed with his long overcoat. He surprised himself by returning to view the painting one last time before leaving the museum that rainy afternoon. In a local paper, he attacked Marie Benoist for painting what he considered to be such a vulgar and repulsive subject.

Four days after the article was published, Count Benoist sat on the edge of his wife's bed with his head in his hands. Marie was propped up on her pillows with her back against the headboard.

"Rumors are spreading throughout Paris that you and our former Queen have similar appetites," he said. Marie reached for him. He pushed her hand away and added, "You'll ruin us."

Silence.

"I could throw her out," he said through his teeth.

"It's not what you think...it's all rumors," Marie whispered.

Her husband snorted, "She's a savage, Marie, just a savage."

Marie's first impulse was to pull her leg up and kick him in the back as hard as she could. But she knew that this sort of violent response would be an admission of both her guilt and her love for Oni. Did she feel guilt? Or only love and defiance? Marie herself wasn't sure.

Hours later, Marie got out of bed, leaving her husband undisturbed. She picked up a candle and slipped out of her room. She felt pulled in the direction of the Oni's tiny room upstairs. As she reached the top of the stairs, she heard the sound of a door opening on the first floor, followed by heavy footsteps. *Is he following me?* she wondered. Turning the corner, she blew out the candle, and leaned against the wall.

"Who's up there?" the cook called out from the foot of the stairs.

Marie waited for the cook to retreat. With one hand on the wall, she felt her way up the second staircase. Before she could reach the top stair, her youngest cried out in his sleep.

"What am I willing to sacrifice?" Marie asked herself in the dark. Her heart raced. *Only everything*, she thought.

❖

One morning after they found themselves entangled in the sheets and each other's legs, Marie asked, "What is the price of our pleasure?"

"Our salvation," Oni whispered.

"And here I thought our pleasure was our salvation."

❖

Oni was always gentle and loving with Marie's children. She tended to their scrapes, helped to bathe them, and brushed the little girl's long brown hair. Late in the winter of 1802, Oni's thoughts of her own daughter began competing with thoughts of Marie for space in her heart.

Lying in bed with Marie's hand on her breast, she said, "I need to go back to Guadeloupe. I waited too long for my mother to wake and walk out of the cane fields. I don't want my daughter dying, thinking I never tried to find her."

Marie did not protest despite the panic she felt pressing down on her chest. She moved to get a closer look at Oni's face.

"My heart is a big enough basket to carry both your loves," Oni said.

Marie knew instantly that if she didn't allow Oni to return to the West Indies, that eventually she risked losing her love. With the help of her brother-in-law, a ship's purser, Marie arranged Oni's passage to Guadeloupe aboard a cargo ship. She was to accompany a wealthy planter's family. Once she found her daughter, she was to return with her to Paris.

Together, they traveled to the seaport, Le Havre, and spent two nights at a local inn. On the last morning, Oni pressed her face to Marie's neck and inhaled deeply, taking in Marie's scent—her powdered skin, the linseed oil, and a faint smell of citrus. They held onto each other like drowning women. When their mouths came together, Marie bit Oni's lip. There was no breath between them, only tears.

Despite the assurance from Marie's brother-in-law that Oni would be given suitable sleeping accommodations, on her first night and the forty that followed, she was forced to share a narrow bunk with another servant. They thought about taking shifts, but it was too dangerous for one of them to be alone on the deck at night. So they remained safer but sleepless in their cramped quarters, surrounded by foul smells and the grunts of strangers.

At first, the rolling seas made Oni sick and weak. She kept little down for days. There was only one long night when Oni regretted leaving Marie and making the journey. It was during a storm they encountered in the middle of the Atlantic. Oni was sure the ship would sink as it pitched and rolled in the darkness. Lanterns were blown out for fear of fire. They were forced to stay below for two full days. She imagined her daughter's fear the morning the child was sold. She recalled how Marie rubbed and washed her feet the night they both returned from the exhibition at the Louvre. These thoughts sustained her. Weeks later, someone spotted Guadeloupe. Oni said a quiet prayer. It was an August afternoon when she walked into the town of Basse-Terre.

Marie threw a plate against the paneled wall and dropped to her knees when she heard the news that Napoleon had reinstated slavery. No one had known. The ministry of the colonies wanted this change to be kept secret. Diplomatic papers passed from hand to hand, arriving on the island in September of 1802. A change of heart in Paris dictated that freedom was not meant for the Negroes. Oni's status was in question. Marie left for her brother-in-law's house without a word to anyone.

Grabbing him by the shoulders, she asked, "Is she a free colored woman or not?"

It would take months for Marie's letter to reach the planter's family, the ones whom Oni had accompanied on the ship. Marie pleaded for word about Oni's welfare.

In late May, the following spring, Marie received a letter from the planter himself. "The Negro woman is dead."

SLAYING THE DRAGON

W. C. Smith

Emile snapped up in bed. Any time a telephone rang in the middle of the night, something generally was wrong.

"Hello?" He tried to sound like he had been awake for hours.

"Emile Abadie?" the voice on the other end asked.

Emile cleared his throat. "Yes, that's me."

"This is Roberta Ann Morrison, George's mother."

Emile paused to think. "Hello, Mrs. Morrison." He had no idea who was on the other end of the phone.

"I'm terribly sorry if I've wakened you." Even half awake, Emile could tell that the voice was small, fragile.

"Don't worry," Emile said. He rolled over to check the clock. It said eight-thirty, not nearly as early as he had thought.

"Oh," she sighed, as if eight-thirty in the morning was late in the day. "I'm still on Montana time. I think we're an hour behind you."

Emile realized who was speaking, and he sat straight up. "You're not in Montana? You're here?"

"Yes. I'm afraid I have some terrible news."

"Yes?"

"George has died."

"George is dead? George Morrison? My George who lives here in New Orleans?" Emile realized he had slipped by referring to him in the possessive. Maybe she didn't catch it. It didn't matter anyway. They hadn't been together for several years.

"Yes, my son, George," she said, reasserting her own possessiveness. "He's gone."

"Are you sure?" Emile asked. He had been out of town on business for ten days and George had been fine when he left.

"I received a call from the New Orleans coroner's office two days ago. They told me he was gone."

At first, the thought struck Emile as odd, even surreal. A woman who lived somewhere in Montana was calling to tell him that a man who lived around the corner, with whom he spoke regularly, had passed away.

"How did he die?" Emile asked.

"I'm not sure yet. It seems as if he had quite a few problems."

"Yes." A few problems was an understatement.

"I just thought you'd want to know." Then after a short pause, "Do you think we might be able to meet for dinner, perhaps tonight? I can let you know what I find out."

"Of course," Emile said, replacing the receiver while still absorbing the shock. George gone? How could it be? Emile slipped on the same clothes he'd worn the previous night. George wasn't sick. What an irony. George was the first person in the Skylark writer's group to die and he wasn't even HIV-positive.

Emile Abadie had met George Morrison in the spring of 1975. Emile was a born-and-bred Cajun boy from Lafayette who had come to New Orleans to supervise his family's property management business. George Morrison grew up in Montana but lived in New York at the time he met Emile. He was an opera singer, trying to establish his career, and had managed to land several minor roles, but he had been mostly successful in securing understudy roles that took him all over the country.

George made his first trip to New Orleans as the understudy for the role of Aeneas in the Berlioz opera *Les Troyens.* Like many other first time visitors tempted by the vibe and the history of the city, he was anxious to explore its nightlife. After the first dress rehearsal, he ventured to the corner of Bourbon and St. Ann where he met Emile in one of the bars. Emile was slightly drunk but not George, who wouldn't let alcohol strain his vocal cords. The next morning, Emile told George that he had never seen an opera, and George immediately invited him, but the performance was sold out and he couldn't secure a ticket.

Emile was entranced with George from the beginning. George was a handsome man despite the wide-frame glasses that made him look older as well as a bit nerdy. He had the remnants of a boy's face, with hazel eyes, a few random freckles, and wavy chocolate brown hair that he frequently brushed back with his hand. He was quick to smile, in a mischievous way. He was tall by most standards, and stocky. He had a stately presence, learned from his years on the stage.

They spent every night together until the day George was scheduled to depart, acknowledging during the course of the week that a bond had formed between them, something that hinted that a future together was a possibility. Emile was surprised but liked it. Perhaps, he thought, this was the person for him. But he didn't push it because he knew he would never move from New Orleans, and he never expected that George would leave a place like New York or abandon a promising career. He was surprised when George brought it up on the final night he was in town.

"I have definitely fallen in love with the city," George said. "And I think I have fallen in love with you."

Emile became flushed, knowing what was coming but unsure whether he should entertain the idea. He pushed back, gently. "Everybody knows long distance romances don't work."

"I know," George responded. "But still, I was wondering if I could live here. I think I could."

Emile wasn't sure what to say. "What about New York? What about your career?"

"Emile, I am on the tail end of my career in opera. The reality is that I probably won't be offered a major role at a major house. It would have happened by now. If I'm lucky, I can transition to teaching, or work in some other capacity for an opera company, but my singing days are coming to an end." He ended the last sentence with a theatrical sigh. "As for New York, it's expensive and competitive, and it can be a very harsh place to live. I doubt if I could afford it. This place is more my speed."

"What about going back to Montana?"

"Not on your life," George said. "I'd never go back there."

"Why not?"

"Because it's Montana for one thing."

"You have family there."

"Just my mother, and that's why I don't want to go back. She's a mean, petty, over-bearing little woman."

"What did she do?"

"I could tell story after story," George said dramatically. "But I just don't want to go into it. Suffice it to say that I won't ever be going back to Montana or to my mother."

Eventually, the distance between them didn't doom them. It became their ally. By the end of summer, they were referring to themselves as 'lovers'. They talked for hours on the telephone, racking up expensive charges before they eventually concocted a plan. George would retire from his waning opera career and move to New Orleans. He would try to find a job in the music industry but if he couldn't, he would get a teaching certificate and become a public school teacher. Emile would provide housing in one of his family's units at no cost until George could get established. They would spend most nights together.

For almost a year, the romance inspired everything they did, and then it simply crumbled. Emile was the one who fell out of love. The relationship, he felt, had become too demanding, too smothering. Emile, the one with the intense countenance and the arctic intensity, found George's whims incomprehensible. George was too capricious, bad at managing money, and easy to pout after a perceived snub. He was moody and became sullen easily.

Emile intended to announce the separation over Sazeracs one evening. He knew George was smart and could see what was coming, but he also knew he would be crushed when it finally happened. After all, George had moved hundreds of miles to be with him, the person he wanted to remain with for the rest of his life.

But then George surprised him by stating that he thought the relationship had run its course, and that he would be fine on his own in this new city. For the next five minutes, George explained why their partnership could not continue, "I love you and I want you to love me but I know it is not to be. I can only be what I am and maybe that's not good enough. Perhaps I am beyond love. I am giving you back your freedom."

Emile stayed in a melancholy mood for months. George moved into a new place. Emile made numerous attempts to contact him but had no luck. George insisted on a clean break, but Emile was skeptical, knowing that in a place like New Orleans, everyone knew everyone else's business, and gossip traveled quickly. He thought that he would run into George somewhere, but he didn't until they ran into each other a couple of years later at the writing class.

Emile learned that George had never really dated anyone since they had been together. He was touched when George expressed genuine concern that Emile had become HIV-positive, but was alarmed that George was no longer the slim and trim man he had met. In fact, George had become quite heavy.

"If you're not positive, why did you decide to come to the writer's group?" Emile asked.

"I know so many people," George said. "I can't just sit by. Looks like I might have to take care of you."

But that wasn't the way it turned out.

Emile was panicked. He showered quickly and was out the door in twenty minutes, making a bee-line for George's house. He had to get there before George's mom, unless she was there already. He tried to reconstruct the conversation with Mrs. Morrison. He hadn't asked where she was staying. Did she have keys to George's house? Unlikely. George still maintained the silent treatment with his mom. She'd never been to New Orleans to visit. Emile recoiled when he remembered that he was supposed to meet Mrs. Morrison for dinner and he regretted that decision, chalking it up to his sleepy state.

Emile believed he was the only one who had an extra key to George's house. George had given it to him soon after they had joined the writer's group and re-established their friendship. Emile suspected that George had hoped that the relationship could be revived, but

George insisted it was an insurance key in case he became locked out. Emile had never used the key and wasn't sure it would work. The bolt inside the lock clicked and Emile sighed with an internal *whoop*.

"George," he said, but caught himself before he could issue a greeting, surprised at speaking out loud. It was dark with the windows closed and the curtains drawn, but Emile knew the place was spotless and filled with the gaudy furniture and knick-knacks of an opera queen.

He remembered a comment made by another member of the writers' group who worked for one of the local oil companies and who had been to George's house: "It's decorated like a small palace in the Middle East, one of those nations that had discovered oil."

Emile sniffed the air when he walked in but couldn't detect the presence of death, only the staleness of uncirculated oxygen. How long had George been dead before his body had been discovered? Who had discovered him? What was the cause of death?

Emile knew what he had to do. He had done it before—the process inelegantly referred to as 'defaggotizing' a friend's apartment after a death, getting there first to clean out the evidence before the family arrived. He would inspect every inch of the apartment for anything incriminating, especially something that would be distasteful to a sixty-five-year-old woman grieving over the loss of her only son. Did she even know he was gay?

In the first hour, he covered the bedroom, den, and bathroom. There were no closets to check, older New Orleans homes didn't have them. He searched it all: under the bed and between the mattresses and sheets, between the cushions, inside the medicine cabinet, and the pockets of shirts and slacks, within the nightstand drawers, and inside the pages of books. He found nothing.

There was no porn and only a few books of fiction with gay themes. There were no sex toys. George had no medications, no pot, no drugs. The house was spotless, not a crumb that would suggest George was anything but a typical man of thirty-seven.

Poppers! George probably didn't have any, but if he did, he probably kept them in the fridge just like everyone else. Emile opened the refrigerator—George called it an 'icebox'—and found it empty, nothing on the inside of the door. No poppers here.

He closed the door and beheld the front of the appliance. Plastered to its front was the timeline of Emile's life, a scrapbook listing the important events of his life in New Orleans. The refrigerator had changed shape since the last time Emile was here, becoming a gigantic flower sprouting buds of Polaroids of friends, invitations, cartoon strips, postcards, clippings from the paper, ticket stubs—ephemera of a lifetime. Marky Mark, clad only in his underwear, peeked over at a photo of Tom Selleck. Madonna smiled out at a snapshot of the members of the Skylark Writer's Group.

Magnets and clips. The collage was held together by ladybugs, hearts, stars, and half-moons. Flat magnets displayed artwork from the Louvre, Prado, Art Institute, and Rijksmuseum. Dorothy and Toto held down naked men from *Playgirl* and a recipe for seafood lasagna. A small Christmas globe tethered an invitation to the Petronius Mardi Gras ball, tickets to JazzFest from two years before, and a Saints game from a year before that. A plastic street sign engraved 'Michigan Avenue' anchored an Ann Landers column, at least three thank you notes, and a TWA boarding pass for a trip to Key West. A red clip held dozens of strips from fortune cookies. Calvin and Hobbes shared a magnet with Chippendales.

Near the bottom of the fridge Emile stopped when he saw a picture of himself taken at some point shortly after he had met George, more than ten years ago. He saw a dark young man with hawk-like features, a head full of black hair. He was wearing a turquoise tank top and he was perspiring, the beads of sweat accentuated his shoulders and arms. He had on a pair of dark yellow shorts that displayed dark, swarthy legs. He was smirking at the camera, his dark brown eyes questioning the picture-taker: *Do you really need to take this photo?*

Next to the older photo was a newer one, taken just months ago, of Emile with George after the weekly writers' group meeting. Emile stared sadly at the photo. It was taken from a greater distance. George had been caught in mid-laugh, his head tilted at the sky and his eyes closed in jubilation. Emile stared at himself and saw that he looked much smaller, partly because of George's weight gain, but also because he appeared to have shrunk. He was thinner, his face had become narrower, and his arms had lost their tone.

Emile sighed but he knew immediately he needed to take the photos with him. In fact, he needed to take it all, everything on the front of the fridge.

Emile went back to the bedroom, reached under the bed and dragged out an abandoned shoe box. He returned to the kitchen, and one by one, plucked the ornaments off the refrigerator, and deposited them into the box until the refrigerator door was bare.

Emile resumed the search in the only room he hadn't checked—the living room. He checked behind the cushions, the backsides of the pictures hanging on the walls, and fanned through every book on the shelves and every magazine on the coffee table. "Where haven't I checked yet?" He looked around the room and remembered a line from his childhood, "Come out, come out, wherever you are."

He moved on to George's record collection and fingered through the records, all devoted to opera, until he came upon something that didn't—the cheesy cover of a Village People album. The record was a gift from Emile to George, something of a joke, but also Emile's attempt to encourage George to explore something besides classical or operatic music. It hadn't worked.

Emile pulled it out of the stack and examined the list of songs on the back. He decided to pop it onto George's turntable and when he pulled the sleeve out of the cover, several sheets of handwritten paper slid out with the album. He checked the top of the pages but he knew he had found what he was looking for—George's handwritten wishes. It wasn't a long document, only two sheets with writing on both sides. He looked it over quickly before stopping at a particular passage. Then he scowled.

George had the distinction of being the only student in the Skylark writer's group who hadn't received the soul-crushing diagnosis that each of the others had experienced. He knew about half of the guys in the group when it began and it was generally assumed that he was there to support the others, to be ready to serve as caretaker when one of them fell, or to serve as a historian, documenting the lives of its participants.

George had stepped on toes when he made it clear that he didn't have much interest in writing about HIV or his friends or the pain they were experiencing. He was interested in writing about food and opera.

"Did you know that the average opera singer loses about five pounds during a live performance?" George had asked Emile after the meeting. "Did you know that opera singers won't eat fried or spicy food because it stresses the vocal chords? Or that 'Trancredi' is known as the rice opera? Or that food plays a role in the plot of 'Tosca'?"

Emile just nodded his head. He didn't know any of it but he was happy that George was enthused. "You're talking about something that's not a memoir, right?"

"Of course," George said, as if Emile should have picked up on this fact automatically. "It's history. It's about Rossini, considered the greatest eater in opera. And Verdi, a great cook. He made his own pasta and knew wines. Beethoven hated food. He ate only enough to survive. Wagner became a vegetarian just two years before he died."

George bustled off to the library to do more research. He ordered books and he called acquaintances to "find out if he was on the right path."

"This is a lot of fun, gathering all this information," he told Emile. Others in the group dismissed George's efforts. He wasn't honoring the true intent of the program. He was mocking them by writing about food, which several of them had no capacity to enjoy any more. Emile dismissed them by stating that George was following his own muse and that he would come around sooner or later.

Emile knew that George was aware of the comments too, but he remained unfazed. He claimed he'd experienced more than enough back-biting in the catty world of opera.

As the writing group continued, George's insensitivity took on a new form. He began to grow fat, a major crime in the gay community where looks and physical appearance meant everything. He had progressed from spare tire to meeting the clinical definition of obesity in a matter of months. He surpassed 300 pounds and began to have trouble walking.

Some members of the group, many who'd known him for years, began to fall away, ignored him, made fat jokes. At one of the writing sessions, someone made a comment about not giving up until the fat lady sings. The others turned and looked at George.

"Ah," said George. "A reference about fat sopranos. How clever. But what does the phrase really mean?" he asked the others in the room. No one answered.

"It means that one shouldn't presume to know the outcome of an event that is still in progress," he said. "It means that things can change. So, I might be fat now but I can lose weight. You think you emaciated boys can get back to normal looking?"

The silence was too huge to measure.

"I didn't think so," he said. "So while you're on the way out, you might want to act like you have a little bit of class."

After that episode, George hadn't been able to count many friends from the group.

❖

Emile grabbed the items he intended to take—the will, the shoebox, a few other mementos. He bolted the two blocks back to his own apartment and was dripping with sweat when he got there. He stood in front of the fan in his living room, holding his arms away from his body, but it offered little relief. *I need a place where I can cool off.*

From two blocks away, Skylark looked like a mirage in the desert, shimmering and glistening and floating in the air. When he opened the door, the cold air hit him. He seated himself, and within ten minutes, he had the lunch special—homemade chicken with noodles with an iced tea—sitting in front of him.

Bella, one of the proprietors, was in the kitchen when he arrived but came to his table when she saw him. He hid the will under the napkin on his lap.

"Emile," she said, settling down in the chair opposite him. "I just heard about George. I am so sorry. I must say, this one caught me off guard."

"Me too," Emile said. "I just found out this morning. I'm still trying to figure it out."

"His mother's alive, isn't she?"

"Yes, but I don't think they were on speaking terms. He didn't have much good to say about her."

"I remember. He described her as something of an ogre. I wonder if she knows yet."

"She's the one who told me."

"What?" Emile thought Bella would fall out of her chair.

"She called me this morning. She's here. But I don't know where."

"His place?"

"No, I was just there. I got there as soon as I knew she was here."

Emile could see that Bella understood the implications and that he didn't have to explain further. "Thank goodness," she said.

"It was clear. George really wasn't much of a party boy."

"Of all people—him," she said. "I bet it was his heart. It gave out from all the weight. At least it was fast. I have grown so weary of seeing these guys linger on and suffer."

They speculated about his last days, who he had talked to, and how long it had taken for someone to find him. Emile learned that it was the mailman trying to deliver an overnighted package who alerted the neighbors.

"Did he leave a will?" Bella wanted to know.

Emile hesitated for a moment and then nodded. "Yes, he left one." He crossed his arms like a Civil War officer in a daguerreotype, a serious pose for someone poised to take on Yankees.

Bella raised her eyebrows.

"It's an olographic will," he said. "It's handwritten. It's considered valid in Louisiana as long as the entire will is in the testator's own handwriting, and is signed and dated, even if it's not notarized."

Bella squinted her eyes and questioned if such a document was really legal.

"Of course it is. In fact, they're pretty common here. All lawyers in Louisiana see these at some point in their careers. Back when we were on closer terms, we talked about wills. He didn't want to spend a lot of money. Olographic wills are free. The court should have no problem with it."

"Did he have much to leave?" she asked.

Emile shrugged. "He did fairly well. He had paid off the house he was living in, plus he had savings and other retirement accounts. It's a nice little chunk of money but I don't know how much he was worth."

"Did he indicate the beneficiary of the will?"

Emile sat still. He didn't know how much to tell her. "That's where we have a problem. George wrote his will many years ago, long before I knew him, and he never updated it."

"Oh," Bella said. "The money should remain here."

Emile saw that she winced when she realized what she had blurted out and he laughed. Bella, who seemed to know all the activities of her eclectic patrons, kept a distance and allowed her men to sort out their own problems, though sometimes with a little behind-the-scenes guidance. She'd been caught out on this one though. It made Emile feel better to know that she felt the same way he did.

"Never mind," she said flatly. "I've already asked too many questions and it's none of my business."

After a pause, she asked, "When do we get to meet her?"

"We're supposed to meet for dinner tonight."

"Where are you going?" Her eyes begged to know. "You must come here."

❖

Early in the romance, Emile had admitted that he'd never seen an opera. George guessed as much, and he had a good time with Emile's confession.

"What?" shouted George. "How could this be?"

"There were not a lot of big opera productions that toured Lafayette."

"You've never seen one on television?"

"Nope."

"What about the radio?"

"Nope."

"Well," George stated, "you need to see an opera and I know how to make it happen."

"How's that?" Emile said. He decided to play along.

"I have two tickets to my favorite opera, The Tales of Hoffman. It's coming to the Orpheum next month. I can hardly wait."

Emile decided to play coy. "I think I'm busy that night."

"You're going to have to change your plans because this night is going to be grand."

"What's so special about this opera?"

"It has one of the best villains in all of opera. His name is Lindorf, Councilor Lindorf. I've been the understudy for Lindorf seven times. He gets to sing some great music. Loved the role."

"But he's a villain. You didn't want to play the good guy?"

"Villains are always great, better than the protagonists. Much more interesting. Lindorf commits fraud by passing off a doll as a human. He kills a courtesan, though that was an accident, but he was trying to convince her to kill Hoffman. He persuades a singer to commit suicide. And then he steals Hoffman's girl in the end."

"That's all?"

"No. He commits forgery too. In fact, that's how the opera opens."

"You really like this guy, don't you?"

"Remember what we were taught in writing class? Satan is always more interesting than God."

Emile spent the afternoon in Skylark, drinking glass after glass of iced tea that Bella kept sending while he wrote a new will for George that made the newly created New Orleans AIDS Task Force the beneficiary. The will specifically stipulated that the monies be given to the organization's buddy program created just two summers before in 1985. He knew George's handwriting and he had the old will in front of him to work from. He examined George's cursive until he felt comfortable to try a first draft. By the sixth draft, he had a document he thought would pass.

Each draft made Emile angrier at George. Why had he never updated his will? It must have been years since he looked at it. How could he allow his mother, a woman he frequently disparaged, to remain as the recipient of his life's earnings? When had he visited her last? When had he spoken to her? The whole thing baffled him.

Emile didn't question his activities. He understood that forging a will probably had a significant penalty attached to it, but the risk of being caught was minimal. Emile already sensed the disease taking a hold inside him. He had lost weight, felt less energy and wondered if the spot between his two larger toes on his right foot was the beginning of the cancer some of his friends had experienced. It was only a matter of time before he ended up like George. What could anyone do to him now?

He looked at the new will and compared it with the old. Not bad, he thought, but what should I do with the old version? He started to wad it up but stopped when he saw Bella approach the table. He didn't want her to see him destroy the original.

"How are things going over here?"

"I'm ready to slay the dragon." Emile replied.

Bella laughed. "When is she due?"

"In about a half an hour."

"Are you going to go home first, freshen up for the big battle? Put on your coat of armor?"

"I hadn't really given it much thought. I guess I'll just face her as I am."

"We're going to need a game plan."

For the next half hour, Bella and Emile discussed strategies for the night, what to say, what not to say, ways Emile could stand his ground, and when to wave the napkin as a signal for Bella to bring more water, or even a cocktail.

"Is she religious?" Bella wanted to know.

"I think she is, but I can't remember."

"You cannot debate the Bible. You will never win. Christianity isn't defined by logic. It is the exact opposite. It defies logic."

"Okay," Emile responded.

"Isn't she a teacher?"

"I think she is."

"What kind? A math teacher? A gym teacher?"

Emile rolled his eyes, signaling an end to the preparation. "She could be a knitting teacher or a karate teacher for all I know."

"Okay," Bella said sarcastically. "I see my work is done. Just remember that she isn't like your family. She's just another one of those people who is incapable of putting the words 'homosexuality' and 'love' and 'compassion' and dignity' in the same sentence. Don't let her get to you."

"Thank you for the pep talk," he said, and meant it.

For the next few minutes, Emile sat in silence, remembering George. He looked around the restaurant, imagining it as a mouse would see it, from the bottom of the world looking up. The curtains swayed lightly in the breeze, giving the impression that the building was breathing. Music was trickling in through the window from a bar down the street, and it sounded more like a fragrance than a collection of musical notes.

❖

Roberta Ann Morrison arrived at exactly the time she said she would—seven o'clock on the dot. Emile watched with humor as the small woman dashed into the restaurant and shut the door quickly behind her, trying to avoid the bug truck that rumbled down the street delivering its toxic load. She waved her hand past her face several times to ward off the fumes.

"That was a close one," Bella said as she greeted her. "You almost got fumigated."

"Yes I did," the diminutive woman said. "Does that happen a lot?"

"More than you would think," Bella said as she extended her hand. "You must be Mrs. Morrison."

Emile could see that Bella was taking her time with their visitor, no doubt trying to get a read on the villainess. She cut her assessment short when another party entered the restaurant. Bella pointed George's mother to Emile's table.

"Emile Abadie?" she asked for the second time that day. "It's a pleasure to meet you."

She was a small, trim woman, no more than five feet tall with grey hair pulled up on top of her head and legs as spindly as pipe cleaners. She was wearing black. When she sat down, Emile could see that she was wearing just a trace of makeup—lipstick and rouge. She had a classy yet down-to-earth look. Her faded, pale blue eyes displayed world weariness and wisdom at the same time. At first, Emile was embarrassed because she'd dressed up for dinner, then he recalled that she was a mother in mourning.

He also remembered all the comments George had made about her and he reminded himself to be on his best behavior around this woman, even if she was the cause for so much of George's pain.

He stood to greet her.

"It's a pleasure to finally meet you," she said, then said spiritedly, "I hope you haven't waited very long. It took me a while to find a cab and then we got stuck in some kind of parade. Then I almost got run over by a bug truck."

Her eyes flashed and Emile knew immediately where George acquired his theatricality.

"No, I haven't been waiting long at all."

Mrs. Morrison sat down, her bullfrog spotted hands clasped in front of her, a knot waiting to be untied. She gazed at Emile for several seconds, studying him, then turned her head, and looked around the restaurant, a look of enchantment on her face as she took it all in.

"This place is so beautiful," she said. "At first, I couldn't understand why he moved to New Orleans," she said. "Now I know. It's so friendly and has so much character. It's a very special place."

"You've never been here?"

"No, never," she said. "I always wanted to." With that statement, Emile knew she'd never been invited.

She opened her menu and looked it up and down. "I don't have a clue what to order."

"We have a saying. 'If it's green, it means trouble, if it's fried, order double'."

She laughed at that. "Apparently my son took that to heart." It was the first reference she had made about his weight.

For the next two hours, Emile and Roberta Ann Morrison talked about New Orleans, Montana, music and education. She was a school teacher after all, a profession that she said gave her great joy. She said the best thing about being a teacher was that she had 'younger friends' and 'to teach is to learn twice'. Emile was polite, careful not to volunteer information that might be misinterpreted.

They spoke about George and when Mrs. Morrison broke into stories about his past, she lowered her voice into a softened baritone that suggested she was telling Emile profound secrets. He could tell that she had made some progress with her wine. She laughed frequently, but Emile could tell that it wasn't easy for her to talk about her son.

Emile realized that she was not the ogre George had made her out to be. She was kind and open-minded, funny and intelligent. She had an appetite for life. Why had he denied her access to his own?

Over dessert, she held a forkful of bread pudding in front of her and studied it, as if waiting for it to send her a message, to explain what had happened between her and George. She stared off into the distance, then back at the fork. Then she blinked and put the fork down, as if the thread of her memory had eluded her once again.

"I just wanted you to know, that I made some mistakes with George when he was younger," she said tearfully. "I just didn't understand. I didn't know how to handle it."

She knew, Emile realized. In the time it took for her to speak, Emile realized what had gone wrong. George had rejected his mother before she could reject him. He had seen it before. He thought back to the night they broke up, when George was the one who officially ended the relationship before he had a chance to do it.

"Was he happy?" she asked through the tears. "Was he happy with you?"

Emile didn't know what to say, so he shrugged, realizing that Mrs. Morrison believed he had shared a life with George. "Yes," he whispered. A little white lie was nothing compared to his activities earlier in the day.

Later it dawned on him that he was now part of an unfortunate triangle. Mrs. Morrison had loved her son, but he had not loved her back. George had loved him, but he did not love him back. Now he was in the same room with George's mother. He decided he would try to explain George to her. She had a right to know.

Emile spotted Bella heading for his table out of the corner of his eye.

"Had so much fun last night you had to come right back this morning?" she asked.

"You know how much I love it here," he responded. He saw her eyeing the document he had in his hands.

"I thought you finished that the other day," she said.

"I did but it needed some revising," he said teasingly, knowing it would confuse Bella. Before she could respond, he stood up and greeted Mrs. Morrison who had stepped into the restaurant.

"Good morning, Emile," she shouted from across the room as she ambled toward his table.

"This is interesting," Bella said under her breath so that only Emile could hear. And then louder, "Shall I get something for you to drink? Some coffee?"

"I'd like a Bloody Mary," Emile said.

"Make that two," Mrs. Morrison said. She giggled as she sat down. "I haven't had a Bloody Mary in years."

Bella shot Emile a glance. *When did the two of you become such close friends?* Emile winked back.

"I know it's only been a matter of hours, but it's so good to see you again," Mrs. Morrison said. "I've been thinking about you and all the things you told me last night and I really appreciate it all. You don't know what it means to me."

"My pleasure," Emile said. "I wanted to tell you that after I left you last night, I had something of an epiphany about the location of George's will. I found it inside one of his records."

He handed her the original document.

"It's an olographic will, which means that he wrote it out by hand. It's signed and dated, so it's perfectly legal. At least in Louisiana."

Mrs. Morrison glanced at the document. "He had such beautiful handwriting, didn't he?"

Emile suppressed a laugh, then nodded. "But what's even more beautiful is that you are the sole beneficiary. He left everything to you."

Mrs. Morrison gasped. "Really? I wasn't expecting that." She studied the document for a few moments, then looked up. "Why didn't he leave anything to you?"

Emile shrugged. "I have plenty," he said. "This is something he wanted for you."

"I don't know what to say."

Emile smiled. He recognized that they had developed a bond, the kind of friendship shared by warriors in the trenches. He knew now that he had made a mistake in judging her, but now that she was off his villain's list, he didn't quite know where to put her.

They sipped their Bloody Marys and ordered breakfast. Deep in the bosom of Skylark, Emile began the process of explaining George to his mother.

BEAUTY MARKS

David James Parr

Mark is breaking up with me. Outside people are playing baseball, bouncing babies, sipping cappuccinos. Traffic lights are turning from red to green then changing their minds. Someone somewhere is whistling a showtune and someone near them is wishing they would stop. But in this cramped, overstuffed living room in this Petri dish of Things Mark and Things Mine, Mark is breaking up with me. That's the long and the short of it and, at the moment, both are inexplicably the same size.

I am sitting on a green velvet chair whose arms have been shredded by the cat's claws. The cat is a Thing Mark, the chair is a Thing Mine. While he is telling me that we are breaking up, Mark is wearing a yellow plaid shirt that I haven't seen before. Usually it's a white shirt to catch the blonde in his hair or a green shirt to show off his eyes, but in the two years we've been together, not yellow and never plaid. "Plaid" is the word we use when we're feeling melancholic but can't explain why.

So after he finishes telling me that he is leaving, the first and only thing I say is, "Where did you get that shirt?"

Mark looks down at the shirt and then back at me as if I'm a story problem, a foreign language, an abstract painting—all things Mark hates. He tosses up his hands like a frustrated French chef whose soufflé is crumbling.

"You never listen to me," he says, but all I'm doing is listening to him. "It's like we're two cars, okay?" he continues. "Two cars going for the same parking space."

"Which one has the right of way?"

"It doesn't matter," he says, but I can't picture it. One of us must have the right of way, but in no way is any of this right. Maybe I need a compass, a protractor, a calculator—all things I hate.

"The one who saw the space first should get it," is my point.

"We both saw it at the same time," he says.

"The one in front should get the space."

Mark shakes his hands impatiently in the manner of swimmers shaking off water, then takes a deep breath as if preparing to dive back in. "I'm the one in front," he counters.

"Okay, then you get the space."

"Thank you," he says, and I realize that I've just agreed to breaking up.

"I don't want that space," I try, shifting in reverse. "If it means us breaking up, then I don't need that space."

"Well," he says resolutely, "I do."

This hits me like an airbag, setting my upper lip trembling. Mark stands in front of me, his head cocked slightly, his expression intense, but not unkind. He looks like the same Mark I first fell in love with, the one with the sweet freckles and the long neck and the hands that stay warm during any season. Not like the one who has just said something so final, so decisive, so heartbreaking. A person should be labeled after making such definitive statements, like the printed warnings on the sides of medications.

A car alarm starts wailing from the street below; it sounds like "Mine! Mine! Mine!" Two states away in Ohio, my little sister, Hope, is taking her final exams, my Mom is picking up a chocolate cake to celebrate, and Jake is thumping his golden brown tail against the floor in the front hallway, waiting patiently by the door for one of them to return. But in this state, my state of New York, my state of shock and disbelief, Mark is breaking up with me.

"I don't know what else," Mark starts to say but stops. He drops his hands like a conductor at the end of a concert.

Meanwhile, I have entangled my fingers in the loose threads of the chair's arm. The color resembles pale grass. I wonder if it has always looked so faded. In the background, one of my favorite songs is playing. Instead of focusing on Mark's new yellow plaid shirt, I'm now thinking that I'll never be able to listen to Nina Simone again without thinking about how awful I feel at this moment.

My mouth is dry but my eyes are wet. I don't look up and I don't speak, because I don't want Mark to know about either condition. I realize the lip tremor, tears, dryness are all also signs of stroke. Maybe Mark isn't really breaking up with me; maybe I'm just having a stroke. His cat, a male calico emasculated by the ridiculously theatrical name Tallulah, is eyeing me from the floor. When I meet his gaze, he meows dramatically as if we are in a scripted scene together.

Mark tires of the view of my scalp and says, "We can talk more later."

I can tell he is mostly done with the talking part. He exits the apartment, leaving the clicking noise of the front door as his end punctuation. I would prefer the sigh of an ellipse or even the deep breath of a semi-colon, but Mark is not one to make promises he doesn't intend to keep. Tallulah bolts after him and begins pawing the door, obviously panicked to be suddenly alone with me.

As am I.

I sit in the green chair with the loose threads for a long time. I'm not sure how long. I'm only sure that I don't know what happens next.

❖

Mark is breaking up with me. I don't know how much longer I can keep phrasing it this way because actually it has been about three weeks. Nineteen days to be exact, but I figure as long as I say breaking rather than broke, it sounds like it is still happening and there is a chance that it will stop.

This is easier said than done, especially when in our bathroom. Well, now it is just my bathroom which makes it seem both bigger and smaller. Mark has left behind his toothbrush, dressed up in navy blue and leaning seductively beside mine in a small glass. He has left behind his used razor, with little commas of his facial hair dotting the blade. He has left behind his robe, white and terry cloth, hanging limply from a hook on the back of the door. One of its belt loops is torn, from when

I aggressively disrobed him, pushing him against the chipped blue tiles, the robe a puddle of lust at our feet. That was only a few weeks ago. Was the breakup in his head already? Was he giving me one for the road? The road without sufficient parking.

I'm not sure exactly why Mark is leaving me, other than that business about the parking space. Maybe it's because we had too many dumb arguments like that one. Maybe it's because I get hung up on language and he gets hung up on real life. Maybe it's because Mark didn't know what a non sequitur was and I did. Mark thought it had something to do with latitude and longitude. "That's why I love you," I told him. I meant because he lived in a less rigid world, where definitions were fluid.

But Mark hates this kind of comment. He immediately looked up non sequitur on his phone, gave me the definition verbatim and then said, "There, are you satisfied?" giving me attitude and longitude. Living with Mark is like a short story collection by a first-time author. You're never sure what you're going to get.

I should have guessed something was wrong the night he brought home handcuffs. "Let's try something," he said. Which was all fine and good until he couldn't find the key and I spent an embarrassing half an hour lying naked in our bed wondering if my dead grandfather could see me sprawled out in a too-small jock strap, while he went back to the same store and bought an identical pair to get a new set of keys.

"What else is in the bag?" I asked while massaging my free wrists.

"Oh, nothing," he shrugged, casually pulling out a bottle of poppers, a set of dildos, and a pair of nipple clamps destined to become Tallulah's favorite toy. I knew our sex life had waxed and waned, but I hadn't realized we'd waned as far as props. In the beginning, all we had needed was saliva and a surface. Well, in the beginning of the beginning, we also had condoms and lubricant. The dildos arranged in increasing sizes resembled Russian dolls.

The first time I took off my shirt in front of Mark, he instantly gravitated to the two large discolorations on my right shoulder blade. "They look like birds," he said with what sounded like wonderment. He meant the birds he had drawn as a child, flying seagulls in the lazy shapes of lowercase m's. I remembered drawing them like that, too.

"Chicken pox," I told him, because I didn't want to say, "Acne."

He kissed each "m" and I promptly told him to stop. "It's ugly," I added, because a previous lover had said as much to me. What the lover had actually said was: "You can get that fixed."

"It's just a beauty mark," Mark whispered, still kissing, his breath warm against my neck.

"You have a strange way of looking at things," I told him, but I was smiling as I said it.

❖

Mark is breaking up with me, and I am breaking up with Mark. Every evening when I get home from my temp assignment, I find another thing missing from the apartment. It is like the game we used to play in first grade where Mrs. Flynn would arrange a collection of objects on her desk and give us all sixty seconds to study them. Then we had to turn around and shut our eyes for another sixty seconds while Mrs. Flynn took away one of the objects. We'd turn back around and have to guess what was missing.

Today it is Tallulah and two of Mark's play anthologies from the bookshelves. I think he is trying to move his things out slowly to make less of a footprint. He is not a bad person. Perhaps he thinks eventually I will just forget that he was ever here, like something accidentally dropped behind a refrigerator.

When he calls to see how I'm doing, I pause for just a second before saying with as much confidence as I can muster, "You look horrible in yellow." I hang up. Which pretty much answers the question of how I'm doing. He doesn't call back, though I clutch my phone for a few minutes hoping it will vibrate.

If he were to call back, instead of "Hello?" I would snarl, "Yellow, yellow, yellow!" This is the kind of plan I hatch these days when I should be doing something practical, such as scouring the bathtub or registering to vote. I've come to realize how much time is actually in a day. The minutes passing uncertainly like disoriented tourists. I've stopped wearing a watch.

❖

The night I met Mark, he was appearing in a bedroom farce so far off Broadway I had to go under a river to get there. It was the type of play set at a posh country estate where everyone starts out in elaborate costumes but then ends up almost naked, popping in and out of doors at the rear of the stage. My friend Peter got me in for free since he was playing the chauffeur, but, even so, I sat near the back of the theatre in case I needed to make a discreet exit. I was just about to when the butler appeared.

He entered Stage Left, or maybe it was Stage Right. I'm not an actor so I don't know these terms, but my program slid off my lap despite Mark's bad Cockney accent that passed in and out like a busy busboy. I realized I was breathing only through my mouth. In Act 2, he appeared clad only in a strategically placed napkin and I fell in love, or at least in a slippery spot near it.

Afterward I hung out with the cast at a bar not far from the theatre where the bartender knew everyone's drinks without them having to order. My friend Peter introduced us. "This is Mark Wood," he said, and I joked, "Would what?"

Mark said without missing a beat, "Pretty much anything."

I knew then and there that I wanted to see him naked again, this time off-stage.

"Mark's from Ohio, too," Peter announced by way of introduction, generously giving us something in common before driving his attention elsewhere. He was still wearing his chauffeur's cap.

It turned out that Mark and I were also both born in the same city. He asked me which school district I was in and suddenly—transfixed by his beauty—I forgot everything about the place where I had lived for eighteen years. I could not recall the name of anything. Not a mall. Not the street where we used to play kickball. Not even the name of the nasty German Shepherd whose bite had left a small scar on my right knee.

Instead I pretended I couldn't hear him because of the noise and excused myself to the bathroom to collect myself.

Mark took a sip of his drink while staring at me with his bright, alert eyes. He set his glass down, sliding it forward across the table so that his fingers eventually grazed mine. "I thought you were going to the bathroom," he said when I hadn't moved a muscle. I was going to, but that would have meant leaving him with other actors nearby. I may not know much about stage directions, but I do know a thing or two about actors.

"I thought I had to go but I don't," I said, shrugging my shoulders in an Isn't Life Funny? sort of way and slurping up the remainder of my martini. "What are you drinking anyway?"

"Scotch," he said. He was wearing a floppy blue fisherman's hat and his face was flushed pink from wiping off his stage makeup. I admire people who can look good in any kind of hat. I always look like something being mashed down.

"I had a roommate who drank scotch," I said animatedly, as if I had had a roommate who cured cancer. But luck was in my favor.

"I had a roommate who drank scotch, too!" Mark said with contagious enthusiasm. "By the gallons!"

It felt like we were in a foreign film, giddily speaking one language while subtitles beneath us revealed something quite different.

"What are the odds of two roommates swilling scotch?" I was trying to be funny. He scanned the bar thoughtfully and answered, "I'd say one in ten. My roomie Dan would drink one before bed every night with lots of ice, and by morning it looked like a glass full of piss."

Usually I think of piss as an ugly word, but on that night it sounded beautiful to me. On that night, I wanted to swim naked in piss. "Your roommate's name was Dan?" I said incredulously. "My roommate's name was Dan." And this was true, though he went by Dan-o.

"Get out!" Mark said.

"I won't," I said back. My right knee was touching his left. If I had swiveled a little, then both of our knees would have been touching, but I didn't want to have too much too soon.

"Have you ever had scallion pancakes?" he asked me.

"Is that a non sequitur?" I asked, and he said, "I don't think so. Where's the non sequitur?"

I said, "In your last question."

He said, "No, I mean: where on the globe?"

I said, "No, I've never had scallion pancakes."

He squeezed my knee and said, "I know a place that serves the best scallion pancakes you'll ever eat, plus a bottle of cheap white wine on ice."

"Really, where?" I asked in a Doesn't That Sound Exciting? voice, though really I was just watching Mark's hand on my knee. I couldn't picture what scallions looked like. To me, they sounded like some kind of fish. Even so, fish pancakes sounded wonderful. I wanted to eat stacks of fish pancakes while swimming naked in piss.

"On Eighth Avenue," Mark said. "I have a friend I take there every time he comes to town."

Immediately, I hated this friend because I was sure this friend was also a lover and I didn't want the competition. I was jealous before our relationship had even begun. "I'd like to go there," I said, leaning forward. I could smell the scotch on his breath and also a hint of garlic. This might seem an unpleasant combination, but at that moment I wanted to spray myself with garlic and scotch before eating a stack of fish pancakes.

"You should definitely try it," Mark said. "You'll thank me later." That was when I swiveled right so that both of our knees were touching. In hindsight, I see I could have swiveled left and saved both of us some trouble.

"General!" I blurted out later, just before our first kiss, remembering the name of the German Shepherd who had bitten me. He didn't seem to mind my outburst and kissed me anyway, turning every single one of my nerve endings into beginnings.

❖

Mark won't tell me where he is moving. He claims we need distance for now. "So does that mean you're in Paris or something?"

"Emotional distance," he says gently.

"I know what you meant."

"I know you know what I meant."

"If you were in Paris, my emotions wouldn't be distant."

"I'm not in Paris," he says. "I'm in my new place."

It would be just like Mark to find some dreamy rent-stabilized apartment with an elevator and a doorman. He is the type of person who could be walking down the sidewalk telling a joke just as a piano came crashing down an inch behind him, and still he would not screw-up the punchline.

That is what is hard about being Mark's boyfriend. You have to constantly be on the lookout for falling pianos.

"I thought we were going to have scallion pancakes on 8th Avenue," I remind him. "We've been together over two years and we've never had those pancakes."

"That place is closed now," he says calmly.

"Figures."

"Think of this as an experiment."

"I flunked Chemistry. I thought this was a parking space."

"You got a 'B' in Chemistry."

"How do you know?"

"Because you told me."

"You were listening?" I feign surprise. Mark is always listening.

"Just give it time, babe."

Babe. Babe. The word dangles in the air, reminding me of all of the others that he would never call me again: sweetheart, honey, muffin. I was someone's babe. I was someone's muffin. I never thought I'd want to be either, but now I think I know what it would be like to be crowned Miss America and then have the crown taken away.

"You really sucked in that play," I say to break the tension. "How's that for a non sequitur, Magellan?"

"Which play?" There have been quite a few, and he's never actually sucked.

"The one you sucked in," I say anyway.

"I'm hanging up," he says but doesn't. Like I said, Mark is not a bad person.

"Do you miss me?" I ask, and immediately regret it. Because both 'Yes' and 'No' would be terrible answers.

"Of course," he says. But of which course does he mean? What course are we on now? This is what I mean about me getting hung up on language instead of real life.

"I miss you, too," I manage. I wonder if I am either making things too easy or too hard for him. Maybe I should make use of his gift and handcuff myself to his ankle the next time that I see him, like radical protestors used to do to historical landmarks and trees marked for demolition.

Mark has nice ankles. They are neither too thick nor too thin, and the anklebones are full and round and easy to put your lips on, like certain fruits. I realize that they are only ankles, but still, it doesn't make things easier knowing I won't be able to kiss them again.

To end the awkward silence on the phone, I steel myself and ask, "Is there someone else?" deciding it might make things easier if there is another boy on deck to push off the deck.

"No, just you," he says softly. I don't think he intends it to sound cruel. "How about I call you tomorrow?"

"I'm busy tomorrow." I'm not. "I'm doing those poppers you bought." I'm not.

And still, he doesn't hang up.

❖

In the shower where it's bright and private as it is nowhere else in New York City, I study my body as if looking for clues to The Mystery of Our Breakup. From above, the scar that General left on my knee looks like a smile. From above, my penis looks harmless, playing dead like a scolded child. When I emerge, the mirror is fogged. Every time I clear a bathroom mirror, I always feel like I'm in a horror movie and when I wipe it, a scary thing will be revealed. But it's only me, though I do notice that Mark's white robe is now missing from the back of the door and his razor is gone.

"How come you've never said anything about the scar on my knee?" I ask him in lieu of "Hello," or "Yellow, yellow, yellow."

"You have beautiful knees," is what he says, unfazed.

"Now you tell me." There is a pause, during which I think he's hung up. "Sorry," and I actually am, for a few seconds anyway. "I guess I'm just feeling plaid."

"I'm back with Dante," he admits after a moment. I suddenly have the vague sensation of falling backward, though I'm leaning against a wall. Dante. Twenty-five. Who believes in astrology. This is pretty much all I know about him. Or cared to know, because I thought Dante was a thing of the past, a closed book, a faded snapshot. I thought he was like Algebra—something I didn't need to learn because I'd never have to use it in real life.

Maybe Dante saw this coming in the stars, but I sure didn't. I want to hang up the phone, but it seems stuck to my hand. The name 'Dante' keeps repeating in my head like an annoying chorus to some infectious Swedish pop song.

"Are you okay?" Mark asks after a moment.

"No," I answer truthfully.

He sighs. "Well, you're the one who asked."

"I asked three days ago."

"I didn't think you were ready then."

I want to say, "Don't," but "Dante, Dante, Dante" is still repeating in my head.

"It's just, we have a history, you know."

"Of what?"

"It's complicated."

"We have a history." Does two years a history make? How much story does there need to be in a history.

"I was driving you crazy."

When I crawled into bed, he no longer immediately turned in his sleep to put his arm around me and pull my body against his. When I woke after him in the morning, there was no longer a fresh pot of coffee waiting. When I came out of the shower while he was brushing his teeth, there was no longer a glance behind him in the mirror, a smile, any naked lingering. There was only abrupt spitting into the sink.

These things were not driving me crazy, exactly, but they were driving me somewhere. An abandoned car park, after dark, in the middle of a town I didn't recognize. The keys dangling from the ignition, Mark nowhere in sight, me with absolutely no idea how to get back.

"Be happy for me," Mark insists. "Please? This is a good thing. For both of us. Really. You'll see."

"I am happy for you," I lie. "I'm just not happy." And then I disconnect, suddenly aware that it may have been my general unhappiness that caused our breakup in the first place.

I did get a 'B' in Chemistry, and I have a vague recollection of how reactions work, what needs to be present, how much of it in order for it to not blow up in your face. I just don't know what elements of personality need to combine in order for a relationship to work the way that you want and not blow up in your face, as mine with Mark clearly has.

I pull on some clothes and head outside, thinking a slap of fresh air might knock the dread out of me. As I'm crossing the intersection in front of my building, a cab comes to a halt about a foot away from me, tires screeching like my Aunt Garnet used to when I tried to steal candy from her secret hiding place.

I start kicking the front fender of the cab repeatedly, shouting "Motherfucker!" in rapid succession.

The cab driver starts shouting "You the motherfucker!" out of his window.

We continue this sweet duet until the driver finally lays on the horn and peels off down Second Avenue, narrowly missing my foot.

This is what is hard about being my boyfriend: you have to constantly be on the lookout for screeching cabs.

Normally, I would not do this kind of thing so I think it might finally be sinking in that Mark and I are breaking up. Maybe one should be given a distinctive uniform during a separation, like hunters or construction workers. A bright orange vest to encourage caution.

To distract myself, I walk to the multiplex movie theatre down the street with 24 screens and buy a ticket for what looks like a big loud teenage comedy, the kind of movie I ordinarily would squirm through because it is "neither clever nor in French," as Mark would say. But somehow I end up in the wrong theatre which is showing a horror film. After the third slaying, I say out loud, "Where are the jokes?" and am shushed by the tense teenage girls in front of me.

I exit the theater before witnessing any more severed limbs, duck into a neighboring pizza place, and order a slice heavy with cloves of garlic and diced red onions because what does it matter how my breath smells now that I live alone and Mark lives with a 25-year-old astrologer named Dante? In the lobby of my building, I run into my downstairs neighbor, Ginny, who works at the hair salon where Mark and I used to go. She is the closest thing either one of us has to a therapist.

"Mark is breaking up with me," I say.

"I know, I saw him walking out with the flatscreen."

"He took the TV but left the DVD player."

"Why don't you come up," she says, and when I do, she immediately starts rolling a joint for us to share. "There are so many reasons people leave," she says with import before lighting it.

"That's just it," I tell her, watching her eyes squint and her lips pucker as she sucks in the smoke. "If it were just insecurity, or boredom, or another boy," I say boy to make Dante sound less threatening, "It would be easier. But it's all of those things, altogether, all at once. I can't fight all of those things. It's like when the Spartans tried to battle—who were they? Those soldiers with the dustpan helmets. Trojans?" And I haven't even taken a hit off of the joint yet.

Ginny passes it to me and says, "I think it was the Persians, but I get what you mean." Then she tries calming me down by playing one of our favorite made-up games, which involves looking up celebrities on-line whom we remember from childhood to see what happened to them. It's sort of a "Where Are They Now?" game, though Ginny refers to it more appropriately as "Dead or Alive?"

"Rodney Dangerfield," Ginny offers while I take another hit.

"I think Mark didn't love me more than he did love me."

Ginny looks up at the ceiling thoughtfully, then says, "Flip that around."

"Mark did love me more than he didn't love me."

"No," she says, taking the joint. "What about you?"

"What about me?" And then I get it. "I'm not sure. I'd have to make a comparison chart. Or one of those circle things where they overlap. What are those called?"

"Edward Asner."

"Venn. A Venn diagram."

"We're playing two different games."

"Welcome to my life," I say, then ask to use her phone since I see my own battery has died. "A metaphor," I tell her while waiting for Mark to pick-up, and she rolls her eyes and throws her charger at me. "Stop thinking in metaphors," she says. "It's like annoying."

It takes five rings before Mark answers, and I say, "You know what, Mark? Your ankles aren't all that great."

"What?" I've woken him up. He has Smoky Sleepy Voice.

"I've seen better is all I'm saying," and then I hang up.

"Dead or Alive?" says Ginny.

"He took his cat but left the litter box."

Ginny, also recently single, nods sympathetically. She has a small mole on the side of her mouth that looks just like Marilyn Monroe's.

When I call it a beauty mark, she says, "You can dress it up in diamonds, but when you get down and dirty with it, it's just a mole."

When I'm sufficiently high and incoherent, Ginny walks me upstairs to my apartment and offers to throw out the litter box because that's the kind of friend she is.

"No thanks," I tell her. "That's something I need to do myself." She nods knowingly like we're in a sad movie together and gives me a hug.

"I'll make you an appointment for tomorrow afternoon," she says. "We'll give you highlights. You'll feel like a brand new person." Ginny looks like a brand new person since coloring her own natural blonde a dark red, or maybe more like her old self redecorated. "Besides, I feel like dyeing." And we laugh and cough like now we're in a funny sitcom together.

"You're on," I tell her. Once she leaves, I call Mark again.

I'm surprised he even answers. I'm hoping to hear Dante in the background, angry, sniping. But it's only Mark's groggy voice that I hear. "You've got to stop," he says.

"I just wanted to let you know that tomorrow I'm getting highlights."

"Please," Mark says flatly. "You've got to stop doing this."

When he hangs up, I'm the one who feels like dying.

"That's not funny," Mom says. "Why does your voice sound froggy? Are you sick?"

"You're missing the pun."

"What fun? What time is it anyway? Are you out dancing?" I'm never out dancing, but she always asks this.

"Pun, Mom. Pun. Put the news on mute for a second." My mom has been through two divorces, and so has a thicker skin when it comes to breakups. But she does mute her television.

"So Hope got straight A's on all of her finals," she tells me, switching topics with the ease of the newscasters she loves. "Even Calculus, which she stressed out about." I'm not in the mood to hear about my little sister's successes, however.

"I don't know why he left," I say.

"Oh, we're back on that," she says.

"It's only been two weeks."

"Right," she says. "Sorry, honey." Then, "You deserve better."

"That's what you said to Mark when you met him."

"I was just trying to be funny. I was just trying to get him to like me."

"I loved him." It's the first time I've said that to my mom.

"I know," she says like she does.

"Does it get any easier?"

"Well, yes and no. Yes, because time helps, and no because—wait. Dyeing and dying. I just got that. You should write that one down."

When I come home from the salon the following afternoon with new blonde highlights, I find that Mark has taken the phone but left the answering machine. I vacuum all of the cat fur from the bedroom rug, and in the process inadvertently suck up the nipple clamps from under the bed. It takes me an hour to untangle them, but mostly because I'm crying while doing it. I take them downstairs to Ginny, my eyes full of tears.

Ginny says that's what I get for cleaning on a Saturday night, because that's the kind of friend she is.

"I think I'm having a nervous breakdown," I tell her.

"No you aren't," Ginny says definitively, lighting us up another joint. She uses the nipple clamp as a roach clip. "If you were having a nervous breakdown you wouldn't be able to tell me you were having it. You would just be having it." She disappears into her bathroom and comes back with a prescription bottle of tranquilizers. Ginny's ex was a pharmacologist. "Here," she says, fishing two tiny yellow pills from inside. "Just in case you are having a breakdown."

"Yellow, yellow, yellow," I say, thinking of Mark's plaid shirt. Ginny pretends to get it.

I wake up on her couch somewhere in the middle of the next morning in the same position as I'd gone to sleep—sitting straight up. Ginny has already left for work but has left me a note with a heart drawn on it. The note reads: Keep passing those open windows. Which I suppose means not to jump.

When I get back upstairs to my apartment, I find Mark walking out with a fern named Fern in one hand and the toaster under his arm. He is wearing the yellow plaid shirt again, which, on second thought, doesn't look so bad on him.

"Wow," he says. "Your hair looks great, babe," even though it is going in a million different directions, none of them forward. Much like our arguments.

"Thanks," I murmur reluctantly. "Does Tallulah miss me?"

Mark sets down Fern and the toaster and gives me an unexpected hug, his warm hands slipping under my shirt, resting in the small of my back where my ON button is located. "I miss you," he murmurs. His day-old whiskers brush against my cheek but they are never bristly. Instead, they are soft and so light they are almost white. His hands slide down to my hips, holding me as if he might lift me to the moon like my grandfather used to do when I was a kid. I believed I'd get there every time.

"Show me that scar on your knee," he whispers.

Suddenly it is as if we have just met all over again, as if I have never felt his tongue in my mouth nor slid down the neat trail of hairs that line his abdomen. We devour one another like children devour candy bars they have stolen—quickly and greedily—before getting caught.

The plug from the toaster digs into my back but I don't mind because what does it matter now that I live alone and Mark lives with an astrologer named Dante? While we both redress, I joke, "Well we both fit nicely into that space, I guess."

Mark's face is once again all business, and the business has nothing to do with my awesome recollection of metaphors. "That shouldn't have happened," he apologizes, his face flushed. "I'm sorry."

"Prove it." I hold up a finger and then drag the litter box from the bathroom. "Take this," I tell him, "And leave that toaster."

"I do love you, you know," he says. Outside, people are running out of gas, growing unwanted hairs, losing keys. But in this hallway we used to share, where we've just had sex, Mark still loves me.

"Then I'll keep feeding the meter," I tell him. He gets a confused look, which I find irritating since he's the one who introduced the stupid parking space analogy in the first place.

After he leaves, I go on-line and find a restaurant that serves scallion pancakes with bottles of white wine on ice. When the waiter starts to clear the place setting opposite mine, I stop him and say with probably too much urgency, "No, I'm expecting someone." I fear that I'm becoming more and more like the irate man I see at my neighborhood bus stop who repeatedly shouts, "Taken!" though there is nowhere to sit.

The scallion pancakes do turn out to be pretty good after all, just as Mark promised. When I get home, I find a long extension cord lying in the middle of the front hallway in the shape of a question mark. Whatever was once attached to it has been disconnected and taken. I make a mental note to follow Ginny's advice and to stop thinking in metaphors. I coil the cord up carefully and put it in a kitchen drawer, because what does it matter now that I live alone and Mark lives with an astrology-spouting 25-year-old named Dante?

It doesn't. It really doesn't.

One should be stamped after a breakup like a passport. That way you can be sure never to return to the same place again, but you'll know exactly where you've been.

BEAR FOOD

Alise Wascom

As the closest childhood friend of Miri, and therefore an honorary, non-blood related family member, some of Tulip's responsibilities included signing the Ketubah, smiling for the photographer, and concentrating on her penmanship. The obligations went on and on. For example, it was essential she choose a dress pretty enough not to ruin pictures, but ugly enough not to upstage either of the brides in this, their interfaith, queer, East Coast wedding. Tulip tried to wear her dress like a beautiful girl wears an ugly name—the ugliness juxtaposing an obvious attractiveness—but she couldn't quite pull it off with confidence. She accepted compliments with grace and a grain of salt.

Tulip let Miri's grandfather kiss both her cheeks, take her arm, and pretend he was escorting her when really she was helping steady him across the grass to the restaurant where they were holding the ceremony and the reception. Miri's grandfather had no sons, only daughters and granddaughters. It was fitting, as he was the kind of man who liked to be surrounded by women. Tulip figured he deserved as many little luxuries as he wanted. He had escaped Nazi Germany for Cuba, where he had lived for five years before immigrating to New York, meeting his wife, making his daughters. Now here was Tulip, finding him scotch even though they were only serving beer and wine.

"Do you want this now? Before the ceremony?"

"I am an old man. I could die any minute."

"Grandfather," she said, as she had called him at his request since she was small.

"I remember you," he said. He touched her face.

"That's a good sign." When they were younger, he was the one who bought her tickets for the high holidays. Miri would join Tulip at her house for Christmas and Easter. If there was a god, they used to joke, all best friends would be a different religion and the same shoe size. Why had they decided, then, there wasn't a god? Was it so hard to imagine an imaginary Father when neither had a physical one present?

"I read my diary entry on the day Miriam was born. I wrote: 6 pounds, 2 ounces. Eight o'clock," he said.

"AM or PM?"

"I didn't put that down."

"I think it's time for the show to start," Tulip said.

"Go." He waved her away with his thick, stiff fingers, like paws. She would have liked to stay with him.

Because of the rain, the tables and chairs in the restaurant had been pushed to the side to quickly create an aisle. It's good luck, everyone complained. The guests were in their assigned seats. First came Miri's aunts, carrying the homemade, quilted chuppah, then Tulip on the arm of Becca's brother, and then an array of flower children with sweaty fistfuls of dried petals. Finally the women of the hour: Miri and Becca in ivory and champagne, looking impossibly in love, if not a little nervous. Nervous, that is, at the attention, the kind of which they weren't used to. Certainly, Tulip knew, not nervous for their lives to come. Not nervous to sign the contract, take the plunge as people are apt to say. But plunge was the wrong word. There was no plummeting here, no nose-dives—just a straight steady walk right into their futures.

If anyone was plunging here, Tulip thought, it was her. Free-falling forward into her future. Sure, there was the wind in her face and the sun at her back, but there was also the fear of where she would ultimately land.

Tulip stood on one foot, and then the other, her feet swollen and pinched in her new heels. They hurt but they were Miri's choice. Anything for Miri, right? Rings were exchanged. Tulip shifted. Left. Right. Left. Fat blisters formed on the backs of her heels and the edges of her little toe. Vows were given, promises made. One of Becca's college friends read from *The Dot & The Line*. Tulip half listened as the Line bent itself into impressive angles and shapes. The overtly-liberal

Justice of the Peace slipped away from her position and behind Tulip. When the JP had discovered Tulip was part Native, she squealed with delight. These kind of reactions always made Tulip suspicious. Now, the JP's whisper was stern and serious. "The light bulb?"

"You don't have it?"

Becca was supposed to break the glass. And the glass was supposed to be a light bulb because it was easier to stomp and made a most satisfying sound.

"No. Do you?"

Tulip grabbed a water goblet and a white cloth napkin from a nearby table. The JP gave her a look, but took them. They didn't have any other choice. The reader choked through the last pages of Juster's love story in lower mathematics. The brides held hands, teary and all smiles.

Since she was not Jewish, Becca had been chosen to break the glass. All these altered traditions and new rules. Tulip sometimes found it difficult to keep up. Becca, honoring Miri's culture—that was the reasoning. And if the glass didn't break? Tulip clutched her bouquet with both hands and held it too high, exactly the way the photographer had instructed her not to.

The JP put the white cloth bundle on the floor. Miri stepped back and Becca-none-the-wiser lifted one foot. She was wearing a pair of delicate gold flats. Almost slippers. Tulip had an image of a shard cutting through the thin sole, going straight into her heel. She calculated the drive to the nearest emergency room. The JP looked pale. But when Becca brought her foot down, there was a pleasing crack and the room of family, of friends, applauded and cheered.

Mazel tov, mazel tov.

Unknown tragedy averted, Tulip and the other guests watched as Miri and Becca shared their first, well-practiced, wedded kiss.

❖

Tulip slipped her shoes off at dinner. She rubbed her feet together underneath the table and drank her wine. She had remained responsibly sober up until this point. Other guests knocked their forks and knives against their glasses and Miri and Becca kissed. Tulip couldn't shake this feeling of being dismissed. Her obligations gone, her duties over. Tulip tried to remind herself that it wasn't a competition but Becca smiled as if she had just won a pie baking contest and Miri was the sweet, pretty slice. It wasn't that Tulip didn't like Becca, it wasn't that she didn't think Becca was good for Miri (she was, she was the best), but they had never gotten close. Their mutual love of Miri never enough to sustain a friendship. Becca was steady where Tulip was uncertain. Becca reliable and Tulip, needy.

The three spent the day in Newburyport, once, when Miri and Becca had just started dating.

"You'll love her, really, you will," Miri had said. At the time, it seemed like something that was important to Miri, Tulip's approval.

Tulip wore her favorite cut-offs and a sheer yellow blouse. She wanted to look bright but the wind at the shore left her feeling uncomfortable and cold. Becca lent Tulip an old college sweatshirt she kept in her car and Tulip felt frumpy wearing it, felt Becca thinking, *you silly girl*.

And Miri, who said, "Oh Tulip, didn't you look at the weather!" when before Miri might have said it was a good excuse to go shopping. Or have said, let's warm up with a glass of wine inside, somewhere. But already, even then, alliances were shifting and it was Becca's approval, not Tulip's that began to count.

The courses kept coming but Tulip didn't have much of an appetite. Everything seemed a little blurred so she walked barefoot to the bar to make it blurrier.

There was a man in line in front of her that she was sure she had met before. Someone from Miri and Becca's parties that she had seen but never really noticed.

"Hello," she said.

"Hey."

"I think,"

"Tulip, right?"

"Yes."

"Les."

"What?"

"My name. Les. It's okay; we met once before but I had a beard."

"Oh, that's right. I remember her. Nice girl."

He looked at her.

"I'm sorry. Bad joke."

"What are you drinking?"

"What works?"

"Ain't that the truth."

She tried to remember any previous conversations they shared, without success. He ordered and handed her wine. He stuffed bills into the tip jar.

"You're Miriam's friend."

"I am. I am the friend of Miri. We are friendly, as they say. We dated in high school. But now, friends. Best friends." *Shut up*, Tulip's brain told her. *Shut up, shut up.*

"Bec's cousin. Second, if you're counting."

"Yes, I know," Tulip said, although she hadn't. She accepted her drink. She drank it.

"I like your dress."

"Don't lie."

"Well," he said. He laughed. "I like your shoes."

She looked at her bare feet and wiggled her toes.

"Would you like to dance?" he asked.

She said she would.

She had been there when Miri made the play list, comforted her as she agonized over the order and appropriateness. It was not the first play list they ever made together but it was the most important, to date. Now she was dancing with Les, yes, Les, keeping the top half of her body still and popping her hips back and forth.

All the other men loosened their ties or took them off. Les kept his perfectly knotted. The song changed. Tulip grabbed his waist.

"Keep dancing," she said.

Miri twirled over with Becca behind her. Les, behind Tulip. Miri and Tulip put their foreheads together.

"Are you having a good time?" Miri asked.

"The best."

"Thank you. For everything."

Tulip smiled.

"Have fun tonight," Miri said.

"Ha."

"He's a good guy," Miri said.

"Not too good, I hope."

Miri winked. She danced away with her wife. Tulip felt her gravity change.

"You want another drink?" Les asked.

"If you're offering."

While he was gone, she spun.

Les brought her more wine. Tulip had had enough but she felt more comfortable with something in her hand. She liked the ritual of bringing it to her mouth, of setting it down on the table. Les brought his beer bottle up under his bottom lip and blew across the top like a flute. He sipped and experimented with the notes.

The music slowed. Everyone got closer together and stopped moving their feet so fast. Tulip wrapped her arms around him. She put her temple on his shoulder, facing away. She watched everyone hold on to each other and sway.

Soon after, a pair of servers in white jackets rolled out the tall, tiered, buttercream cake. Becca sliced first and fed Miri. The idea of being fed was appealing to Tulip, but not like this. The scene, too predictable, too ordinary to really satisfy.

Miri swallowed and the guests applauded and snapped photos and, soon after, began to gather their things together.

Tulip asked Les if they could go.

"Now? No after party?"

"Right now."

When they got to the door she looked down at her feet.

"Your shoes," he said.

She shook her head. "They hurt too much."

He picked her up and fireman-carried her up over his shoulder. Tulip laughed and slapped at his ass. She stole his wallet from his back pocket and looked through it, upside-down.

"Need some money?" he asked.

"Just checking your birthday."

He opened his passenger side door with one hand and dropped her inside the car. He didn't even bump her head. Les pulled the seatbelt across her waist, pulled at the strap and let it snap hard against her chest.

"Ow," she said and laughed.

The drive was black with bits of light now and then. Tulip crossed her legs in his bucket seat and pressed the buttons on his stereo, not finding what she was looking for.

"Everything will be different now," she said.

But he misunderstood. He said, "They'll be fine. It's just a piece of paper, really."

Tulip shook her head but didn't try to explain. How could she? All she had was this sinking feeling and feet full of blisters. Gone, she thought. Miri is gone now.

They were staying at the same hotel. In retrospect, it wasn't an amazing coincidence.

Les carried Tulip through the hotel lobby and down the bleak hotel-colored halls, one arm under her knees and the other under her shoulder blades.

"I can walk," she said and laughed but pushed her face into his chest and slipped her arms around his neck. She curled herself up tighter to fit through the door. She wondered, if she stayed with him, if he would always carry her everywhere like this. If her legs would atrophy and become as useless as a mermaid fin on land.

He set her down easy.

"Wow," she said when she saw the four-post bed, the Jacuzzi tub, the gas fireplace. She had been happy when her own room had a blow dryer. He sat in the armchair, legs crossed and hands folded in his lap. Tulip took off her dress, made a show of it, the way one does.

"Aren't you going to come over here?" she asked.

"Is that what you want?"

She stood dumbly in the center of the room.

"Why don't you come here?" he said, so she went and sat on his lap.

He kissed her a little but she pulled away and squirmed. "No," she said. "No. *No*. Don't be nice." And then she stared at him until he knew she meant it.

He stood up fast and she fell off his lap and onto the floor landing hard on her tailbone.

"Stand up," he said.

She stood. They looked at one another and he raised his arm up over his head and slapped her fast, across the face. The sound was deeply satisfying.

Tulip put her hand on her jaw. "Thank you," she said. She went to kiss him but he held her at arm's length.

He put her on the bed, belly down. He went to his duffle bag and un-did the straps. She heard the nylon swoosh swoosh in two easy tugs and then felt it being tied around each of her ankles, on to each post. Les took off his belt and tied her wrists together above her head. He was strong, quick, efficient. With his confidence, she felt more comfortable than she had all night. She kept her eyes closed and pushed her face into the mattress. She heard him walk around, heard him clear his throat and drag his keys off the dresser. Heard the lights snap off and saw the dots behind her eyelids change. She heard the door open and click shut and then she heard nothing at all. The room was still; Tulip was alone.

When she was little, there was a story Tulip's Grandpa used to tell her about when he lived on the reservation.

"Don't scare her, Dad," Tulip's mother would say.

"I'm not scared!" Tulip would shout back.

"What? She's not scared," her Grandpa would repeat.

Looking back, Tulip supposes he needed to tell these stories because his life was so different from that of his own daughter and granddaughter. Or perhaps he just felt that pull, storyteller. A desire not just to speak, but to be heard.

When her Grandpa was growing up, he had four older brothers. They were darker and bigger and faster than him. As the baby, he felt a lot of pressure to keep up. Poverty had made these brothers very tough. They were always hungry and there were holes in the soles of their shoes. They didn't go to school because the nuns beat them and called them half-breeds. They didn't stay home because their father beat them and called them bastards. So they roamed around the woods and trapped squirrels and rabbits and groundhogs, which they would bring home for their mother and sisters to make into a stew. Every day, her

Grandpa would follow his brothers all over the mountains, all through the woods.

Somehow, they had gotten a hold of a gun. It was long and heavy and made him nervous. His brothers had bad tempers, each one more hot headed than the next. He didn't trust them. But they shared the gun and learned to shoot. They were able to bring more game home to their mother, which made her very happy and, in turn, made him very happy. Everyone's bellies were a little more full.

One day they saw a doe in the woods. She was tall with big, soft ears. His brothers gave him the gun. "Shoot," they told him.

Her Grandpa brought the gun to his shoulder and closed one eye the way he had seen his brothers do it. The doe was very still, very close. Close enough to see her hindquarters twitch when a fly landed on her fur.

"Shoot, dummy," the brothers said.

Her eyes were wide and brown, a little watery. The doe looked straight at her Grandpa.

"Kill her," the brothers told him. "Kill her or we'll kill you."

But her Grandpa hesitated too long and the deer sprinted away.

The brothers were angry, they were the angriest her Grandpa had ever seen. He was certain they would make good on their promise. They shouted and pushed him. They kicked him in the shins. They found some rope and tied one end around his belly and the other around a tree.

"They left me there," her Grandpa told her. "I don't know where those boys learned to tie knots but do you think I could have wiggled my way out? I worked it until my palms bled. Those brothers, they left me for bear food."

Les smoothed back Tulip's hair, waking her gently. Her hands tingled and her feet were pins and needles. The sun had come up, but just barely. She didn't remember her dreams, but then again, when did she ever?

"I am going to un-do this," he said "but don't move too fast or you'll hurt yourself. You have to give your blood a chance to get flowing again, okay?"

Tulip nodded. Her mouth felt dry. He unwrapped his belt from around her wrists but she left her hands above her head like he said. He undid the nylon straps from her ankles and she pulled her legs together.

"I'm cold," she said.

He took the white bathrobe from the closet and covered her with it like a blanket.

"I brought you this," he said and knelt at the edge of the bed. He brought a to-go cup with a bent plastic straw to her mouth. Orange juice, pulpy, sweet and not too cold. Perfect.

Of course, she wondered where Les had gone. She imagined, of course, he ended up with someone else, another woman, or maybe at a party with other wedding guests, but that's not the scenario that upsets her. It's the idea that he spent the night alone and her imagining his contentment with that. The possible peace of his loneliness is something Tulip fears she will never have.

"Do you want to try to sit up now?"

She moved slowly. Her head spun a little, but she was fine. They sat on the bed in silence. Tulip finished her orange juice and watched the light change through the gauzy curtains.

At her Grandpa's funeral, Tulip asked her great-Uncles which one of them had finally untied him. They were big, stoic men who normally didn't say much.

"What do you mean?" they asked.

She repeated the story: the doe, the gun, the tree.

Her uncles laughed.

"Your Grandpa told you this?" they sang.

Tulip didn't like the way they snickered and snorted. She wanted to stomp on their toes.

"Look how mad she is—just like him!"

Her Great-Uncle Blackie pulled her up on his lap. She squirmed and scratched his arms but he was much stronger than her.

"Listen to me," he said. "Your Grandpa was the meanest, toughest little boy I ever knew. Almost as mean and tough as you."

"Liar," Tulip said. "You left him in the woods for bear food."

"Your Grandpa ran away every day. Worried our poor mother sick. Jesus help whoever found him and had to bring him home. Look at this," he said. He showed her a half-moon scar on his right hand. "Bit almost straight to the bone. I needed fourteen stitches."

Tulip started to cry a little. She was eight years old and had never been to a funeral before.

"Now, now," he said and rocked her back and forth.

In the end, he didn't try to fuck her. She wasn't surprised, not really, but felt slightly wounded. She wanted him to, but if she had to ask, it wouldn't feel the same.

Tulip stayed in bed, looking out the window, while Les gathered some of his things together. She was bored and disheartened.

"Breakfast?" he said.

He seemed foolish to her. Ordinary. "No."

"Come on, my treat."

Tulip stood up and put her ugly dress back on. The fabric was awful, stiff and itchy. It was fitted too loose on top, giving her a baggy, matronly look but the sleeves were too tight, restricting the full motion of her arms. She couldn't get comfortable.

She stood in front of the mirror. Dark eyes, all pupils. She pulled her hair back. Still blonde, even though everyone said it would darken. A regular Goldilocks. This bed is too hard and this bed is too soft. She looked at Les. She had tried his porridge. Not 'just right,' not even close.

What was Goldilocks doing, anyway, stumbling into someone else's house, someone else's life, uninvited? What had she been looking for?

Tulip found her bag, her phone.

"You're leaving?"

What did she expect from him? What did she want? At first she thought her desire was never ending, that inside of her was a deep, empty well that could never be filled. The thought frightened her, but that wasn't true. There had been moments, times in her life where she felt full and satisfied. There were good meals, rich conversations, books that made her toes curl. She was not insatiable; she was simply disappointed with what she had been presented so far.

"I am."

"Tulip, listen, you asked—"

She put her hand up and he stopped. Whatever he was going to say was certain to embarrass her, and she didn't want to hear it.

"You're a strange one."

"The strangest," she said. She kissed him full on the lips. She left.

❖

Tulip walked barefoot down the hall. Eyes down, she made a game of stepping on the squares in the rug.

"Well look who's still in her party dress."

Miri was showered, her wet hair pulled back off her face. She was wearing a yellow cardigan. She looked fresh, bright. Awake.

"Where are your shoes?"

"I don't know. At the restaurant. I think. Where's Becca?"

"She's driving her brother to the airport. How was Les?"

Tulip wrapped her arms around Miri's waist, she put her head on Miri's shoulder, pushed right into her neck.

"Hey," Miri said. "Hey." She ran her fingers along Tulip's scalp and tugged on her hair the way it seemed only girls knew how.

Tulip didn't let go. She held on tighter.

"Okay. It's okay. You want to come back with me? Come on, let's go to my room."

Tulip let Miri lead her to the honeymoon suite. They crawled into the big, honeymoon bed, just like they used to before, in high school, gossiping under the covers, sharing the same pillow.

"What's wrong?" Miri asked. She poured them each a glass of champagne from an open bottle on the nightstand.

"I don't know," Tulip said. The wine was flat and sweet. "I don't feel right. Something's wrong. I think. I think something's wrong."

Miri put her hand on Tulip's cheek. "Was it Les?"

"No. Yes. No. I don't know."

Tulip pressed under her eyes with the heels of her palms. The pressure felt good.

"Miri. I hate this dress."

Miri laughed and laughed.

Tulip laughed too. They laughed until tears ran down their cheeks. They laughed until they thought they would pee, until they were gasping for breath, laughing silently, mouthing Stop, Stop.

Eventually they composed themselves and Tulip sat up fast, swung her legs off the side of the bed. She had the urge to flee, wanted to go before Becca came back. Not that Becca would be angry or upset, Tulip just didn't want to feel what she knew was true: that in level of importance, she had slipped down a peg in Miri's life. Tulip was tired of loving people more than they loved her.

Intuitive Miri, Miri who knew her so well, was suddenly quiet and serious. "You are going to be okay."

At her most cynical, Tulip thought Miri was only trying to comfort and convince herself. That she didn't want to be responsible for Tulip anymore. At her best, Tulip liked to believe it. There were moments. There were times she felt full.

❖

This is what we know: Goldilocks finds the bears' house in the woods. She goes in, explores and figures out what she likes and doesn't like. In the midst of her exploration, she is discovered by the bears.

We don't know why Goldilocks enters the house, but we can assume. She is searching. She is seeking. What? We do not know.

The bears come home. From where? The forest, most likely, but we do not know.

They are appropriately upset that someone has been poking around their residence. Unsettled, certainly, to have found she was in their beds—a disturbing, intimate detail. Angry, she ate their food, broke a chair, violated their privacy.

Still, there is no bloody massacre. Three bears against one blonde girl; it could have been worse. In its most gruesome version, Goldilocks leaps out the window. Possible suicide. But this version is seldom told; over time, this ending has fallen out of fashion.

Goldilocks disappears back into the forest that she came from. Where does she go? Does she find what she so desperately seeks?

This is not a story for answers.

This is a story for those who are still looking.

CONTRIBUTOR BIOS

ELLIS ANDERSON's first book, *Under Surge, Under Siege* (2010), garnered several recognitions, including the Eudora Welty Book Prize. As a freelancer, she has written for many publications, including MSNBC and Salon. A North Carolina native and longtime resident of New Orleans, Anderson now resides in Bay St. Louis on the Mississippi Gulf Coast, where she is publisher of a hyperlocal online magazine, The Shoofly.

LOUIS FLINT CECI's poetry has been published in Colorado North Review and read on the air as part of PRI's Living on Earth. His short stories have appeared in Diseased Pariah News, Trikone, and Jonathan, and in the anthologies *Queer and Catholic* and *Gay City Volume 4: At Second Glance*. His first novel, *Comfort Me*, was published by Prizm Books in 2009. In 2000, he launched Beautiful Dreamer Press. It has published several collections of poetry and prose since, including 2016's visual anthology *Not Just Another Pretty Face*, which pairs photos of go-go boys with stories they inspire.

MICHAEL CHIN is a recent alum of the MFA program in creative writing at Oregon State University. He has previously published or has work forthcoming with journals including *The Normal School, Passages North, Iron Horse*, and *Bayou Magazine*, and currently works as a contributing editor for *Moss*. In his spare time, he blogs about a cappella music and professional wrestling. You can visit him on the web at miketchin.com and follow him on Twitter @miketchin.

DALE CORVINO found his confessional voice at live readings, recounting his kept boy youth. Under a pseudonym, he blogged advice for rentboy. com (now shuttered by the Feds) and appeared with Dan Savage. Under his government name, he's written about Marilyn Monroe (Salon), Blondie (*ImageOutWrite*), and kink (the Rumpus). His short stories have appeared in *Jonathan* and *Chelsea Station*. He's participated in live storytelling (*RISK!*) and received the 2015 Christopher Hewitt Award for Fiction.

DEBRA CURTIS is a cultural anthropologist who lives and works in Rhode Island. Her first book *Pleasures and Perils: Girls' Sexuality in a Caribbean Consumer Culture* is taught at universities across the United States and in the UK. Her research on sex toys was mentioned on the front page of the *New York Times*. She has completed her first novel, which is set in New England and on the grasslands of Mongolia.

J. MARSHALL FREEMAN is a writer, musician, cartoonist, and graphic designer. His activist teen adventure novel, *Teetering*, was published in October 2016. He is currently finishing a queer YA novel entitled *The Dubious Gift of Dragon Blood*. Mr. Freeman is a graduate of the University of Toronto and proudly wears epithets thrown at him online, including: Bleeding Heart, Pussy, Tree-hugger, and Social Justice Warrior. Please visit his website, jmarshallfreeman.com, for more information.

WILLIAM MOECK worked in the restaurant business while earning a doctorate in British Literature at City University of New York. His scholarship reached broad audiences through the New York Public Library, where he curated exhibitions about Milton and Dickens. The story, "Gay Restaurants of New York," was adapted from an unpublished novel, and he currently teaches LGBTQ literature at SUNY Nassau, where he often starts the semester with Tennessee Williams's "One Arm."

Sheila Morris is a lesbian activist who was born and raised in rural Grimes County, Texas in the days long before Will and Grace. She is the author of four nonfiction books and the editor of a fifth work being published by the University of South Carolina Press in 2017, *Southern Perspectives on the Queer Movement: Committed to Home.* She and her wife Teresa Williams live in Columbia, South Carolina with their two dogs.

David James Parr is the author of the novel *Violet Peaks* and of a collection of short stories titled *How to Survive Overwhelming Loss & Loneliness in 5 Easy Steps.* His play *Slap & Tickle* has been produced in New York, Chicago, St. Petersburg and Provincetown. His comedy-drama *Eleanor Rigby Is Waiting* premiered at the New York International Fringe Festival and is now an independent feature in post-production.

A native New Yorker, James Penha (@JamesPenha) has lived for the past quarter-century in Indonesia. He has been nominated for Pushcart Prizes in fiction and in poetry. His essay "It's Been a Long Time Coming" was featured in *The New York Times* «Modern Love» column in April 2016. Penha edits *The New Verse News*, an online journal of current-events poetry.

William "Chris" Smith is a public relations/communications professional who has worked at the American Dental Association, Louisiana State University, Tulane University, Sierra Club, New Orleans Museum of Art, and the Southern Food and Beverage Museum. He holds a degree in English from Westminster College, Fulton, Missouri, a Master of Arts degree in liberal arts from the University of Chicago, and a Master of Arts degree in Arts Administration from the University of New Orleans. He lives in New Orleans.

P.D. Walter (pdwalterbooks.com) writes novels, short stories and screenplays from his home in Toronto. His writing gravitates toward the alternately hilarious, head-scratching and downright tragic contradictions of contemporary urban life through the lenses of LGBTQ identities, parent-child relationships, or anything else that attracts his interested fascination. "Temporary Adhesions" (a title drawn from the memoirs of Gore Vidal) is excerpted from the as-yet-unpublished novel *Twilight of the Adults*.

ALISE WASCOM holds a BFA in writing, literature and publishing from Emerson College and an MFA from Lesley University in Cambridge. She is a 2013 Phipps-Massey fellowship winner for the Tomales Bay Writing by Writers conference. Her essays have appeared in *Publishers Weekly* and *Fiction Southeast* and her fiction has appeared in *Merrimack Valley Magazine* and the Francesca Lia Block edited anthologies *Love Magick* and *Rough Magick*. She lives in southeast Louisiana, where she studies Library Science at LSU and is completing her first novel.

THOMAS WESTERFIELD is, for better and for worse, still a son of Kentucky despite having lived the last twenty-three years in San Francisco. His story "Mr. Sissy in Sin City" was published in the 2016 Saints & Sinners Anthology, and he continues to work on a collection of short stories. An award-winning and produced playwright, he was named as one of the "25 Unsung Heroes of the Gay Community" in 1988 by The Advocate magazine.

A longtime journalist, JOHN MORGAN WILSON broke into fiction writing in 1996 with the publication of *Simple Justice*, winning an Edgar from Mystery Writers of America for best first novel. Three other titles in the eight-book Justice series won Lambda Literary Awards for best gay men's mystery. John's short fiction has appeared in *Blithe House Quarterly*, *Ellery Queen Mystery Magazine*, *Alfred Hitchcock Mystery Magazine*, and several anthologies, including *Saints & Sinners: New Fiction from the Festival 2011*.

ABOUT THE EDITORS

AMIE M. EVANS has published over 57 short stories and essays as well as one novella. She is a creative-nonfiction and literary erotica writer. Evans is the co-editor of eight volumes of *Saints + Sinners: New Fiction from the Festival* with Paul J. Willis and the anthology *Queer and Catholic* with Trebor Healey. She also writes gay male erotica under a pen name. Evans is on the board of directors of the Saints and Sinners Literary Festival. She has worked at Harvard University for over 17 years. She is currently the EA to the Dean of Harvard Extension School. She has a collection of lesbian short stories coming out in 2016. She is currently working on a memoir about food, religion, and mothers as well as a satirical novel about saving lesbian sex.

PAUL J. WILLIS has over 21 years of experience in non-profit management. He earned a B.S. degree in Psychology and a M.S. degree in Communication. He started his administrative work in 1992 as the co-director of the Holos Foundation in Minneapolis. The Foundation operated an alternative high school program for at-risk youth. Willis has been the executive director of the Tennessee Williams/New Orleans Literary Festival since 2004. He is the founder of the Saints and Sinners Literary Festival (established in 2003), and has edited various anthologies including the award-winning *Love Bourbon Street* with his partner Greg Herren.

OUR FINALIST JUDGE

MICHAEL THOMAS FORD is the author of numerous books, including *Lily, Sharon Needles and the Curse of the Devil's Deck, Suicide Notes, Jane Bites Back, What We Remember,* and *Alec Baldwin Doesn't Love Me and Other Trials of My Queer Life.* A 5-time winner of the Lambda Literary Award, he also received the Jim Duggins Outstanding Mid-Career Novelist Prize, is a member of the Saints and Sinners Hall of Fame, and has been a finalist for prizes including the Horror Writers Association's Bram Stoker Award and the Maxwell Award presented by the Dog Writers Association of America. He lives in rural Maryland with 7 dogs, 6 horses, and 4 cats. Things he likes include rescue dogs, Tarot cards, scuba diving, coffee, making a mess in the kitchen, creepy clown films, Christmas ornaments, 80's pop music, Doctor Who, and tattoos. He does not like to shave. You may visit him at www.michaelthomasford.com.

Saints + Sinners Literary Festival

The first Saints and Sinners Literary Festival took place in May of 2003. The event started as a new initiative designed as an innovative way to reach the community with information about HIV/AIDS. It was also formed to bring the LGBT community together to celebrate the literary arts. Literature has long nurtured hope and inspiration, and has provided an avenue of understanding. A steady stream of LGBT novels, short stories, poems, plays, and non-fiction works has served to awaken lesbians, gay men, bisexuals, and transgendered persons to the existence of others like them; to trace the outlines of a shared culture; and to bring the outside world into the emotional passages of LGBT life.

After the Stonewall Riots in New York City, gay literature finally came "out of the closet." In time, noted authors such as Dorothy Allison, Michael Cunningham, and Mark Doty (all past *Saints'* participants) were receiving mainstream award recognition for their works. But there are still few opportunities for media attention of gay-themed books, and decreasing publishing options. This Festival helps to ensure that written work from the LGBT community will continue to have an outlet, and that people will have access to books that will help dispel stereotypes, alleviate isolation, and provide resources for personal wellness.

The event has since evolved into a program of the Tennessee Williams/New Orleans Literary Festival made possible by our premier sponsor the John Burton Harter Foundation. The NO/AIDS Task Force of New Orleans provides volunteer and special event support with a percentage of profits from these events going back to directly benefit NO/AIDS community initiatives. The Saints and Sinners Literary Festival works to achieve the following goals:

1. to create an environment for productive networking to ensure increased knowledge and dissemination of LGBT literature;
2. to provide an atmosphere for discussion, brainstorming, and the emergence of new ideas;
3. to recognize and honor writers, editors, and publishers who broke new ground and made it possible for LGBT books to reach an audience; and
4. to provide a forum for authors, editors, and publishers to talk about their work for the benefit of emerging writers, and for the enjoyment of readers of LGBT literature.

Saints and Sinners is an annual celebration that takes place in the heart of the French Quarter of New Orleans each Spring. The Festival includes writing workshops, readings, panel discussions, literary walking tours, and a variety of special events. We also aim to inspire the written word through our short fiction contest. Each year we induct individuals to our Saints and Sinners Hall of Fame. The Hall of Fame is intended to recognize people for their dedication to LGBT literature. Selected members have shown their passion for our literary community through various avenues including writing, promotion, publishing, editing, teaching, bookselling, and volunteerism.

Past year's inductees into the Saints and Sinners Literary Hall of Fame include: Dorothy Allison, Carol Anshaw, Ann Bannon, Lucy Jane Bledsoe, Maureen Brady, Rob Byrnes, Patrick Califia, Bernard Cooper, Jameson Currier, Brenda Currin, Mark Doty, Jim Duggins, Amie M. Evans, Otis Fennell, Michael Thomas Ford, Katherine V. Forrest, Nancy Garden, Jewelle Gomez, Jim Grimsley, Tara Hardy, Ellen Hart, Greg Herren, Kenneth Holditch, Andrew Holleran, Candice Huber, Fay Jacobs, G. Winston James, Michele Karlsberg, Joan Larkin, Susan Larson, Lee Lynch, Jeff Mann, William J. Mann, Marianne K. Martin, Stephen McCauley, Val McDermid, Mark Merlis, Tim Miller, Rip & Marsha Naquin-Delain, Michael Nava, Achy Obejas, Felice Picano, Radclyffe, J.M. Redmann, David Rosen, Carol Rosenfeld, Steven

Saylor, Carol Seajay, Kelly Smith, Jack Sullivan, Cecilia Tan, Patricia Nell Warren, Jess Wells, Edmund White, and Paul J. Willis.

For more information about the Saints and Sinners Literary Festival including sponsorship opportunities and our Archangel Membership Program, visit: www.sasfest.org. Be sure to sign up for our e-newsletter for updates for future programs. We hope you will join other writers and bibliophiles for a weekend of literary revelry not to be missed!

"Saints & Sinners is hands down one of the best places to go to revive a writer's spirit. Imagine a gathering in which you can lean into conversations with some of the best writers and editors and agents in the country, all of them speaking frankly and passionately about the books, stories and people they love and hate and want most to record in some indelible way. Imagine a community that tells you truthfully what is happening with writing and publishing in the world you most want to reach. Imagine the flirting, the arguing, the teasing and praising and exchanging of not just vital information, but the whole spirit of queer arts and creating. Then imagine it all taking place on the sultry streets of New Orleans' French Quarter. That's Saints & Sinners—the best wellspring of inspiration and enthusiasm you are going to find. Go there."

Dorothy Allison, National Book Award finalist
for *Bastard Out of Carolina*, and author
of the critically acclaimed novel *Cavedweller*.

Lightning Source UK Ltd.
Milton Keynes UK
UKOW04f2354020817
306567UK00001B/24/P

9 781635 550047